The Definitive Guide to SugarCRM

Better Business Applications

T0210427

John Mertic

Apress®

The Definitive Guide to SugarCRM: Better Business Applications

Lead Editor: Steve Anglin
Technical Reviewer: Matt Heitzenroder, Roger Smith, Collin Lee
Editorial Board: Clay Andres, Steve Anglin, Mark Beckner, Ewan Buckingham, Tony Campbell, Gary Cornell, Jonathan Gennick, Michelle Lowman, Matthew Moodie, Jeffrey Pepper, Frank Pohlmann, Ben Renow-Clarke, Dominic Shakeshaft, Matt Wade, Tom Welsh
Copy Editor: Jim Markham
Coordinating Editor: Katie Stence
Compositor: MacPS, LLC
Artist: April Milne

Distributed to the book trade worldwide by Springer-Verlag New York, Inc., 233 Spring Street, 6th Floor, New York, NY 10013. Phone 1-800-SPRINGER, fax 201-348-4505, e-mail orders-ny@springer-sbm.com, or visit http://www.springeronline.com.

For information on translations, please contact Apress directly at 2855 Telegraph Avenue, Suite 600, Berkeley, CA 94705. Phone 510-549-5939, e-mail info@apress.com, or visit http://www.apress.com.

Apress and friends of ED books may be purchased in bulk for academic, corporate, or promotional use. eBook versions and licenses are also available for most titles. For more information, reference our Special Bulk Sales–eBook Licensing web page at http://www.apress.com/info/bulksales.

The source code for this book is available to readers at http://www.apress.com.

Contents at a Glance

Contents at a Glance

Contents

About the Author

 **John Mertic** is a software engineer at SugarCRM, and has several years of experience with PHP Web applications. An avid writer, he has been published in php|architect, IBM Developerworks, and in the Apple Developer Connection, and has been a speaker at several developer conferences. He has also contributed to many open source projects, most notably the PHP project where he is the creator and maintainer of the PHP Windows Installer. John is happily married to his lovely and exceptionally supportive wife Kristy. Together they have a daughter Malloryand a dog Dominic.

About the Technical Reviewers

 **Roger Smith** is currently an Engineering Manager and Staff Engineer at SugarCRM. Prior to SugarCRM, Roger held Software Engineering positions at StrikeIron, a Web Services company focused on providing commercial data as a service. He also served as a Software Engineer at Cisco Systems on their E-Commerce and Government Solutions teams. Roger holds a Masters degree in Machine Learning from Columbia University and a BS in Mathematics from the University of North Carolina at Chapel Hill.

 **Collin Lee** has been working at SugarCRM as a platform developer for over three years. He has also previously worked for IBM and Xerox Corporation. In his spare time, he enjoys cooking, running, and experimenting with software technologies. He currently lives with his wife in New York City.

 **Matthew Heitzenroder**, SugarCRM's Community Manager, is a fanatic about the power of community and democratization of software. Four years ago, Matt joined SugarCRM's Support team, dedicating himself to provide an outstanding customer support experience. He made a transition to become a Senior Professional Services consultant, implementing SugarCRM in some the companies largest clients and most demanding projects. Today, Matt's passion for Open Source and it's ideals has naturally lead to a career of empowering and advocating the SugarCRM community of developers, consultants, and users. He happily lives life with his wife in sunny Miami, Florida, sailing and diving every chance he gets.

Acknowledgments

One thing that I've learned over the past 8 years is software development is hard work. But I never realized that writing about software development is even harder.

Looking back on writing this book, I am simply amazed at the gift God has given me to accomplish such an amazing feat. He stuck by my side, even when it was 2 a.m. and I was trying to make it through a few more paragraphs, and for that I am the most grateful. There is also an amazing group of individuals that he put here who I am in tremendous debt to that made this book possible.

I'll begin by thanking the entire team at SugarCRM for all their help and support with the book. I'd like to personally thank SugarCRMS's founders, John Roberts, Clint Oram, and Jacob Taylor, for starting the project and the entire company from scratch five years ago. I want to personally thank the reviewers Matt Heitzenroder, Roger Smith, and Collin Lee for giving me great advice and direction in making the book such a resounding success. And, I want to thank all those at Sugar who have put their time and energy into developing SugarCRM into a world class application. My hope is that this book puts a light to the high quality engineering that has been put into the product.

I would also like to thank Apress, especially Steve Anglin, Michelle Lowman, James Markham, and Dominic Shakeshaft for giving me the opportunity as a new author to write this book. The group at Apress put a ton of effort into making this book a reality, even when the schedule seemed to work against us at times.

And last, but certainly not least, I would like to thank all my friends and family that have provided me support and encouragement over the years, especially during the writing of this book. The biggest thank you goes to my exceptionally supportive wife Kristy, who put up with all the long writing nights and weekends (and family vacation) in my efforts to put together this book. I could never have done this without you.

Introduction

I started this book with the intention of bringing a new side of SugarCRM to light. Since I began working at SugarCRM, I saw the flexibility and extensibility that the application could provide. I looked back on my previous position developing internal business applications, and saw that many of the features I added and design issues I would wrestle with were problems that SugarCRM had already solved. The engineering team at SugarCRM had built the application to solve this problem, yet few developers outside of SugarCRM really knew how powerful the underlying platform was. I knew there were other developers in this same boat, and that if I could reach them it would make their jobs much easier.

What a CRM application does or doesn't do isn't authoritatively defined; instead, its goal is to fill in the gap where a company needs to solve problems in their relationships with their customers. Sometimes this means keeping track of meetings and phone calls. Other times, this means tracking the progress of an ongoing project. It could also mean managing support cases and product defects. Yet sometimes an application may not completely cover this. Just as every business or organization is unique, so must be what CRM will mean to them. Up until SugarCRM, this application space was full of players who thought they had the CRM problem solved, and built large proprietary applications that were expensive to implement and support and notoriously difficult to customize to meet their needs. SugarCRM came in and changed that scene, making CRM something that is inexpensive to implement, easier to customize, and more approachable for end-users to work with. It's designed to be a CRM that your users won't hate, which is the philosophy that the founders of SugarCRM set as their paramount goal when building it.

This book is designed to take this easy-to-use and customizable application and show you what you need to do with it. The contents of this book are unique as they come directly from the engineering experience of SugarCRM, giving you as the reader an insight into the application that you can't find anywhere else. I've broken the book down into three distinct parts:

- Part 1: The SugarCRM Platform
- Part 2: Customizing SugarCRM Out of the Box
- Part 3: Building New Functionality on Top of SugarCRM

While this book is designed to be read from beginning to end, it's also useful as a general reference manual when developing on SugarCRM. Once you have the knowledge of how the application works internally, you can go back to the book easily to pick up any tidbit of information you might need as you work with the platform. All of the information contained within is current with SugarCRM version 5.5, and most of the examples are built upon the community edition of SugarCRM. I encourage you as you read through the book to download and install SugarCRM on your local machine and try the examples out to see how easy it is to work with. This book is only the tip of the iceberg in what can be done with SugarCRM. Therefore, I also encourage you to also visit the Sugar Forums (http://www.sugarcrm.com/forums) and the Sugar Developer Zone (http://developers.sugarcrm.com) for more about what Sugar can do for you and where we are going in the future.

Thanks for picking up this book and taking a chance on SugarCRM. My hope is that it can help you out in your future applications for your business or organization.

PART 1

■ ■ ■

The SugarCRM Platform

is first part of the book, you'll learn all about SugarCRM; from the company and ommunity to the various features of the platform. You'll see in depth how the MVC nd metadata frameworks drive the core of the application. You'll also see how you an integrate SugarCRM with various other applications using the feature rich web services platform, and learn about many other features the Sugar platform offers the user and the developer.

CHAPTER 1

■ ■ ■

What Is SugarCRM?

SugarCRM is a commercial open source company. It's not often that "commercial" and "open source" go together. When we think of commercial software we think proprietary, closed-source software. On the flipside, when we think of open source software, we think of free or "libre" software that is community driven and community oriented. SugarCRM is unique in that it breaks the expectation of how commercial software works, leveraging the best of how open-source software is designed and built to create a product that is focused on the end-users and developers, creating a positive experience for both groups. But it also has the advantages of a commercial company, which includes world-class support, comprehensive end-user training, and end-to-end quality assurance testing to ensure high product stability.

Let's look at SugarCRM from a few different perspectives: as a company, product, and community.

The Company

SugarCRM was founded in 2004 as an open source project on SourceForge, http://www.sourceforge.net, one of the Internet's largest open source development sites. SugarCRM's three founders, John Roberts, Clint Oram, and Jacob Taylor, had a combined experience of over 50 years building proprietary Customer Relationship Management (CRM) applications for Silicon Valley companies. They had grown frustrated with the lack of innovation in CRM and the high failure rates of proprietary CRM applications. SugarCRM's founders took an unusual approach in building a CRM solution. Rather than write the code in secret and keep the product proprietary, the founders released the code with an open source license and allowed for any interested party to download, modify, and redistribute SugarCRM.

In just a few months, the application was downloaded 50,000 times and translated into ten languages. In November 2004, the Sugar Open Source Project was selected as Project of the Month by SourceForge.net. The popularity of the application allowed SugarCRM founders to incorporate a business around the open source project and receive $2 million in venture capital funding from Draper Fisher Jurvetson, a leading Silicon Valley venture capital firm.

Rapid Growth—Harnessing Open Source and SaaS

The popularity of SugarCRM on SourceForge and an infusion of capital from Silicon Valley investors allowed the company to begin expanding. SugarCRM established a headquarters in Cupertino, CA and began building out its engineering team. In early 2005, SugarCRM introduced Sugar On-Demand, which is a "Software-as-a-Service" (software is provided for a user via a hosting service) that allows customers to use Sugar without installing software on premise.

The adoption of an Open Source and On-Demand product offering positioned SugarCRM at the nexus of two major technology waves. The first—On-Demand— promotes more flexibility and control over how the application is installed, customized, and used. The second—On-Demand—gives users the ability to use CRM software without having technical expertise in-house.

SugarCRM's innovation in the marketplace was to champion both approaches. Previously, companies had offered On-Site or On-Demand, rarely both. In all cases, the code was kept proprietary which means it was very difficult for customers to understand what they were purchasing, and nearly impossible to modify the code without large investments in professional services and long project timelines.

The Product

Customer Relationship Management is a well-established industry that has evolved over the past two decades. Simply put, CRM is about using information technology to gain a better understanding of customers and deliver a differentiated customer experience across the entire relationship. Think of it as turning your customers inside out, giving businesses a tool to learn what their history is, buying trends are, and interactions have been, allowing you to use this knowledge to plan ahead for your interactions with them. CRM suites, such as SugarCRM, provide tools to all customer-facing employees—marketing, sales, customer support—as well as provide collaboration tools to ease communications and reporting functionality, so managers can understand what is happening in their business. CRM suites also provide administration tools to manage users, information flow, customizations, and other "behind-the-scenes" operations of the CRM system.

SugarCRM began as a sales force automation tool and quickly expanded to include marketing automation functionality and customer support, as well as collaboration and reporting across all parts of the application. It is a web-based application written mostly in the PHP programming language, supporting version 5.2.1 and greater as of SugarCRM version 5.5.0, as well as using the latest javascript and flash techniques to enhance the user experience. It supports running on the MySQL, Microsoft SQL Server, and Oracle database servers (Oracle is only supported in the Enterprise Edition) as well as deployments on Windows, Linux, Mac OS X, and Solaris. Being a browser-based application, it allows the end-users to use either Internet Explorer, Mozilla Firefox, or Apple's Safari browser.

SugarCRM comes in three product editions: Sugar Community Edition contains core CRM functionality designed for small businesses. Sugar Professional contains additional functionality to manage the needs of small-and-medium-sized business. Sugar Enterprise contains the CRM features and support for large enterprises. The following discusses each edition in detail:

- *Sugar Community Edition*: A Free Open Source Software (FOSS) licensed under the GNU General Public License Version 3 (GPLv3), the newest and one of the many prevalent open source licenses in the software world. Sugar Community Edition is available for free download at SugarCRM's development environment at `http://www.sugarforge.org`. Customers are free to download, modify, and use Sugar Community Edition without restriction.

- *Sugar Professional*: SugarCRM's flagship product, targeted at small and medium-sized businesses. It contains additional functionality, such as team management, access control, reporting, and wireless device access. It is offered under a commercial license. Sugar Professional is offered under an annual subscription.

- *Sugar Enterprise*: Contains enterprise-grade functionality for large enterprises. It adds additional features that most large scale deployments require, such as Oracle database support and Advanced SQL reporting. It is also commercially licensed and offered under an annual subscription, just like Sugar Professional.

Figure 1-1 provides a graphical outline of what is included with the various editions of SugarCRM.

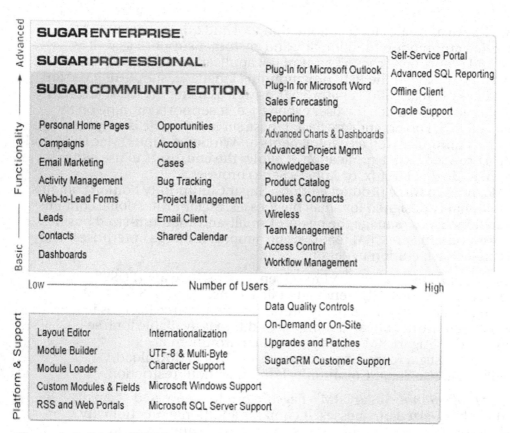

Figure 1-1. SugarCRM Product Matrix

SugarCRM is further customizable by allowing multiple deployment options, which allows even companies without IT expertise to use SugarCRM.

- *Sugar On-Demand*: Allows users to set up and run SugarCRM within minutes, using SugarCRM Managed Data Centers. Advantages include guaranteed uptime and management of your SugarCRM instance, which takes away all the upgrade and server maintenance worries.

- *Sugar On-Site*: Allows users to install SugarCRM on their existing hardware. In addition, SugarCRM has a Faststack installer that is designed to install all the required components (Web Server, Database Server, PHP) for SugarCRM as well.

The beauty of flexible deployment options is that even users using Sugar On-Demand can customize how SugarCRM works through the powerful, yet easy-to-use Module Builder and Studio tools. (We'll learn more about these in Parts 2 and 3 of this book.) This allows anyone using SugarCRM to customize it to meet their needs without having the burden of supporting a server and installation. In addition, they can leverage both the On-Demand and On-Site deployment options at no additional charge. This is handy so that one system can be used as a backup of the other, or one can be used as a development/staging system and the other as a production system.

SugarCRM's growth has continued month after month since being founded as an open source project in 2004. To date, SugarCRM has been downloaded over 5.2 million times, with over 55,000 active systems in over 195 countries supporting nearly half a million users. In addition, SugarCRM has 4,500 paying customers that use the commercial versions of the product to power their enterprise.

The Community

The key to SugarCRM's success lies in the large community of users and developers around the world. Their feedback and contributions have helped shape the product, and have been an invaluable resource for helping SugarCRM grow. SugarCRM as a company has recognized this and have built several tools for the community to interact with SugarCRM and other users of SugarCRM around the world. Let's take a look at them.

Sugar Forums and Wiki

The easiest place to interact with the Sugar community is at the Sugar Forums (http://www.sugarcrm.com/forums/). Here is where members of the SugarCRM team, end-users, partners, and developers interact to discuss issues with the product, learn about upcoming features and releases, and learn how others are using SugarCRM within their industry. The forums are driven by both members of the SugarCRM team and community volunteers and is the easiest way to participate with the SugarCRM community.

The Sugar Wiki (http://www.sugarcrm.com/wiki/) is an invaluable resource for tips and tricks when working with SugarCRM. This is a mostly community-driven wiki, but also provides official SugarCRM documentation on the product and podcasts from SugarCRM team members on a variety of SugarCRM and industry topics.

SugarExchange and SugarForge

SugarExchange (http://www.sugarexchange.com/)is the SugarCRM marketplace where any Sugar user wishing to extend core Sugar functionality can choose among hundreds of module extensions, themes, and language packs provided by Sugar community members and partners. It is the go–to place when you are looking for functionality that can be easily added to your SugarCRM instance. SugarExchange contains both free and non-free add-ons to SugarCRM. While SugarExchange is facilitated by SugarCRM, all transactions and support for the add-ons offered is completely independent of SugarCRM, which provides a forum for the SugarCRM developer community to showcase add-ons to the product.

SugarForge (http://www.sugarforge.org/) is the developer side of the SugarExchange, which provides developer and project collaborations tools for those developing on the SugarCRM platform. This is designed to offer features similar to SourceForge or Google Code, and provides forums, and documentation space for your add-ons. It is often used in conjunction with SugarExchange, where SugarExchange is used to help feature the add-ons to the Sugar Community as a whole. There are over 600 active projects on SugarForge to date, including over 80 language translations offered for free download.

Sugar Developer Zone

If you do any development on top of SugarCRM, this is the place to be. It is a comprehensive resource for any Sugar developer, with links to the official SugarCRM developer guide, developer forums, and tutorials on common customizations and topics. It also features a blog that is run by the SugarCRM team, which provides developers insight on upcoming developer features in SugarCRM or tips and tricks on developing applications with SugarCRM.

As you can see, SugarCRM isn't like typical commercial software, but it has the more polished feel of typical open source software. This book focuses on this distinction, so in Part 1 we will take an in-depth look at the SugarCRM platform and the features of the product that make it ideal for building a business application.

Getting SugarCRM

In order to best follow along with the examples in the remaining chapters, you should probably download and install SugarCRM. The community edition of SugarCRM is available for download at http://www.sugarcrm.com/crm/download/sugar-suite.html. You have two options for installing SugarCRM from this site. One option is to download the zip archive that contains the application, and install it on your local machine or Web Server. In order to do this, you'll need the following components installed and configured:

- *Web Server*: Either Apache 1.3 or later or IIS 6 or later with FastCGI installed if you are using Windows.

- *PHP*: Version 5.2.1 or later installed and configured to be used with the above Web Server.

- *Database Server*: Either MySQL 5.0 or later or SQL Server 2005 or later.

To install SugarCRM, simply open a web browser and point it to the location where SugarCRM was unzipped. If you unzipped it into the sugar directory in the root of the Web Server on your local machine, point your web browser to `http://localhost/sugar`, and then the Sugar interactive installer will guide you to the remainder of the setup process.

To make it easier to get the stack installed, SugarCRM provides several "faststack" installers that will install SugarCRM along with the complete Apache, MySQL, (or SQL Server Express for Windows), and PHP stacks, so you can be ready to run in no time.

Summary

In this chapter, you looked at SugarCRM, and saw how the open source and community-driven nature of the company has helped the product grow into such a success. You then looked at the product, learning the various editions available as well as the many different ways that SugarCRM can be deployed and used by businesses. Next, you turned toward the SugarCRM community, seeing how the SugarCRM as a company and the Sugar community can interact through both forums and wikis to add-on package repositories and marketplaces. Finally, you took a brief look at installing Sugar, so you can follow through with the examples in the remainder of this book.

Let's continue on with a deep dive into SugarCRM's underlining platform. In Chapter 2, you'll look at the MVC framework that Sugar is built upon.

■ ■ ■

MVC Architecture

With the advent of SugarCRM 5.0, a new MVC architecture was born. This architecture was designed to eliminate the painful tasks in building a module in SugarCRM. Instead of having to manually lay out templates and set up object interactions and relationships, you can easily leverage the framework by using standardized templates and definition files for building the various views. The system is also very extensible, allowing new views and custom templating to be built on top of it as well.

Before digging into how the SugarCRM MVC model works, let's take a step back and see what MVC actually is.

What Is MVC?

MVC stands for Model View Controller, and is a very common architectural pattern used in both web and desktop application design. The goals of using the MVC pattern is to separate the user interface logic from the application logic, having a layer in between to facilitate the communication between them. Each one of the Model, View, and Controller components are tasked with handling certain roles within an application (see Figure 2-1).

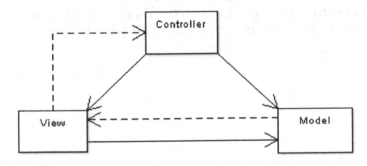

Figure 2-1. Diagram of the MVC pattern

The model layer represents the application logic layer. The goal of this layer is to handle the communication with any external resources, such as databases, Web Services, and files. It also contains any business logic in the application, such as ways to calculate field values. A good model provides a clean interface to the guts of the application, providing methods and functions to easily interact with the lower level services and provide any needed transformation or interpretation so that other parts of the application can easily use it.

The view layer represents the user interface. This is where any display logic is dealt with, such as form layout and data display. It is also designed to how it's consumed, so for a web application a view would be a typical web page. The view layer is specific to what role it is meant to have, so a data entry view would be different than a record display view, even though they may represent the same model.

The controller layer is the glue between the model and view layer. A good controller will accept the request from the user, calls upon a model for the information it needs, and then calls upon a view to return that information to the user. This layer is meant to be a thin layer. It shouldn't contain business logic, communicate with a database directly, or deal with the how to display information to the user.

Sugar has used the MVC pattern to replace the aging architecture used before version 5.0. Although it was based upon many of the principles of the MVC architecture, it was not truly optimized in a way to really take advantage of it. Let's look now at how SugarCRM does MVC.

MVC the Sugar Way

Sugar uses the MVC pattern to handle requests from the users. Each request to the primary entrypoint (index.php) will specify HTTP request variables indicating the module (which maps to the MVC definition of controller) and the action (which maps to the MVC definition of view) as follows:

`http://servername/index.php?module=Contacts&action=EditView`.

For the preceding URL, the request to Sugar would return the EditView action of the Contacts module. Figure 2-2 shows what happens internally when that request is made.

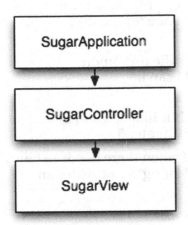

Figure 2-2. *Sugar MVC flowchart*

Let's take a look at each component in the MVC flowchart.

SugarApplication

The first step in the request handling happens at the SugarApplication level. This class handles much of the prerequisites needed for the Sugar application, including session checking, user authentication, setting the theme, and making the connection to the database. It also handles much of the preprocess logic of the application. For example, setting the user time zone on first login and letting the user know when their password is expired. The class is not designed to be modified or extended by developers. However, a preprocess method does exist in the SugarController class which allows developers to interject logic into the handling of the request before the controller is executed.

After loading the controller, the following tasks are done before executing the controller:

- User authentication takes place. If the user is already authenticated then you'll continue on with the request, otherwise you'll redirect the login form so the user can authenticate. I'll talk in more detail about user authentication in Chapter 5.

- Using the settings from the user, any Access control list (ACL) rules are applied for the cases of what modules to expose to the user.

- Any preprocess rules from that are defined on the application level or are applied by the controller. Setting the time zone for the user on their first login is handled here.

- The correct language strings are loaded, as set by the user upon login. In Chapter 5, I'll talk about how SugarCRM can be internationalized for any language.

- The theme that is currently selected by the user is initialized and loaded. I'll talk more about how themes work in Chapter 5.

The preProcess() method in the controller is best used when there needs to be some initial logic before you do anything with a module. Listing 2-1 provides an example of what that would be.

Listing 2-1. Example of a preProcess() Method in the Controller

```
public function preProcess()
{
    global $current_user;

    if ( !is_admin($current_user) ) {
        echo 'This module is for admin use only!';
        sugar_die();

    }

}
```

You would use this if the module is going to be an admin-only module, so you could check initially in the controller to see if the user has access to it or not. This avoids the need to add this logic to every view in the module.

Once all of these prerequisites are handled, you can then move on to the SugarController, which is designed to take the request and execute it.

SugarController

The SugarController class handles the main flow of the request, and is designed to control all requests for the module specified. The SugarController implementation maps very well to the MVC model's interpretation of what a controller will do, and contains several action hooks for common actions you would have in a typical module. These actions, available out of the box by default, include complete implementations for DetailView, EditView, ListView, and saving and deleting records. Several of these have definition files, or metadata, that is used to define what they look and act like, which you'll learn more about in Chapter 3.

The SugarController will provide representation for each of the views of the module for which it controls. It does this is by providing two ways of handling the mapping to a view. The first way is by having an actual action method in the controller class which represents the action and transfers control over to the view. At a minimum, this method will specify the view to use with this action, but it can also do some logic at this level that isn't really related to the view layer. Listing 2-2 shows an example view, which I'll call 'getthemail'.

Listing 2-2. action_getthemail()

```
public function action_getthemail()
{
    if ( mailExists() )
        $this->view = 'getthemail';
    else
        $this->view = 'hasnomail';
}
```

The action hook will first add a check to see if mail exists before redirecting to the 'getthemail' view. If there is no mail, then it will use 'hasnomail' view instead. This kind of situation is a common one, and can provide hooks to direct different views to use depending upon the state of the application or the type of request being made. For example, you could have different views based upon whether json or HTML data is being requested, but the core logic could use the same action hook.

If you have additional controller logic that needs added, such as handling extra request parameters, you can subclass the SugarController class by naming it *Modulename*Controller and saving the file as controller.php in the module's directory. Listing 2-3 is an example where you will override the Meetings module EditView action to allow marking a meeting completed by passing the request variable 'close'.

Listing 2-3. *MeetingsController Class*

```php
<?php

class MeetingsController extends SugarController
{
    public function action_editview()
    {
        if ( isset($_REQUEST['close'] )
            $this->bean->status = 'Held';

    }
}
```

In the preceding, you simply added a new piece of logic to the EditView action which will set the status of the Meeting to 'Held', if you have requested to close it. The bean object corresponds to the data record of the module being requested. The record id is grabbed from the request variable 'record', and it is initialized and loaded automatically in the SugarController class as a part when it processed the request, prior to calling the actual action logic.

Sometimes you may want to be selective about overriding a controller action, by adding logic before or after the action is called. The SugarController class provides hooks for this, by having pre_*action()* and post_*action()* methods for each action, which are called before and after the action is called, if they are defined. There are multiple uses for this. Listing 2-4 shows an example where you will check for a changed value of the status field during a save of a Bugs module record in the BugsController class.

Listing 2-4. *BugsController Class*

```php
<?php

class BugsController extends SugarController
{
    protected $_prevStatus = '';

    public function pre_save()
    {
        $bugFocus = new Bug;
        $bugFocus->retrieve($_REQUEST['record']);
        if ( isset($bugFocus->id) )
            $this->_prevStatus = $bugFocus->status;

        parent::pre_save();
    }

    public function post_save()
    {
        if ( ($bugFocus->status != $this->bean->status)
```

```
                && ($this->bean->status != 'Closed') ) {
            // do something now that the bug is closed
        }

        parent::post_save();
    }
}
```

In the pre_save() method, you will save the value of the status of the bug in the private class variable $_prevStatus, and then you'll check to see if it's changed to 'Closed' in the post_save() method. It's important here to call the parent pre_save() and post_save() methods, since there is logic for those in the SugarController class.

Another use for the pre_*action()* and post_*action()* methods is to give options for extending the logic needed for an action without needing to override the main action method. This is handy so that you split the logic of an action into multiple parts. Then, if it needs to be overridden by a subclass, you only have to override the part that needs changed. Let's say you want to override the BugsController in Listing 2-4 with another check for a different status type. Listing 2-5 shows how this is done.

Listing 2-5. CustomBugsController Class

```
<?php

class CustomBugsController extends SugarController
{
    public function post_save()
    {
        if ( ($bugFocus->status != $this->bean->status)
                && ($this->bean->status != 'Pending') ) {
            // do something now that the bug is pending
        }

        parent::post_save(); // call the parent class BugsController
    }
}
```

Now you've added an additional check into the post_save() method for bugs that are pending, so in this case you may e-mail it to a QA engineer for verification or a team lead to know that the engineer has fixed the issue.

If you have no additional controller logic to add, you can simply create a mapping from the action name to the view to be called in the action_view_map.php file. This file can be specified at the application level in the custom/include/MVC/Controller directory or in the module level at the root of the module directory or module custom directory. It is simply defined as an associative array with the key as the action name given and the value as the view file to call. Listing 2-6 shows an example of this code.

Listing 2-6. action_view_map.php File Example

```php
<?php

$action_view_map['myspecialview']= 'edit';
$action_view_map['myreallyspecialview']= 'edit';
```

Using the preceding action view mapping file for the Cases module will map to the Cases EditView.

SugarView

After the controller code is processed, and if a valid view is specified, the appropriate SugarView derived class is called. This class provides any view handling needed, such as setting up the display template. By default, the Sugar application ships with many views out of the box designed to handle certain types of views. Table 2-1 specifies those views.

Table 2-1. Some of the Default Views in Sugar

View File	View Name	Description
view.edit.php	ViewEdit	Handles displaying the EditView to the user using the metadata framework
view.detail.php	ViewDetail	Handles displaying the DetailView to the user using the metadata framework
view.list.php	ViewList	Handles displaying the ListView to the user using the metadata framework
view.ajax.php	ViewAjax	Used to return ajax data back to the user client
view.popup.php	ViewPopup	Handles displaying the popup record selector to the user using the metadata framework
view.classic.php	ViewClassic	Displays view created using the pre-MVC style view files
view.json.php	ViewJson	Returns json data directly to the user without any other markup
view.noaccess.php	ViewNoaccess	Called when the user doesn't have permission to access the given action
view.vcard.php	ViewVcard	Returns the given object's data as a vCard

You'll learn more about how the metadata framework works in Chapter 3.

Each of the previous views are also customizable as well by extending the view class and adding the functionality you need. Normally when overriding a view, there are two methods you'll want to change: the display() method is designed to handle the actual display logic of the view. It is by default an empty method, so you can customize the output to whatever you need it to be (calling a template, outputting straight html, or returning a json string). There is also the preDisplay() method, which is used for handling any non-display logic code, and also is often used in the base views previously listed. This allows the base views to define display logic in such a way so that if they are subclassed, the child class can just override the display method and not have to worry about making sure the display() method of the parent class is called as well.

You can also define your own views as well. This is a two-part process: part one involves adding either an action method in the respective controller that specifies the view to call, while part two is adding an entry in the action_view_map.php to direct the called action to the view to execute. Listing 2-7 shows an example action call in the controller (you'll call it the helloworld view).

Listing 2-7. *action_helloworld() Controller Method*

```php
public function action_helloworld()
{
    $this->view = 'helloworld';
}
```

The key here is to make sure the view property of the controller is set to the name of the view to call. From there, you can create your own view, which is defined in either the custom/include/MVC/View/views directory for the case of an application level view (available to all modules) in the module/modulename/views, or custom/module/modulename/views directory for those views only defined at the module level. Listing 2-8 is an example of creating your own view for the action helloworld.

Listing 2-8. *view.helloworld.php*

```php
<?php

class ViewHelloworld extends SugarView
{
    var $message = 'Hello World!';

    public function __construct()
    {
        parent::SugarView();
    }

    public function preDisplay()
    {
```

```php
        if ( isset($_REQUEST['message']) )
            $this->message = $_REQUEST['message'];
    }

    public function display()
    {
        echo "<p>{$this->message}</p>";
    }
}
```

If you would call the previous view, defined as a base view for the application, and specify the helloworld view with no arguments, you would have the message 'Hello World!' outputted to the display. If you specify the message to display in the request variables, it would override the default message in the preDisplay() method and be output to the user in the display() method.

You can also add view customizations to existing views in the custom directory. This is handy if you are looking to customize a module that defines many of its own views, but does so in an upgrade safe way that does require you to code and paste a bunch of code. Listing 2-9 shows how you can extend the following Calls EditView.

Listing 2-9. *Customize a Module Defined View*

```php
<?php
require_once('modules/Calls/views/view.edit.php');

class CustomCallsEditView extends CallsEditView
{
    public function __construct()
    {
        parent::CallsEditView();
    }

    public function display()
    {
        // code to add

        parent::display();
    }
}
```

Anytime you extend a class, be sure to call the parent method as well to ensure you are leveraging any logic it adds. Of course, that assumes the customization you are doing isn't re-writing the entire method.

Entrypoints

Sometimes certain actions in the application don't really apply to the normal module-action model. Many times this code doesn't require authentication to the application, such as tracking images that are inserted into HTML email. For these situations, the entire process flow of the normal MVC framework either won't work or isn't needed, which is why a different entrypoint in the application is often needed. However, there is still quite a bit of code that needs to be set up and several security related measures that need to be taken care of. Because of this, Sugar has always been particular to which files are granted the privilege of being able to be an initial file requested from the browser, or entrypoint, so that those cases are taken care of properly.

To help streamline the use of entrypoints, Sugar 5.1 added the ability to directly handle them though the MVC framework. This is done in two parts: the first part is an entrypoint registry, which is defined at include/MVC/Controller/entry_point_registry.php, and specifies the available entrypoints, where they exist in the filesystem, and if it requires authentication or not. Listing 2-10 shows part of the standard entry_point_registry.php file that ships with SugarCRM.

Listing 2-10. entry_point_registry.php

```php
$entry_point_registry = array(
    'download' => array('file' => 'download.php', 'auth' => true),
    'export' => array('file' => 'export.php', 'auth' => true),
    'image' => array('file' => 'modules/Campaigns/image.php', 'auth' => false),
    'acceptDecline' => array('file' => 'modules/Contacts/AcceptDecline.php',
 'auth' => false),
    'removeme' => array('file' => 'modules/Campaigns/RemoveMe.php', 'auth' => false),
    'process_queue' => array('file' => 'process_queue.php', 'auth' => true),
    'process_workflow' => array('file' => 'process_workflow.php', 'auth' => true),
```

The key of the $entry_point_registry registry array is the entrypoint name, which will be given as a part of the URL. The value is an array with two elements: the file element is the path to the entrypoint file to call, and the auth element indicates whether the entrypoint requires authentication or not. The registry can be overridden by developers as well simply by adding the same entry_point_registry.php in the custom/include/MVC/Controller/ directory.

Now that the entrypoint is defined, you can now access it from the browser. Pointing your browser to the following URL formatted will direct the request to the entrypoint: http://servername/index.php?entryPoint=entrypoint.

If you are converting an entrypoint that existed before Sugar 5.1 into the new module, be sure to change:

```
if(!defined('sugarEntry'))define('sugarEntry', true);
```

to:

```
if(!defined('sugarEntry') || !sugarEntry) die('Not A Valid Entry Point');
```

at the top of the previous entrypoint file.

Also, you can still maintain your entrypoints in the previous way by pointing the URL at the file directly. This is helpful if there is some technical reason why changing it would not work, such as if the application that uses the URL doesn't work nicely with URL parameters (the vcal.php entrypoint is one example of this, since Outlook doesn't like the parameters in the URL request for some reason). However, it is highly recommended that you change to the newer style entrypoints if at all possible, since it will greatly simplify your code by setting up most parts of the environment for you.

What About the Model?

The model layer is sometimes the forgotten part of the MVC paradigm. For SugarCRM, ea module represents one primary table. This in turn is represented by a bean class, derived from the main bean class called SugarBean (defined at data/SugarBean.php) which each bean derives from. The SugarBean provides an interface to the lower level database calls which control storing, retrieving, and deleting data from the database, as well as a tool for interpreting the structure of the table underneath it, defined in a vardefs.php file in each module.

The core concepts of the model layer in SugarCRM revolve around the bean classes, the vardefs, and the database layer. Let's start off by looking at the bean classes.

Bean Classes and SugarObjects

The bean class is the primary place that the model layer of the Sugar MVC framework interacts with the database or any other data stores. Its purpose is to provide all the methods you need in the controller to interact with the module. It comes with several methods by default, such as handle saving, deleting, and retrieving records, as well as helper methods for the standard views that ship with SugarCRM (Detail, Edit, and List views).

One thing most people notice as they build modules in SugarCRM is that often times they will share the same or similar fields with other modules. These modules may also be objects that represent the same kind of entity. For example, a Students and Teachers module would probably both have similar address and phone number fields. Because of this sort of situation, several module templates exist that you can base your module on. They are listed in Table 2-2, and are located in the include/SugarObjects/templates directory.

Table 2-2. SugarObject Template Names and Descriptions

Template Name	Description
Basic	A basic template with only fields for a name and description, plus those "behind the scenes" fields, like id, the deleted flag, and created/modified timestamps. This template is intended to be the base of all the following templates.
Company	Fields that would normally be used with a company, such as name, address, phone, web site, industry, etc.
File	Used when the object stores files that the user uploads.
Issue	For modeling an issue or job tracking system.
Person	Fields that represent a person, such as name, address, phone, email, etc.
Sale	Used when the object is for sales transactions or forecasting.

In addition, you can apply the assignable or team_security (for SugarCRM Professional and Enterprise only) fields to any of the previous modules to enable records to be assigned to a person or a team. These aren't full-fledged templates like those listed previously which contain bean files, starter metadata, and other specific code, but rather are just additional sets of fields that a module can use.

Let's see how simple it is to build a new module based upon one of these templates. If you want a module to track applicants for a company, the person template very closely models this example. The new bean definition would look something like Listing 2-11.

Listing 2-11. Applicants Bean Class

```php
<?php

require_once('include/SugarObjects/templates/person/Person.php');

class Applicants extends Person
{
    public function __construct()
    {
        parent::Person();
    }

    //
    // here we would add any other bean class methods we would need
    //
}
```

By simply extending the template class you now inherit the special actions and properties of it. There's one other part to making the module a true descendent of the templated class, which you'll see in the next section when you look at vardefs.

Vardefs

Vardefs define how the data fields should exist in the database, plus provide properties of each field on how Sugar should deal with it. It is defined as an associative array, and it contains several pieces. At the top level, you find information about the table as a whole, such as table name, whether the table provides auditing and global search capabilities, and a description of the table's purpose. This is defined at the top level of the associative array.

Fields

Field definitions are defined in the `'fields'` attribute of the array. Each field is a key in this array and has several properties, as shown in Table 2-3.

Table 2-3. Attributes in the Fields Array Key of the vardefs

Attribute	Default Setting	Description
name	--	The name of the field should be set to the same value as the key to this fielddef.
vname	--	The language pack id for the label of this field. This is used in the metadata layer to provide a display label for the field.
type	--	The type of the attribute: `'relate'` represents a field in a related bean. `'datetime'` is a date and time value. `'bool'` is a boolean value. `'enum'` is an enumeration field; the values are specified from the from the language pack. `'char'` is a character array. `'assigned_user_name'` is a linked user name. `'varchar'` is a variable sized string. `'link'` provides a relationship to another module.
table	--	The table this field comes from.
comment	--	A description of what the field should represent.
isnull	True	Set this to false if the field is not allowed to store null values.
len	--	Length of the field.
dbType	same as type attribute	The database type of the field; only specify if it needs to be different than the `'type'` attribute.
reportable	True	Set this to false if this field should not show up in the list of fields for the reporting module (only applies to modules that are used in the reporting module).
required	False	Set this to true if this field is a required field. In the EditView, the field will be indicated as required and must have a valid value in order to save.
Default	--	The default value for this field.
massupdate	True	Set this to false if you do not want this field to show up in the Mass Update section at the bottom of the List views.

Attribute	Default Setting	Description
Unified_search	false	Set to true if you want this field searched when doing a unified search on this module. Only applicable if the module vardef has the `'unified_search'` attribute set at the top level of vardef array.
rname	--	The field from the related module that contains the value for this field. (Used only when field type is relate.)
id_name	--	The field from the module that stores the id for the related module. (Used only when field type is relate.)
source	Db	Set this to `'non-db'` if the field value does not come from the database. This is designed to be used for the calculated field or if the value for the field can be retrieved in some other way.
sort_on	--	If this field represents concatenated values in the database, this will specify what database field you should sort by.
fields	--	If this field represents concatenated values in the database, this is an array containing the fields that are concatenated. For example: `'fields' => array('first_name','last_name')`.
db_concat_fields	--	If this field represents concatenated values in the database, this is an array containing the fields to concatenate in the DB. For example: `'db_concat_fields' => array('first_name','last_name')`.
importable	True	Set this to `'false'` (either the string `'false'` or the boolean false) if the field is not able to be imported into, or set to `'required'` if the field is required for importing into.
options	--	If the field is an enum type, this will be the key in the language pack that specifies the enumerated values to use.
relationship	--	For link type fields, this will be the name of the relationship definition used to build this link.

Listing 2-12 provides a sample of a few fields that would be defined in the fields section of the vardefs for the Applicants module you have begun to previously define.

Listing 2-12. Fields in the Applicants Module As Defined in the vardefs.php File

```php
<?php

$dictionary['Applicants']['fields']['first_name'] = array(
    'name' => 'first_name',
    'vname' => 'LBL_FIRST_NAME',
    'type' => 'varchar',
```

```
        'len' => '100',
        'comment' => 'First name of the applicant',
        );
$dictionary['Applicants']['fields']['last_name'] = array (
        'name' => 'last_name',
        'vname' => 'LBL_LAST_NAME',
        'type' => 'varchar',
        'len' => '100',
        'comment' => 'Last lname of the applicant',
        );
$dictionary['Applicants']['fields']['name'] = array (
        'name' => 'name',
        'rname' => 'name',
        'vname' => 'LBL_NAME',
        'type' => 'name',
        'fields' => array('first_name', 'last_name'),
        'sort_on' => 'last_name',
        'source' => 'non-db',
        'group'=>'last_name',
        'len' => '255',
        'db_concat_fields'=> array(0=>'first_name', 1=>'last_name'),
        'importable' => 'false',
        );

$dictionary['Applicants']['fields']['referral_source'] = array (
        'name' => 'referral_source',
        'vname' => 'LBL_REFERRAL_SOURCE',
        'type' => 'enum',
        'options' => 'referral_source_dom',
        'len' => '100',
        'audited' => true,
        'comment' => 'Referral source of the application ( Recruiter, Existing Employee,↵
  etc )',
        'merge_filter' => 'enabled',
        );

$dictionary['Applicants']['fields']['position_id'] = array(
        'name' => 'position_id',
        'vname' => 'LBL_POSITION_ID',
        'type' => 'id',
        'isnull' => 'true',
        'reportable' => false,
        'massupdate' => false,
        'duplicate_merge'=> 'disabled',
        'comment' => 'ID field of the position in the Positions module'

    );


$dictionary['Applicants']['fields']['position_name'] = array(
  'name' => 'position_name',
  'rname' => 'name',
  'id_name' => 'position_id',
```

```
'vname' => 'LBL_ACCOUNT_NAME',
'type' => 'relate',
'table' => 'positions',
'isnull' => 'true',
'module' => 'Positions',
'dbType' => 'varchar',
'len' => '255',
'source' => 'non-db',
'unified_search' => false,
'comment' => 'Name field of the position in the Positions module'

);
```

You have defined the first and last name fields in the table, and also have added a field for the name field which should be the concatenation of the first and last name fields. However, this field is only available in the bean and will not be stored in the database. You also defined an enum field for storing the referral source, which comes from a preset list that is in the `'referral_source_dom'` entry in the language pack. You then created a related field to the Positions module. The position_id field will be stored in this table and will be used to reference the position this applicant is related to. The position_name field value will come from the Positions module.

Indexes

Index definitions are in the `'indices'` key of the array, and represent all of the indexes in the table. Each of the array entries in this list does not have keys. Table 2-4 outlines the specification of the attributes for the index definitions.

Table 2-4. *Attributes in the Indices Array Key of the vardefs*

Attribute	Description
Name	Name of the index, as you want it to exist in the database.
Type	primary is the primary index for table, there should only be one of these.
	unique adds a constraint that only unique values are allowed for the fields this index uses.
	index is a standard index on table, useful for speeding up searches and sorting alternate_key, same as index.
	foreign is a key that links a field in one table to a field in another, adding a constraint to the values that can be used in the field. If the database or table does not support foreign keys then a regular index will be created instead.
	fulltext is a fulltext index, useful for doing full text searches on a table. If the database or table does not support fulltext indexes then the index will be skipped.
Fields	An array that specifies the field that makes up the index, in the order you want them indexed. For example: `'fields' => array('id','name','deleted'),`.
Db	Set to one of mysql, mssql, or oracle if you only want the index in that respective database. Defaults to setting the index in all databases.

Listing 2-13 is an example of some indexes for the aforementioned applicants module, as they would be defined in the vardefs files.

Listing 2-13. *Sample Indices in the vardefs.php File*

```php
<?php

$dictionary['Applicants']['indices'][] = array(
        'name' =>'applicantspk',
        'type' =>'primary',
        'fields'=>array('id')
    );

$dictionary['Applicants']['indices'][] = array(
        'name' =>'idx_applicants_name',
        'type' =>'index',
        'fields'=>array('last_name','first_name'))
    );
$dictionary['Applicants']['indices'][] = array(
        'name' =>'idx_applicants_name_unique',
        'type' =>'unique',
        'fields'=>array('last_name','first_name','position_id'))
    );
```

You defined three indices for the table. The first one is your primary index, which is on the id field, and is the main identifier for the record in the table. Next, you create an index on the applicant's name in last_name then first_name order. Finally, you add an unique index to the table which incorporates the applicant name plus the id of the position he is applying for, which will help you avoid having duplicate records in the database.

Relationships

Relationships are in the 'relationships' array key, and show the relationships from this module into other modules in the application. Each relationship listed in Table 2-5 should have a link field also in the 'fields' section of the vardefs to reference it.

Table 2-5. *Attributes in the Relationships Array Key of the vardefs*

Attribute	Description
lhs_module	The module on the left-hand side of the relationship.
lhs_table	The table on the left-hand side of the relationship.
lhs_key	The primary key column of the left-hand side of the relationship.
rhs_module	The module on the right-hand side of the relationship
rhs_table	The table on the right-hand side of the relationship.
rhs_key	The primary key column of the right-hand side of the relationship.
relationship_type	The type of relationship, which can be one of one-to-one, one-to-many, many-to-one, or many-to-many.
relationship_role_column	The type of relationship role.
relationship_role_column_value	Defines the unique identifier for the relationship role.
join_table	For many-to-many relationships, this specifies the name of the join table.
join_key_lhs	For many-to-many relationships, this is the key in the join table that joins to the lhs_key in the lhs_table table.
join_key_rhs	For many-to-many relationships, this is the key in the join table that joins to the rhs_key in the rhs_table.
relationship_role_column	One-to-many relationships set an additional field in the rhs_table to be used to match the record. This is most commonly used in flex relate fields, where one field is used to provide a relationship to several different modules. You'll learn more about flex relate field when you build your sample application in Chapter 11.
relationship_role_column_value	For one-to-many relationships, used in conjunction with the 'relationship_role_column' field. It sets what the value should be of that additional field in the rhs_table, which is used to match the record.

Let's build a few relationships for the Applicants module you have been working with in this section. Listing 2-14 shows how you would define them in the vardefs.

Listing 2-14. Sample Relationships Defined in the vardefs.php File

```php
<?php

$dictionary['Applicants']['relationships']['applicants_modified_user' ] = array (
    'lhs_module' => 'Users',
    'lhs_table' => 'users',
    'lhs_key' => 'id',
    'rhs_module' => 'Applicants',
    'rhs_table' => 'applicants',
    'rhs_key' => 'modified_user_id',
    'relationship_type' => 'one-to-many',
);

$dictionary['Applicants']['relationships']['applicants_notes'] = array (
    'lhs_module' => 'Applicants',
    'lhs_table' => 'applicants',
    'lhs_key' => 'id',
    'rhs_module' => 'Notes',
    'rhs_table' => 'notes',
    'rhs_key' => 'parent_id',
    'relationship_type' => 'one-to-many',
    'relationship_role_column' => 'parent_type',
    'relationship_role_column_value' => 'Applicants',
);
```

The first relationship is a standard one, setting the one-to-many relationship between the Users and Applicants table for the purpose of tracking the user who last modified the record. The second relationship allows you to assign notes to the applicants records. Since the Notes module uses a flex relate field so that you can specify more than one type of module to relate the note to, you specify the role column and value of 'Applicants' to help further qualify the relationship.

Database Layer

SugarCRM supports three different database management systems (DBMS) by default: MySQL, Microsoft SQL Server, and Oracle. Sugar provides an abstraction layer to each of the PHP interfaces to the individual databases. This enables database agnostic programming in each of the bean classes.

As of Sugar 5.5, the following database extensions listed in Table 2-6 are supported.

Table 2-6. *Supported Database Extensions*

Extension	Description	Notes
mysql	PHP mysql driver	Designed for MySQL 4.0 and earlier, but will work with any version of MySQL.
mysqli	PHP mysql improved driver	Designed for and works with MySQL 4.1+.
oci8	Oracle OCI8 driver	
mssql	PHP Microsoft SQL Server driver	Does not support full UTF-8 character set; deprecated.
dblib	FreeTDS driver	Can be downloaded at http://www.sugarforge.org/frs/?group_id=6.
sqlsrv	Microsoft SQL Server Driver for PHP	Added in Sugar 5.5; does not have complete UTF-8 support, but will in the future.

As stated earlier, the database layer is designed in such a way that it is very agnostic, so you should never need to make calls to the actual database later functions, but rather use the exposed class methods for doing all the work needed. In Listing 2-15 shows an example of making a query from the users table, iterating through the results, and making and updating the records if needed.

Listing 2-15. *Iterating Through the Users Table Using the Database Layer Methods*

```php
<?php

$db = DBManagerFactory::getInstance();

$res = $db->query("select * from users");

while ( $row = $db->fetchByAssoc($res) ) {
    // remove the admin privilege from any non-active users
    if ( $row['status'] != 'Active' ) {

        $db->query("update users set is_admin = 0 where id = '{$row['id']}'");

    }
}
```

The query method of the database object executes a query to the database, returning back a resource handle for the result. Then you can iterate through the result set, grabbing each row using the fetchByAssoc() method. One handy part of this method is that by default the html encodes any data coming back to the user, which can be disabled if this is not needed. This eliminates another headache by preventing cross site scripting (XSS) attacks when the content may include dangerous javascript code that is invisible to the user.

Sugar Before MVC

Sugar modules are often referred to in two categories, MVC and pre-MVC. The pre-MVC modules are part of Sugar 4.5.1 and earlier, and didn't use the very structured application structure for routing the request. While the request URL would look the same using index.php as the entrypoint and the request variables `'module'` and `'action'` to route the request, it would rely on a PHP file existing in the root of the module directory to point the request to. This made a lot of extra work for creating very common views, as I'll talk about in the Chapter 3.

One nice part about the transition from pre-MVC to MVC modules in Sugar is that the pre-MVC style is still supported in SugarCRM versions 5.0 and later. You can also mix and match styles within a module, with some actions using the pre-MVC style and others using the MVC style. This gives module developers some flexibility in the transition to the newer module design. However, it is recommended to not build new modules or enhance older ones using that pattern since it may be dropped in the future.

Summary

In this chapter, you learned about the MVC framework, both what traditional MVC design pattern is and how Sugar does MVC with the application. You took an in-depth look at the request flow of the application through a request, and saw how easy it is to customize this to meet your needs. You also took a look at what Sugar offers out of the box in terms of actions, so that you can reuse these in your modules easily. You finished up by taking a look at entrypoints in the application and how you can use those with the MVC framework as well.

The MVC framework is one very major aspect of the overall SugarCRM platform. In Chapter 3, you'll look at the metadata framework, which aims to simplify the building of common views in the applications, such as the Edit, Detail, and List views, removing the need for us to build and maintain them manually.

CHAPTER 3

■ ■ ■

Metadata Layer

Often times, the core of what a module does follows the Create, Retrieve, Update, and Delete (CRUD) pattern. These modules also use the same basic forms for each of these actions. Frequently, developers copy and paste the exact same basic code to handle each time they create a new view, just changing the names input types of the actual fields shown. This can be very cumbersome and tedious, and updates to certain field types (such as a calendar widget) would have to be made across the codebase, which can be quite an undertaking.

Up until Sugar 5.0, this is what the developer had to deal with when building the most common views in use: the EditView, DetailView, and ListView. With the advent of Sugar 5.0, this model was changed so the layout of these common views can be defined in a metadata file, so that it is easier to build and maintain these forms. I'll talk about the metadata layer in regard to the various ways it is used. This model also hooks in directly with the visual development tools of Studio and Module Builder, which I will talk more about in Chapters 6 and 9.

Let's start with the prime example where metadata is used to define the DetailView and EditView.

DetailView and EditView

The main data entry form for SugarCRM is known as the EditView. This form serves the purpose of both creating new records and updating existing records. Upon a successful save, it redirects to the DetailView, which is a read-only view at the record. Both of these forms work in conjunction with one another to provide the primary way to interact with a record for a module. Both the Detail and Edit views within the Sugar MVC model are predefined to use metadata to build the forms that display to the user. They do this by using the EditView class (defined at include/EditView/EditView2.php) for the EditView, and then extends that class into the subclass DetailView (defined at include/DetailView/DetailView2.php) for building the DetailView. Each of these classes work the same way.

The first step is to set up the view by loading the metadata file. It is structured as an associative array that is part of the global $viewdefs array. The schema has two parts: the templateMeta section lays out some general parts to the form, as shown in Table 3-1. The other part is the form section, which is in the next section.

Table 3-1. The templateMeta Section of the Edit and Detail viewdefs

Parent Attribute	Attribute	Default	Description
preRow		none	HTML code to insert before the form element.
form	buttons	`array('SAVE','CANCEL')` for the EditView `array('EDIT','DUPLICATE', 'DELETE')` for the DetailView	An array of buttons that appear at the top of the form. The following buttons are predefined and available by specifying the string as the array value: `'SAVE'`: Save button (EditView only). `'CANCEL'`: Cancel button (EditView only). `'DELETE'`: Delete current record button. `'DUPLICATE'`: Duplicate the current record (DetailView only). `'EDIT'`: Go to the Editview for the current record (DetailView only). `'CONNECTOR'`: Button to enter the wizard for merging in data from a connector. If you want to use custom code to define your button, you can do so in an array and specify the `'customCode'` attribute to specify your button's code. Example: `array(    'customCode' => '<input type=.....',)`.
form	hidden	`array()`	Array of html hidden input elements to put in the form.
form	hideAudit	false	True if you want to hide the audit button.
form	headerTpl	null	Set to the path of the header template file you want to use in place of the default.
form	footerTpl	null	Set to the path of the footer template file you want to use in place of the default.
form	links	`array()`	Array of links to put at the top of the form.
maxColumns		2	Number of columns of fields for the form.

Parent Attribute	Attribute	Default	Description
widths		Auto-calculated based upon the number of columns in the forms.	Defined as an array, one element for each column, and a `'field'` key for the width of the field and a `'label'` key for the width of the label. Example: `array(  '0' =>` `array('label'=>'10','field'=>'30'),` `'1' =>` `array('label'=>'10','field'=>'30'), ).`

The next part of the viewdefs contain the field definitions. These are also defined in associative arrays, but are grouped by sections and then by rows. Grouping by sections allows you to make a multi-section form, grouping together fields that are in common. Furthermore, grouping by rows gives users the ability to dictate the exact placement of the elements on the form. If you've defined your form to be two columns wide and have two sections, the `'panels'` section of the vardefs for the Accounts detailview would look something like Listing 3-1.

Listing 3-1. Fields Section of viewdefs for Two Column Form

```php
<?php
$viewdefs['Accounts']['DetailView']['panels'] = array(

    'default' => array(
        array(
            'name',
            'phone_office'
        ),
array(
            'parent_name',
            'account_type'
        ),
    ),
    'lbl_account_information' =>  array(
        array(
            'ownership',
            'rating'
        ),
        array(
            'industry',
            'sic_code'
        ),
        array(
            'employees',
            'annual_revenue'
        ),
```

```
    ),
);
```

The preceding would have two sections to the form, one would be the `'default'` section while the second would use the string `'lbl_account_information'` from the module language strings. The layout would be two columns wide, with the main information in the top of the form and the rest in the second section of the form. When rendered, it would look similar to Figure 3-1.

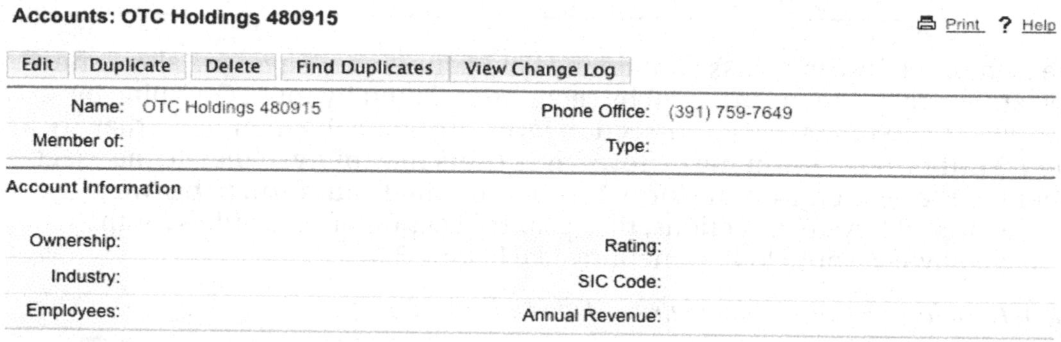

Accounts: OTC Holdings 480915   🖶 Print ❓ Help

| Edit | Duplicate | Delete | Find Duplicates | View Change Log |

| Name: OTC Holdings 480915 | Phone Office: (391) 759-7649 |
| Member of: | Type: |

Account Information

Ownership:	Rating:
Industry:	SIC Code:
Employees:	Annual Revenue:

Figure 3-1. *Accounts Detail View as customized by viewdefs in Listing 3-1*

Now that you see how easy it is to build a form layout for a module, let's look at how the internals of the DetailView and EditView rendering work.

How the DetailView and EditView Classes Work

The control of the layout of these forms is driven by the DetailView2.php and EditView2.php files which contain the DetailView and EditView classes. (Note that there are also DetailView and EditView classes in the DetailView.php and EditView.php classes as well, but these are used for the pre-5.0 DetailView and EditView templates.) It does the job of parsing the viewdefs, building the templates files, and populating the fields in several steps. Figure 3-2 is a diagram showing how the basic flow works.

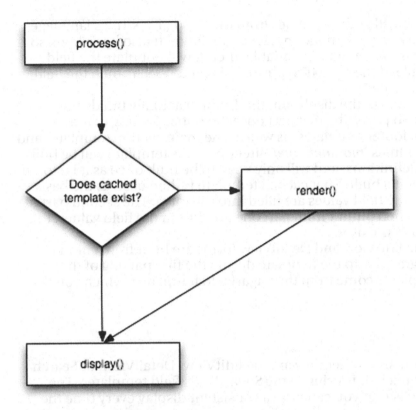

Figure 3-2. EditView/DetailView class flow

The first part of the work occurs in the render() method, which is called at the beginning of the process() method. This method will do the actual processing of the viewdef file, which it will begin by going through and laying out all the panels and fields as they have been defined. It will also calculate the column widths so that the form layout will be consistent across the form. This only occurs once, however, when the form is ready to be displayed. The main rendering is stored in the cache/modules/*modulename*/ directory when the form is processed by Smarty (http://www.smarty.net), which is an html template tool.

Next let's look at the process() method, where the request variables and the module's vardefs are processed. The first part handles the request variables, setting certain ones such as 'return_module', 'return_action', and 'return_id' to class variables which will be later set as hidden form values in the template. The next part iterates through the fields, formatting it for the display as each field type requires. Date and time fields are formatted and converted to be in the correct date and time format and in the correct time zone. For enum and multienum fields, the process() method will go through and populate the options that are part of the select dropdown that displays on the form; it will grab the values from the $app_list_strings language pack array based upon the key given in the 'options' attribute. It also has a hook so that if the field name is passed as a request variable, then it will populate the field with that value. For example, if the $_REQUEST['name'] is set to 'John' then the field in the form will be set to that value.

Finally, the last part occurs in the display method, which actually builds the template. This is done in two parts: the first part does the initial parsing of the templates (the header and footer templates, as well as the main section template) and outputs it to the cache/modules/*modulename*/ directory. This template will be built according to the viewdef definitions, and will only need to be built once as it is stored in the cache directory after it's built. That cached template is then used as the basis for the second part, where the field values are filled into the form. The second part of the build then takes the cached output from part one and fills in the field values; this template will be displayed to the user.

Each of the fields in the EditView and DetailView forms are built from common templates, which are integrated into the template during the first parsing of the template. These field templates come from the SugarField templates, which you'll look at next.

SugarFields

Each field shown in the forms, whether they are the EditView, DetailView, or Search Form is built for the type of field it is using in the SugarFields field templates. The nice part about this system is that you can have a consistent display every time the field type is displayed.

The SugarFields are located in the include/SugarFields/Fields/ directory. Each field is based off of the Base field definition, which has default templates for each of the EditView, DetailView, and SearchForms widgets, as well as class named SugarFieldBase. The hooks display the correct template depending upon the view that is requesting it. Other fields are based upon this definition, but only need to specify what's different from the base template or the template that the field is derived from. For example, the 'Phone' field type only specifies an override for the DetailView template, if the Skype integration is enabled so the display will be a link instead of just text. Listing 3-2 shows the code.

Listing 3-2. Phone SugarField DetailView Template

```
{if !empty({{sugarvar key='value' string=true}})}
{assign var="phone_value" value={{sugarvar key='value' string=true}} }
{sugar_phone value=$phone_value }
{/if}
{{if !empty($displayParams.enableConnectors)}}
{{sugarvar_connector view='DetailView'}}
{{/if}}
```

In the same way, you can also modify the display of any of the built-in field types, by simply dropping a copy of the corresponding file inside the custom/include/SugarFields/Fields/*fieldname*/ directory. For example, if you would want to change the way the 'Link' field displays on the DetailView, you would simply add the code in Listing 3-3 to the file custom/include/SugarFields/Fields/Link/DetailView.tpl.

Listing 3-3. DetailView Template Override for the 'Link' Field Type

```
{if !empty($vardef.value)}
<a href='{$vardef.value}' target="_blank">{$vardef.value}</a>
{/if}
```

The previous code would always have links opened in a new window, regardless of any settings that may be in the vardefs.

In the same way, you can also define custom field types. Let's say instead of changing the default link template code, you want to define a different type of link field that always defaults to opening the link in a new page. To do this, you could simply create a new directory in the custom/include/ SugarFields/Fields/ directory called Newpagelink, and copy the DetailView.tpl template shown in Listing 3-3 to that directory.

Relate, one type of SugarField, is used when specifying a record to relate the current record to. Part of this field is a 'Select' button, which displays a popup window to select the record to relate to. The Popup form you see is also very definable through metadata, as you'll see in the next section.

ListViews

The default view for most modules is the ListView, which provides a listing of records currently in the module. It also has both a basic search for quickly locating records, as well as a more in-depth search form for building more detailed queries, which gives an option to save the search terms for later use. Using the ListView form it is also possible to do mass updates of records with ease (see Listing 3-4).

Listing 3-4. Listviewdefs.php for the Calls Module

```
$listViewDefs['Calls'] = array(
    'SET_COMPLETE' => array(
        'width' => '1',
        'label' => 'LBL_LIST_CLOSE',
        'link' => true,
        'sortable' => false,
        'default' => true,
        'related_fields' => array('status')),
    'DIRECTION' => array(
        'width' => '10',
        'label' => 'LBL_LIST_DIRECTION',
```

```
                'link' => false,
                'default' => true),
          'NAME' => array(
                'width' => '40',
                'label' => 'LBL_LIST_SUBJECT',
                'link' => true,
                'default' => true),
          'CONTACT_NAME' => array(
                'width' => '20',
                'label' => 'LBL_LIST_CONTACT',
                'link' => true,
                'id' => 'CONTACT_ID',
                'module' => 'Contacts',
                'default' => true,
                'ACLTag' => 'CONTACT'),
          'PARENT_NAME' => array(
                'width'          => '20',
                'label'          => 'LBL_LIST_RELATED_TO',
                'dynamic_module' => 'PARENT_TYPE',
                'id' => 'PARENT_ID',
                'link' => true,
                'default' => true,
                'sortable' => false,
                'ACLTag' => 'PARENT',
                'related_fields' => array('parent_id', 'parent_type')),
          'DATE_START' => array(
                'width' => '15',
                'label' => 'LBL_LIST_DATE',
                'link' => false,
                'default' => true,
                'related_fields' => array('time_start'),
                ),
          'ASSIGNED_USER_NAME' => array(
                'width' => '2',
                'label' => 'LBL_LIST_ASSIGNED_TO_NAME',
                'default' => true),
          'STATUS' => array(
                'width' => '10',
                'label' => 'LBL_STATUS',
                'link' => false,
                'default' => false),
);
```

Table 3-2 outlines the many things you can customize.

Table 3-2. Listviewdef Attribute Options

Attribute	Description
width	Width of the field.
label	Language pack label to use for the column header.
link	True if this field will be a link; defaults to false.
default	True, if this field is in the default ListView. False, if it's not in the default ListView, but can be added later.
sortable	False if this column is not sortable, defaults to true.
related_fields	Array of fields that are used in conjunction with the given field to display it. A common use is for relate fields to list the other fields needed to help grab the field values.
Id	For relate fields, this is the id in the current module that provides a link to the other module.
dynamic_module	For flex relate fields, this is the field containing the module name you are relating to.
module	For relate fields, this is the name of the module to relate to.
ACLTag	This is the module used to verify if the user has access to the related module according to the ACL.

Sortable and default attributes are used most often. Having the sortable attribute set to false can be very handy for fields that are calculated, since often these field are impossible to sort correctly using SQL statements in the Listview. The default attribute allows you to set up a list of 'default' and 'available' fields, so that the user is presented by default with the most sensible list of fields to have, yet has the ability to tweak the layout as needed. The user can tweak the fields he or she wishes to show or hide using a special section inside the Advanced Search search panel (Figure 3-3).

Figure 3-3. *Customizing the ListView*

The first two columns control the display and hidden columns for the ListView. You can also set the default sort order and direction in the `'Order by column'` and `'Direction'` fields. Once you have the search set where you want it, you can then save it here as well.

Speaking of the search form, this is also a part of the ListView that can be easily customized. Let's see how it works.

Defining Search Fields

One major component of the ListViews is the search boxes at the top of the list. The search forms allow you to filter down records in the ListView below it, as well as save these parameters for later use.

SugarCRM's search implementation has two sets of search boxes: a basic search with a small number of common used fields and an advanced search that provides more exhaustive search options. There's no restriction on the usage of these sets of search fields, but the intention is to have the default set of search fields consist of only those that are most commonly used, such as searching by name. The advanced search view is designed to provide a more exhaustive search, with options for searching by most of the fields existing in the table. The advanced search page will also contain a widget for changing the fields displayed in the ListView form, as well as saving the current search so that it can be accessed later. However, it is recommended to add database indexes for any fields you plan to search on, which you learned how to do back in Chapter 2.

The searchdefs.php metadata file looks very similar to the editviewdefs.php and detailviewdefs.php file, as you can see in Listing 3-5, which shows the searchdefs.php file for the Accounts module.

Listing 3-5. *Searchdefs.php Metadata File for the Accounts Module*

```
$searchdefs['Accounts'] = array(
    'templateMeta' => array(
        'maxColumns' => '3',
        'widths' => array(
            'label' => '10',
            'field' => '30'
```

```
                ),
            ),
    'layout' => array(
        'basic_search' => array(
            'name',
            'billing_address_city',
            'phone_office',
            array('name' => 'address_street', 'label' =>'LBL_BILLING_ADDRESS', 'type' =>↵
'name' , 'group'=>'billing_address_street'),
            array('name'=>'current_user_only', 'label'=>'LBL_CURRENT_USER_FILTER',↵
'type'=>'bool'),
            ),
        'advanced_search' => array(
            'name',
            array('name' => 'address_street', 'label' =>'LBL_ANY_ADDRESS', 'type' =>↵
'name'),
            array('name' => 'phone', 'label' =>'LBL_ANY_PHONE', 'type' => 'name'),
            'website',
            array('name' => 'address_city', 'label' =>'LBL_CITY', 'type' => 'name'),
            array('name' => 'email', 'label' =>'LBL_ANY_EMAIL', 'type' => 'name'),
            'annual_revenue',
            array('name' => 'address_state', 'label' =>'LBL_STATE', 'type' => 'name'),
            'employees',
            array('name' => 'address_postalcode', 'label' =>'LBL_POSTAL_CODE', 'type' =>↵
'name'),
            array('name' => 'billing_address_country', 'label' =>'LBL_COUNTRY', 'type' =>↵
'name', 'options' => 'countries_dom', ),
            'ticker_symbol',
            'sic_code',
            'rating',
            'ownership',
            array('name' => 'assigned_user_id', 'type' => 'enum', 'label' =>↵
'LBL_ASSIGNED_TO', 'function' => array('name' => 'get_user_array', 'params' =>↵
array(false))),
            'account_type',
            'industry',
            ),
        ),
    );
```

Just like the editviewdefs and detailviewdefs, you can just specify the name of the
vardef field to use, or specify it as an array if you need to make changes to the default
implementation of the field in that view. The array options are the same as the
detailviewdefs and editviewdefs. The big difference with the searchdefs.php
metadata file is that there is a 'layout' attribute instead of the 'panels' attribute,
which has two options of 'basic_search' and 'advanced_search' for specifying the
fields on those search forms.

Field Overlays"

Sometimes you would like to deliver a bit more information to the user about a record, but do not want them going to DetailView to get to it. Fortunately, the ListViews allow you to define text that would appear in a popup when the user hovers over a field in the ListView, which can pull its contents from the current record's field values.

This metadata file works differently than the other ones. You will specify a function to call, whose name is in the format of `additionalDetailsobjectname` which will return back an array. The array attributes, shown in Table 3-3, will provide the definition of the field overlays.

Table 3-3. additionalDetails Function Return Array Attributes

Attribute	Description
String	The text to show in the field overlay.
width	Optional, the width of the field overlay popup. Defaults to 300px.
editLink	Optional, the link to go to when clicking on the 'edit' button in the field overlay title.
viewLink	Optional, the link to go to when clicking on the 'view' button in the field overlay title.
fieldToAddTo	Name of the field in the EditView to add the field overlay to.

On the ListView page, you'll see a dropdown arrow icon, which indicates the additional details overlay available.

The reason this metadata file works differently than the others is that often the `string` attribute is a calculated value. The function is passed an array of the values of the various fields in the module for that record, so in turn you can build the text to show in the popup. Listing 3-6 shows an example of this function, in this case the one used to build the field overlay for the Bugs module.

Listing 3-6. additionalDetails.php Metadata File for the Bugs Module

```php
function additionalDetailsBug($fields)
{
    static $mod_strings;
    global $app_strings;
    if(empty($mod_strings)) {
        global $current_language;
        $mod_strings = return_module_language($current_language, 'Bugs');
    }

    $overlib_string = '';

    if(!empty($fields['DATE_ENTERED']))
        $overlib_string .= '<b>'. $app_strings['LBL_DATE_ENTERED'] . '</b> ' . ↵
$fields['DATE_ENTERED'] . '<br>';
    if(!empty($fields['SOURCE']))
        $overlib_string .= '<b>'. $mod_strings['LBL_SOURCE'] . '</b> '↵
. $fields['SOURCE'] . '<br>';
    if(!empty($fields['PRODUCT_CATEGORY']))
        $overlib_string .= '<b>'. $mod_strings['LBL_PRODUCT_CATEGORY'] . '</b>↵
' . $fields['PRODUCT_CATEGORY'] . '<br>';
    if(!empty($fields['RESOLUTION']))
        $overlib_string .= '<b>'. $mod_strings['LBL_RESOLUTION'] . '</b>↵
' . $fields['RESOLUTION'] . '<br>';
    if(!empty($fields['DESCRIPTION'])) {
        $overlib_string .= '<b>'. $mod_strings['LBL_DESCRIPTION'] . '</b>↵
' . substr($fields['DESCRIPTION'], 0, 300);
        if(strlen($fields['DESCRIPTION']) > 300)
                $overlib_string .= '...';
        $overlib_string .= '<br>';
    }
    if(!empty($fields['WORK_LOG'])) {
        $overlib_string .= '<b>'. $mod_strings['LBL_WORK_LOG'] . '</b>↵
' . substr($fields['WORK_LOG'], 0, 300);
        if(strlen($fields['WORK_LOG']) > 300)
                $overlib_string .= '...';

    }

    return array('fieldToAddTo' => 'NAME',
        'string' => $overlib_string,
        'editLink' => ↵
"index.php?action=EditView&module=Bugs&return_module=Bugs&record={$fields['ID']}",
        'viewLink' => ↵
"index.php?action=DetailView&module=Bugs&return_module=Bugs&record={$fields['ID']}"
    );
}
```

Figure 3-4 shows the final product of the additionalDetails.php file in the Bugs module Listview. It is activated by clicking the down arrow icon at beginning of the row.

Figure 3-4. *Additional Details field overlay*

Subpanels

As you learned in Chapter 2, modules can be related to other modules in many kinds of ways. One-to-one relationships are typically expressed using a related id field in each module, providing one record to another. One-to-Many relationships for the child module are usually expressed the same way, providing an id field for holding the id of the parent module's record in the child module's record. Working with these kinds of relationships will often use the 'relate' or 'parent' field type in the DetailView, which I showed earlier in this chapter when I talked about the various field types.

However, when expressing a many-to-many relationship, or the showing related child records in a parent module's record in a one-to-many relationship, you need to use a different paradigm that can show all the related records to the current record. For this, you will recycle the ListView used before, but this time make it part of the DetailView form. This allows working with the ListView to be more interactive. Figure 3-5 shows the various relationship types available.

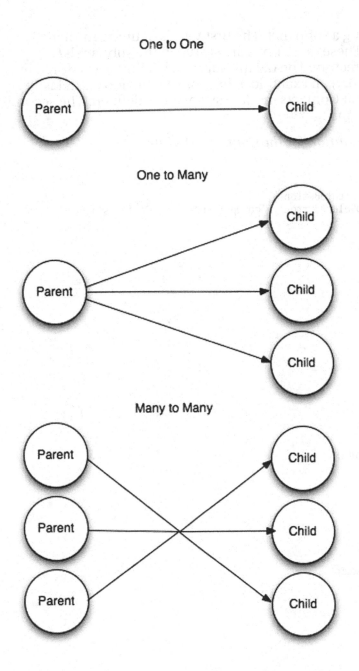

Figure 3-5. Diagram illustrating the different relationship types available

There are two parts to building a subpanel. The first part is defining the actual structure of the subpanel itself. These definitions are stored in the subpanels/ directory inside the metadata directory. The default subpanel definition is stored in the default.php file in that directory; an example of how one would look is in Listing 3-7, where you see how the default Contacts module subpanel is defined. The second part is discussed in the next section.

Listing 3-7. Default Subpanel Definition for the Contacts Module

```
$subpanel_layout = array(
'top_buttons' => array(
array('widget_class' => 'SubPanelTopCreateButton'),
array('widget_class' => 'SubPanelTopSelectButton', 'popup_module' => 'Contacts'),
),

'where' => '',

'list_fields' => array(
'first_name'=>array(
'name'=>'first_name',
'usage' => 'query_only',
),
'last_name'=>array(
'name'=>'last_name',
'usage' => 'query_only',
),
'name'=>array(
'name'=>'name',
'vname' => 'LBL_LIST_NAME',
            'sort_by' => 'last_name',
            'sort_order' => 'asc',
'widget_class' => 'SubPanelDetailViewLink',
'module' => 'Contacts',
'width' => '23%',
),
'account_name'=>array(
'name'=>'account_name',
'module' => 'Accounts',
'target_record_key' => 'account_id',
'target_module' => 'Accounts',
'widget_class' => 'SubPanelDetailViewLink',
'vname' => 'LBL_LIST_ACCOUNT_NAME',
'width' => '22%',
'sortable'=>false,
),
'account_id'=>array(
'usage'=>'query_only',
),
'email1'=>array(
'name'=>'email1',
'vname' => 'LBL_LIST_EMAIL',
'widget_class' => 'SubPanelEmailLink',
```

```
'width' => '30%',
'sortable'=>false,
),
'phone_work'=>array (
'name'=>'phone_work',
'vname' => 'LBL_LIST_PHONE',
'width' => '15%',
),
'edit_button'=>array(
'vname' => 'LBL_EDIT_BUTTON',
'widget_class' => 'SubPanelEditButton',
'module' => 'Contacts',
'width' => '5%',
),
'remove_button'=>array(
'vname' => 'LBL_REMOVE',
'widget_class' => 'SubPanelRemoveButton',
'module' => 'Contacts',
'width' => '5%',
),
),
);
```

There are three distinct parts to the subpanel definition:

- 'top_buttons' *attribute*: An array defining the buttons to appear at the top of the subpanel grid. These come from the templates in the include/generic/SugarWidgets/ directory, as specified by the 'widget_class' attribute.

- 'where' attribute: A string that allows the subpanel to pass an additional condition to the WHERE clause of the underlying SQL query that will build the subpanel.

- 'list_fields' *attribute*: An associative array of the fields to show in the subpanel. It follows a similar pattern to the detailviewdefs.php and editviewdefs.php.

There are a few interesting things to note in the subpanel definition. First off, each field that is not just displaying text must indicate which SugarWidget it is using to render the field. The most common SugarWidget used is the 'SubPanelDetailViewLink', which is used to provide a link to the given record or to a related record. In the case of a related record, the 'target_module' field is used to specify the related field's module, and the 'target_record_key' field is used to provide the id record in the current module that relates to the other module. One thing you may have noticed is that this field is also in the subpanel definition, even though it is not shown. It is used in the building of the query that populates the subpanel fields, so give the option 'usage' and set it to 'query_only' to be sure that you don't show it in the table. The edit and remove buttons also have their own widgets.

Once you have the subpanel definition built, you can now add a reference to it in the subpaneldefs.php file, which is located in the module's metadata/ folder. This is an associative array, that is keyed off the $layout_defs global variable. For each subpanel you wish to have, you'll add an entry to it in the subpaneldefs.php file. Listing 3-8 shows an example of an entry in this file. In this case, it is for the Quotes subpanel in the Contacts module.

Listing 3-8. *Quotes Subpanel As Defined in the Contacts Module subpaneldefs.php File*

```
$layout_defs['Contacts']['subpanel_setup']['quotes'] => array(
    'order' => 50,
    'module' => 'Quotes',
    'sort_order' => 'desc',
    'sort_by' => 'date_quote_expected_closed',
    'subpanel_name' => 'default',
    'get_subpanel_data' => 'quotes',
    'add_subpanel_data' => 'quote_id',
    'title_key' => 'LBL_QUOTES_SUBPANEL_TITLE',
    'get_distinct_data' => true,
    'top_buttons' => array(array('widget_class' => 'SubPanelTopCreateButton'))
);
```

The preceding subpanel definition is rather straightforward. You indicate the link field (quotes) and module you are relating to (Quotes). You also specify a default sort field and order in to use when displaying the subpanel. Of course, this can be changed by the user just as he or she can change the sort order of a ListView by clicking the column header. You also have an opportunity to change the buttons which will be displayed at the top of the form, in case you want to change from the 'top_buttons' attribute as in the subpanel definition.

Sometimes, the module subpanel may want to be displayed differently depending upon the situation in which it is used. For this, you can define an additional subpanel definition file with a different name in the same subpanels/ directory, and then from the subpaneldefs.php file, you can reference this by name. Listing 3-9 is an example of the Contracts subpanel in the Documents module.

Listing 3-9. *Contracts Subpanel As Defined in the Documents Module subpaneldefs.php File*

```
$layout_defs['Contacts']['subpanel_setup']['contracts'] => array(
    'order' => 20,
    'sort_order' => 'desc',
    'sort_by' => 'name',
    'module' => 'Contracts',
    'subpanel_name' => 'ForDocuments',
    'get_subpanel_data' => 'contracts',
    'add_subpanel_data' => 'contract_id',
    'title_key' => 'LBL_CONTRACTS_SUBPANEL_TITLE',
    'top_buttons' => array(),
);
```

You specify the subpanel definition file to use by giving its file name in the 'subpanel_name' attribute.

Pulling it all together, you have a complete subpanel built. Figure 3-6 shows an example of the Contacts subpanel in the Accounts module.

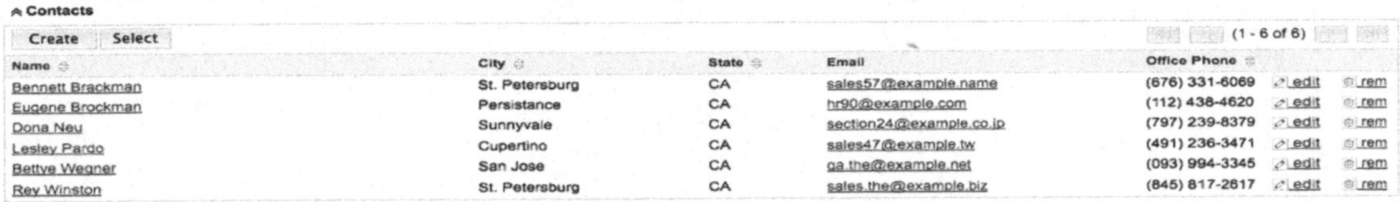

Figure 3-6. Contacts subpanel in the Accounts module

Summary

In this chapter, you explored the major parts of the metadata framework. You began by looking at the editviewdefs.php and detailviewdefs.php files, and saw how those build the main forms used in the module. You then looked at ListViews, saw how they are built, as well as looked at the additional components of them, such as the Search boxes and the additional details field overlays. You finally looked at the subpanels, showing how to construct them in the module, as well as add them to the desired related module's DetailView form.

You have looked at the two major components in the platform, the MVC and metadata framework. Let's now move on to learning how SugarCRM can interact with other applications using its rich Web Services framework.

CHAPTER 4

▪ ▪ ▪

Web Services

One of the biggest questions about any application built in the last few years revolves around Web Services. Does the application support it? How can an application interact with it? What methods are supported? Web Services are one of the most popular ways to not only have your application interact with other applications, but they also serve as tools for the outside world to interact with you.

What Are Web Services?

A Web service is defined by the W3C as "a software system designed to support interoperable machine-to-machine interaction over a network." You usually use Web Services in terms of an API that can be accessed over a network. In the old days, this incorporated technologies such as Object Management Group's (OMG) Common Object Request Broker Architecture (CORBA), Microsoft's Distributed Component Object Model (DCOM), or SUN's Java/Remote Method Invocation (RMI). As the web has grown in the last few years, newer protocols have grown to take the place of these outdated technologies.

With this growth of Web Services, a few different standards have emerged. One standard is the Simple Object Access Protocol (SOAP) standard, which allows calls towed services just like they were local objects and libraries. It's a very popular Web Service protocol since it is very easy to integrate at the code level, and because most languages have SOAP support which treats the SOAP calls just like they are normal local function calls. It's a highly structured standard, however, using XML as a messaging format that is quite verbose. It's often considered very heavyweight for many tasks, since the actual response is a small portion of the returned payload.

Another major standard is Representational State Transfer (REST), which is a much leaner Web Services format. It's actually considered more of software architecture, but is most commonly used in the Web Services context when using the HTTP verbs of GET, POST, and DELETE to interact with another application. It's a very loosely defined standard. There's no explicit requirement to use any sort of messaging format or structure for the data being transferred. The formats are more often determined by the application requirements. Formats such as HTML and JSON are often used when interacting with other common web applications since it's easy to consume, while XML is many times used when specifying an external API.

SugarCRM is built in mind with being "open," both in terms of allowing other applications to access SugarCRM data and also allowing SugarCRM to consume data from other applications. To do this, SugarCRM has provided a SOAP API for quite some time, and in Sugar 5.5 has enhanced that API and also added a REST API to the mix. In addition, Sugar 5.2 added a Connectors framework, which opens SugarCRM to the infinite amount of consumable data existing on the web. Let's take a look at how this framework works, and how you can add new Web Services to be able to be consumed by SugarCRM.

Connectors

The Cloud Connector framework is designed to provide an abstract layer around a connector, so essentially your own databases would just be considered another connector alongside any SOAP or REST connector. By abstracting out the connector layer they can then be swapped in and out seamlessly. These connectors can then be loaded by a factory and returned and called based on their interface methods. In the Community Edition, the framework will allow the placement of "hover" icons on fields in a record's DetailView. These "hover" icons may link to external Web Services or widgets to retrieve additional information. It also includes support for LinkedIn's Company Insider widget in the Community Edition release. In the Professional Edition and Enterprise Edition, the system will also contain additional connectors (both contain connectors for Hoovers and Jigsaw) and have the ability to merge the data into existing records.

The main components for the connector framework are the factories, source, and formatter classes. The factories implement the Factory pattern, returning the appropriate source or formatter instance for a connector. The sources are responsible for encapsulating the retrieval of the data as a single record, or a list of records, of the connectors. The formatters are responsible for rendering the display elements of the connectors.

Let's see how a connector is built.

Building the Connector Source

The sources are the centerpiece of the connector framework" . The class name of the source should be prefixed with either "ext_soap_" or "ext_rest_" because the "_" character serves as a delimiter into the file system for the class to be found. For example, a SOAP implementation for a source we call "Test" will have the class name "ext_soap_test" and a REST implementation will have the class name "ext_rest_test". There are two categories of sources, one for REST and one for SOAP, which the connector class must extend from.

The connector class has two methods it must implement: getItem() and getList(). The methods work just as you would expect; getList() will return a list of records for the given arguments passed to it, while getItem() returns a single record passed upon the same argument criteria. The important thing for your connector is to be able to identify a unique identifier for each record provided by the service. This may be an actual unique id like a GUID, an email address, or specially formatted record. What's important is that each record can be uniquely indentified. This is important for the getList() method since the returned array is multidimensional, and expects each record array key to be that unique identifier. It's also important for the getItem() method, since this method will often be called when you know the exact record you want, and will specify it by id. Listing 4-1 shows an example of how your connector might look for simple rest-based service that returns json data.

Listing 4-1. Sample Connector Source Definition

```php
require_once('include/connectors/sources/ext/rest/rest.php');

class ext_rest_sample extends ext_rest
{
    protected $service_url = 'http://example.com/rest/';

    public function getItem($args=array(), $module=null)
    {
        $curl = curl_init($this->service_url.'item/');
        curl_setopt($curl, CURLOPT_RETURNTRANSFER, true);
        curl_setopt($curl, CURLOPT_POST, true);
        curl_setopt($curl, CURLOPT_POSTFIELDS, $args);
        $curl_response = curl_exec($curl);
        curl_close($curl);

        return json_decode($curl_response);
    }

    public function getList($args=array(), $module=null)
    {
        $curl = curl_init($this->service_url.'list/');
        curl_setopt($curl, CURLOPT_RETURNTRANSFER, true);
        curl_setopt($curl, CURLOPT_POST, true);
        curl_setopt($curl, CURLOPT_POSTFIELDS, $args);
        $curl_response = curl_exec($curl);
        curl_close($curl);

        $ids = json_decode($curl_response);
        $returnArray = array();
        foreach ( $ids as $id )
            $returnArray[$id] = $this->getList(array('id'=>$id));
```

```
        return $returnArray;
    }
}
```

Here you use the PHP curl library to make the REST calls. There are two REST services: `http://example.com/rest/list/` is used for getting a list of records and `http://example.com/rest/item/` is used for grabbing a particular record, both using HTTP POST. You make the calls, then translate the results back to a PHP array using the json_decode() function. For the getList() method, you actually leverage the getItem() method to help fill in the individual record array's values.

As mentioned earlier, these functions expect the records formatted a certain way. For the getItem() method, the returned array would look like Listing 4-2.

Listing 4-2. *getItem() Array*

```
Array(
    ['id'] => 19303193202,
    ['recname'] => 'SugarCRM, Inc',
    ['addrcity'] => 'Cupertino',
)
```

The getList() array is very similar, only adding another dimension to the array that acts as a container to the array.

Listing 4-3. *getList() Array*

```
Array(
    [19303193202] => Array(
        ['id'] => 19303193202,
        ['recname'] => 'SugarCRM, Inc',
        ['addrcity'] => 'Cupertino',
    ),
    [39203032990] => Array(
        ['id'] => 39203032990,
        ['recname'] => 'Google',
        ['addrcity'] => 'Mountain View',
    )
)
```

One other option is to provide a test interface for your connector. This is an optional step where you may wish to provide functionality for your connector so that it may be tested through the administration interface under the "Set Connector Properties" section. It's valuable to have since sometimes a Web Service may go down or has changed its parameters, so this method can do a simple test to make sure connectivity can be made to the Web Service. To enable testing for your connector, set the connector class variable $_has_testing_enabled to true in the constructor and provide a test() method implementation, as shown in Listing 4-4.

Listing 4-4. Providing Testing Functionality for a Connector Source

```php
require_once('include/connectors/sources/ext/rest/rest.php');

class ext_rest_sample extends ext_rest
{
    protected $service_url = 'http://example.com/rest/';
    protected $_has_testing_enabled = true;

    public function getItem($args=array(), $module=null)
    {
        $curl = curl_init($this->service_url.'item/');
        curl_setopt($curl, CURLOPT_RETURNTRANSFER, true);
        curl_setopt($curl, CURLOPT_POST, true);
        curl_setopt($curl, CURLOPT_POSTFIELDS, $args);
        $curl_response = curl_exec($curl);
        curl_close($curl);

        return json_decode($curl_response);
    }

    public function getList($args=array(), $module=null)
    {
        $curl = curl_init($this->service_url.'list/');
        curl_setopt($curl, CURLOPT_RETURNTRANSFER, true);
        curl_setopt($curl, CURLOPT_POST, true);
        curl_setopt($curl, CURLOPT_POSTFIELDS, $args);
        $curl_response = curl_exec($curl);
        curl_close($curl);

        $ids = json_decode($curl_response);
        $returnArray = array();
        foreach ( $ids as $id )
            $returnArray[$id] = $this->getList(array('id'=>$id));

        return $returnArray;
    }

    public function test()
    {
        $item = $this->getItem(array('id'=>'1'));
        return !empty($item['firstname']) && ($item['firstname'] == 'John');
    }
}
```

Defining the Fields from the Web Service"

Just like you defined a vardefs.php file for the database table in Chapter 2, you also will define one here to describe the fields coming back from the connector.

Each key value in the array from the getList() and getItem() methods should be mapped to this vardefs.php, and it is contained within the source. The format is similar to the one before, as you can see in Listing 4-5.

Listing 4-5. vardefs.php for a Connector

```php
<?php
$dictionary['ext_rest_test'] = array(
    'comment' => 'vardefs for test connector',
    'fields' => array (
        'id' => array (
        'name' => 'id',
        'vname' => 'LBL_ID',
        'type' => 'id',
        'hidden' => true
        'comment' => 'Unique identifier'
        ),
    'addrcity' => array (
        'name' => 'addrcity',
        'input' => 'bal.location.city',
        'vname' => 'LBL_CITY',
        'type' => 'varchar',
        'comment' => 'The city address for the company',
        'options' => 'addrcity_list',
        'search' => true,
        ),
    )
);
?>
```

One difference from the vardefs.php you used with database tables is the addition of the 'input' key for the addrcity entry. The 'input' key allows for some internal argument mapping conversion that the source uses. The period (.) is used as a separator to map the input value into an Array. In the example of the addrcity entry, the value bal.location.city will be translated into the Array argument ['bal']['location']['city']. The 'search' key for the addrcity entry may be used for the search form in the connector data merge wizard screens available for the professional and enterprise editions.

You can also define a mappings.php file, which helps with the mapping process of the fields as they come from the connector to how they exist in the database. One way this is done is by specifying the mapping of source values for a field to how you use them in the database. You'll note the `'options'` key for the addrcity entry. This `'options'` key maps to an entry in the mapping.php file. The mappings.php also can specify specific module field mappings, in case the fields would map differently based upon the module you are using. Listing 4-6 shows an example mappings.php file.

Listing 4-6. Sample mappings.php File

```
$mapping = array (
    'beans' => array (
        'Contacts' => array (
            'id' => 'id',
            'addrcity' => 'primary_address_city',
        ),
        'Accounts' => array (
            'id' => 'id',
            'addrcity' => 'billing_address_city',
        ),
    ),
    'options' => array (
        'addrcity_list' => array (
            '001' => 'sjc', //San Jose
            '032' => 'sfo', //San Francisco
        ),
    ),
);
?>
```

Here you change your field mapping based upon which module the connector will be using. In the case of the Contacts module, the `'addrcity'` field will map to the `'primary_address_city'` field. However, this field does not exist in the Accounts module, so you'll map to the `'billing_address_city'` field instead. In addition, you have provided a way to map given addrcity values to those you would use inside Sugar.

Formatters

The optional formatter components are used by the connector framework to render the 'Cloud View' window that may display additional details and information. Out of the box, they are shown in the DetailView screens for modules that are enabled for the connector. Like the source class, the formatter class has a corresponding factory class (FormatterFactory). The formatters also follow the same convention of using the "ext_rest_" or "ext_soap_" prefix. However, to distinguish conflicting class names, a suffix "_formatter" is also used. Formatters extend from default_formatter.

By default, the formatter will look for a default.tpl in the tpls/ directory of the connector, which it will render in the first field of the DetailView. It's a simple Smarty template that can supply the information the record is connected to inside the DetailView. (As you may remember from Chapter 3, these are templates SugarCRM uses for handling displaying the user interface to the client.) Listing 4-7 shows the formatter used for the LinkedIn connector.

Listing 4-7. LinkedIn Connector Formatter

```
<div style="visibility:hidden;" id="linkedin_popup_div"></div>
<script src="{{$config.properties.company_url}}" type="text/javascript"></script>
<script type="text/javascript" src="{sugar_getjspath↩
 file='include/connectors/formatters/default/company_detail.js'}"></script>
<script type="text/javascript">
function show_ext_rest_linkedin(event)
{literal}
{

var xCoordinate = event.clientX;
var yCoordinate = event.clientY;
var isIE = document.all?true:false;

if(isIE) {
    xCoordinate = xCoordinate + document.body.scrollLeft;
    yCoordinate = yCoordinate + document.body.scrollTop;
}

{/literal}

cd = new CompanyDetailsDialog("linkedin_popup_div", '<div id="linkedin_div"></div>',↩
 xCoordinate, yCoordinate);
cd.setHeader("{$fields.{{$mapping_name}}.value}");
cd.display();
linked_in_popup = new LinkedIn.CompanyInsiderBox("linkedin_div",↩
 "{$fields.{{$mapping_name}}.value}");
{literal}
}
{/literal}
</script>
```

The default_formatter class will scan the tpls directory for a Smarty template file named after the module that is being viewed. For example, the file *formatters/ext/rest/linkedin/tpls/Accounts.tpl will be used for the Accounts popup view if the file exists. If the module named template file is not found, it will attempt to use a file named default.tpl.

Localization

The connectors support localization through the use of language files placed in a folder named language under the connector's root folder. The file should declare a key/value Array named $connector_strings. The vardefs.php entries will use the standard 'vname' key to denote the label key in the language file. The configuration labels shown in the administration screens use the key value in the config.php files to render the label. Listing 4-8 provides an example of how this file would look.

Listing 4-8. Localization File for a Connector

```php
$connector_strings = array (
    //vardef labels
    'LBL_ID' => 'ID',
    'LBL_FIRST_NAME' => 'First Name',
    'LBL_LAST_NAME' => 'Last Name',
    'LBL_JOB_TITLE' => 'Job Title',
    'LBL_IMAGE_URL' => 'Image URL',
    'LBL_COMPANY_NAME' => 'Company Name',
    //Configuration labels
    'url' => 'URL',
    'api_key' => 'API Key',
);
```

Pulling It Together

Sources also need to provide a config.php file that may contain optional runtime properties, such as the URL of the SOAP WSDL file and API keys. These runtime properties should be placed under the 'properties' array. At a minimum, a 'name' key should be provided for the source (see Listing 4-9).

Listing 4-9. Sample config.php

```php
<?php
$config = array(
    'name' => 'Test', //Name of the source
    'properties' => array(
        'TEST_ENDPOINT' => 'http://test-dev.com/axis2/services/AccessTest',
        'TEST_WSDL' => 'http://hapi-dev.test.com/axis2/test.wsdl',
        'TEST_API_KEY' => 'abc123',
    ),
);
?>
```

At this point, the directory structure for a rest based connector named 'test' should look like the following:

custom/modules/Connectors/connectors/sources/ext/rest/test/test.php

custom/modules/Connectors/connectors/sources/ext/rest/test/vardefs.php custom/modules/Connectors/connectors/sources/ext/rest/test/config.php

custom/modules/Connectors/connectors/sources/ext/rest/test/mapping.php (optional)

custom/modules/Connectors/connectors/sources/ext/rest/test/language/en_us.lang.php (default English language file for localization)

custom/modules/Connectors/connectors/formatters/ext/rest/test/test.php

custom/modules/Connectors/connectors/formatters/ext/rest/test/tpls/test.gif (optional)

custom/modules/Connectors/connectors/formatters/ext/rest/test/tpls/default.tpl (optional)

You would exchange out `'soap'` for `'rest'` in the preceding pathnames if you were building a SOAP-based connector.

Web Services API

The other half of the Web Services support in SugarCRM is the Web Services API, which provides a way for external applications to interact with your Sugar instance. SugarCRM has a SOAP API, which has opened up access to the internals of SugarCRM in such a way where any application or programming language with a SOAP library or SOAP capabilities can connect to Sugar. You'll see shortly how in Sugar 5.5 it has undergone a major transformation, greatly simplifying the interface, allowing it to be easily customized, and adding a REST interface to complement the existing SOAP interface.

One big step forward in your Web Services API in Sugar 5.5 is the addition of a versioning and extensibility framework. With this, you can make changes to the Web Services API that will not break any existing applications, since your application can target a particular version of the API whose interface will remain constant. It also makes it easier to customize the Web Services API with additional methods and change the existing method definitions. These revisions can be tagged with a certain version that will remain constant, even through upgrades to the application. Since this is a separate framework from the SOAP API that existed in previous versions of SugarCRM, Sugar 5.5 will continue to support backwards compatibility for Version 1 of your Web Services API.

All the classes used to implement the Web Services live in a service directory. The service directory contains the following subdirectories:

- *core/*: Contains all the core classes that the Web Services API are derived from.

- *REST/*: Contains all the REST classes used for returning data in a particular format, such as JSON, Serialized data, or RSS.

- *v2/*: Contains all the version 2 specific classes for SOAP and REST implementation of the Web Services API.

In the v2/ directory, you will define the new entrypoints for the Web Services API. The entrypoint code will look similar to Listing 4-10, which is the code used to define the v2 SOAP entrypoint.

***Listing 4-10.** Web Service API Entrypoint for v2 SOAP Web Service*

```
chdir('../..');
// name of the web service class
$webservice_class = 'SugarSoapService2';
// location of the above class
$webservice_path = 'service/v2/SugarSoapService2.php';
// name of class that is responsible for registering all the complex data types↵
 and functions available to call
$registry_class = 'registry';
// path to the above class
$registry_path = 'service/v2/registry.php';
// name of the implementation class for all the functions
$webservice_impl_class = 'SugarWebServiceImpl';
// location of the SOAP entrypoint ( should be the URI to this script )
$location = '/service/v2/soap.php';

require_once('service/core/webservice.php');
```

To access the new version of the Web Services you will use the URL http://sugar_root_url/
service/v2/soap.php to connect.

Now let's look at how you can connect to the new Sugar Web Services API using SOAP and REST.

SOAP

SOAP is probably the most used Web Services protocol. It provides a way of exchanging structured information of application functionality. A SOAP interface can be defined by its Web Service Description Language (WSDL) file, which simply provides the definitions of all available methods to the client. One of the biggest attractions to using SOAP as a Web Service over lighter weight services, such as REST, is that it makes interacting with remote Web Services as seamless as making local function calls. It can do this because SOAP support in various languages mimic object method calls, allowing use of built-in data types with them automatically making the needed conversions between the data provided by a method to those used in the class itself

I'll focus on the newer version of SOAP interface in this book. SugarCRM will continue to support backwards compatibility of the previous SOAP interface, which has been in use for many versions now. I recommend you upgrade to the newer libraries because they are much more efficient than the older libraries (less calls needed to accomplish the same end results in the newer library versus the old), as well as make it easier to write custom SOAP methods.

Let's look at a few common actions and how to do them with the SOAP interface. You'll use the nusoap PHP SOAP library for all of the following examples, but they should translate easily into the language/library of your choice.

Make a Connection

To begin, you need to connect to the service. You start this process by initializing the SOAP object with the URL of the SOAP instance, then using the login method to authenticate against the Sugar instance. Listing 4-11 provides the implementation.

Listing 4-11. Connecting to the Sugar Instance Using SOAP

```
// Create the SOAP client instance
$soapclient = new nusoapclient('http://sugar_root_url/service/v2/soap.php?wsdl', true);
// Login to the server
$result = $soapclient->call('login',array('user_auth'=>array('user_name'=>$user_name,↵
'password'=>md5($user_password), 'version'=>'.01'), 'application_name'=>'SoapTest'));
$session = $result['id'];
// Get the user_id of the logged on user
$user_id = $soapclient->call('get_user_id',array('session'=>$session));
```

You pass the credentials that you are using to login to the instance using the 'user_auth' parameter of the login method. The array key 'user_name' specifies the user name and the key 'password' specifies the password, which you need to pass md5 encoded for added security. Returned from this method call, among other things, is the session_id, which is returned as in the 'id' key element of the array. This key is important, since you'll need to pass it along as the first argument to all further soap function calls.

One performance issue you have seen is when dealing with the WSDL file. Loading it on every SOAP client call can degrade performance considerably. I have seen up to 40 percent performance improvement by simply caching the WSDL file locally, instead of loading it from the remote source every time. NuSOAP provide a class to do such a thing, called wsdlcache, which integrates nicely into the NuSOAP client (see Listing 4-12).

Listing 4-12. Caching the WSDL File with NuSOAP

```
$cache = new wsdlcache("C:\temp", $cachelifetimeinseconds);
$wsdl = $cache->get("http://localhost/soap.php?wsdl");
if (is_null($wsdl)) {
    // Retrieve the WSDL file and store it in the cache
    $wsdl = new wsdl("http://localhost/soap.php?wsdl");
    $cache->put($wsdl);
} else {
    $wsdl->debug_str = '';
    $wsdl->debug('Retrieved from cache');
} // else
// instantiate the soap client using the cached wsdl file
$soapclient = new nusoapclient($wsdl, true);
```

You can see in Listing 4-12 how to establish a WSDL cache location and check to see if the WDSL file you need is in the cache. If it isn't, you can use the put() method of the wsdlcache object to store the retrieved WSDL file. Finally, you specify the wsdlcache object instance instead of a URL as the first parameter to the nusoapclient constructor to use the cached WSDL file, rather than retrieving it from the remote source every time. Note that using WSDL files are not required by this SOAP service. It's merely provided as a convenience. You could always choose not to pull the WSDL file when you initiate the SOAP connection (in NuSOAP, you would pass false to the second argument of the nusoapclient constructor).

Get Lists and Counts of Records

Now that you can establish a connection to the SOAP server, let's try to actually query the data there. A good place to start is by trying to get a count of records available for a module. In Listing 4-13, you'll do this for the Accounts module, returning the number of non-deleted records back to you.

Listing 4-13. Get a Count of Records in a Module

```
// Create the SOAP client instance
$soapclient = new nusoapclient('http://sugar_root_url/service/v2/soap.php?wsdl', true);
// Login to the server
$result = $soapclient->call('login',array('user_auth'=>array('user_name'=>
$user_name,'password'=>md5($user_password), 'version'=>'.01'),
  'application_name'=>'SoapTest'));
$session = $result['id'];
// Get the count of records
$result = $soapclient->call('get_entries_count',array('session'=>$session,
  'module_name' => 'Accounts', 'query' => '', 'deleted' => 0));
$count = $result['result_count'];
```

You initialize your SOAP instance and login, and then make the get_entries_count SOAP call. You'll pass the session id as a parameter, as well as the name of the module which you are querying. The query parameter to the call allows you to add extra conditions to the records being counted. For example, you could set it to 'array('industry = 'Banking')' to return only accounts in the Banking industry. The deleted parameter at the end specifies that you only want non-deleted records counted.

Extending this example, let's now actually get the records for a module. The SOAP call you'll use here is get_entry_list, which returns an array of fields for the given parameter specified. Listing 4-14 shows an example of this in action for retrieving all Contacts in the Sugar instance.

Listing 4-14. *Get All Contacts in a Module*

```
// Create the SOAP client instance
$soapclient = new nusoapclient('http://sugar_root_url/service/v2/soap.php?wsdl', true);
// Login to the server
$result = $soapclient->call('login',array('user_auth'=>array('user_name'=>$user_name, ↵
'password'=>md5($user_password), 'version'=>'.01'), 'application_name'=>'SoapTest'));
$session = $result['id'];
// Get the list of records
$result = $soapclient->call('get_entry_list',array('session'=>$session,'module_name'=>↵
'Contacts','query'=>'', 'order_by'=>'','offset'=>0,'select_fields'=>array(),↵
'link_name_to_fields_array' => '', 'max_results'=>10,'deleted'=>-1));
$records_returned = $result['result_count'];
$next_offset = $result['next_offset'];
$field_list = $result['entry_list'];
```

The actual records retrieved will be in the $field list array. The $records_returned and $next_offset integer values are handy if you want to page the returned results—in case you expect the result set to be large and want to handle it chunk by chunk (just like the SugarCRM ListViews only deal with 20 records at a time). To handle the paging, you can specify the 'offset' parameter to the get_entry_list method to the result given by $next_offset, limiting the page set size by the 'max_results' parameter. You'll know when you've reached the end when the method call returns no records or the $records_returned is less than the value used for 'max_results'.

Add a New Record

Adding a record is a fairly straightforward exercise. The set_entry method call is used here, where you will specify an array of name/value pairs that each record should be set to. Listing 4-15 has the code for this example.

Listing 4-15. *Add a New Record with set_entry*

```
// Create the SOAP client instance
$soapclient = new nusoapclient('http://sugar_root_url/service/v2/soap.php?wsdl', true);
// Login to the server
$result = $soapclient->call('login',array('user_auth'=>array('user_name'=>$user_name,↵
```

```
'password'=>md5($user_password), 'version'=>'.01'), 'application_name'=>'SoapTest'));
$session = $result['id'];
// Add the new record
$result = $soapclient->call('set_entry',array('session'=>$session,'module_name'=>↵
'Contacts', 'name_value_list'=>array(array('name'=>'last_name' , 'value'=>"Mertic"),↵
 array('name'=>'first_name' , 'value'=>'John'))));
$id = $result['id'];
```

The 'name_value_list' parameter you use is an array with each field specified. The 'name' key in the subarray is the name of the field you'll be setting, while the 'value' field is the value. The resulting record id is returned back in the 'id' key of the $result array, which you quickly grab and store in a local variable.

You use the same method for also updating records. In this case, you just need to specify what the id of the record to update is. Assuming the previous record was successfully created in Listing 4-15, you'll extend that example to update the newly created Contact record with a title in Listing 4-16.

Listing 4-16. Add a New Contact Record and Then Update It

```
// Create the SOAP client instance
$soapclient = new nusoapclient('http://sugar_root_url/service/v2/soap.php?wsdl', true);
// Login to the server
$result = $soapclient->call('login',array('user_auth'=>array('user_name'=>$user_name,↵
'password'=>md5($user_password), 'version'=>'.01'), 'application_name'=>'SoapTest'));
$session = $result['id'];
// Add the new record
$result = $soapclient->call('set_entry',array('session'=>$session, 'module_name'=>↵
'Contacts', 'name_value_list'=>array(array('name'=>'last_name' ,↵
 'value'=>"Mertic"), array('name'=>'first_name' , 'value'=>'John'))));
$id = $result['id'];
// Now change a field in the newly created record
$result = $soapclient->call('set_entry',array('session'=>$session,'module_name'=>↵
'Contacts', 'name_value_list'=>array(array('name'=>'id' , 'value'=>$id),↵
 array('name'=>'title' , 'value'=>'Author'))));
$id = $result['id'];
```

Let's say you have a bunch of records to update or create in one shot for a module. Instead of having to do several set_entry calls in a row, you can save yourself the extra network time and use the set_entries method (notice that it's plural) to do several changes in one shot. The biggest difference is that now the 'name_value_list' parameter becomes 'name_value_lists' (again, plural). Listing 4-17 has all the code details.

Listing 4-17. Creating Multiple Records with set_entries

```
// Create the SOAP client instance
$soapclient = new nusoapclient('http://sugar_root_url/service/v2/soap.php?wsdl', true);
// Login to the server
$result = $soapclient->call('login',array('user_auth'=>array('user_name'=>$user_name,↵
'password'=>md5($user_password), 'version'=>'.01'), 'application_name'=>'SoapTest'));
```

```
$session = $result['id'];
// Specify the list of records to add
$name_value_lists[] = array(array('name'=>'last_name' , 'value'=>"Mertic"),↵
 array('name'=>'first_name' , 'value'=>'John'));
$name_value_lists[] = array(array('name'=>'last_name' , 'value'=>"Mertic"),↵
 array('name'=>'first_name' , 'value'=>'Dominic'));
$name_value_lists[] = array(array('name'=>'last_name' , 'value'=>"Mertic"),↵
 array('name'=>'first_name' , 'value'=>'Mallory'));
// Now add all the new records
$result = $soapclient->call('set_entries',array('session'=>$session,'module_name'=>↵
'Contacts', 'name_value_lists'=>$name_value_lists));
$ids = $result['ids'];
```

You specify the records to create or update the same way as before, but this time wrap them in one more array, using that array as the value for the 'name_value_lists' parameter in the SOAP method call. The returned result is similar as well, this time returning an 'ids' key with the array list of ids created or updated.

Saving and Retrieving Attachments

Don't let simple record creation stop you in your SOAP integration. You can also upload and retrieve attachments as well, such as those used in the Notes module. You do this as a secondary call instead of using set_entry, like you would for normal record data. Here you use the set_note_attachment method to upload the actual file to the Sugar instance record. Listing 4-18 shows you how to do this for the Notes module.

Listing 4-18. Add a New Notes Record with an Attachment

```
// Create the SOAP client instance
$soapclient = new nusoapclient('http://sugar_root_url/service/v2/soap.php?wsdl', true);
// Login to the server
$result = $soapclient->call('login',array('user_auth'=>array('user_name'=>$user_name,↵
'password'=>md5($user_password), 'version'=>'.01'), 'application_name'=>'SoapTest'));
$session = $result['id'];
// Add the new note record
$result = $soapclient->call('set_entry',array('session'=>$session,'module_name'=>↵
'Notes', 'name_value_list'=>array(array('name'=>'name' , 'value'=>"My new note"),↵
 array('name'=>'description' , 'value'=>'This is a note with a file attached to it'))));
$id = $result['id'];
// Now attach the file to the newly created note
$file = base64_encode(file_get_contents('attach.txt'));
$result = $soapclient->call('set_note_attachment',array('session'=>$session,↵
'note'=>array('id'=>$id, 'filename'=>'attach.txt','file'=>$file) ));
$id = $result['id'];
```

You create the file attachment from the local file named `'attach.txt'`. You grab the contents of it and base64 encode it for transport in the SOAP method call, passing it under the parameter `'file'`. You also need to specify the actual name of the file as it should be stored on the server in the `'filename'` attribute.

What comes in must come out as well, so the get_note_attachment method call provides this functionality. Here you'll assume the existence of record in the Notes module already, and you'll assume you already know the id of that record (which is provided in the $id variable). Listing 4-19 shows the details on the more interesting parts of the file retrieval process.

Listing 4-19. Grab a Given Notes Record Attachment

```
// Create the SOAP client instance
$soapclient = new nusoapclient('http://sugar_root_url/service/v2/soap.php?wsdl', true);
// Login to the server
$result = $soapclient->call('login',array('user_auth'=>array('user_name'=>$user_name,↵
'password'=>md5($user_password), 'version'=>'.01'), 'application_name'=>'SoapTest'));
$session = $result['id'];
// Grab the given record's attachment
$result = $soapclient->call('get_note_attachment',array('session'=>$session,↵
'id'=>$note_id ));
$file_contents = base64_decode($result['note_attachment']['file']);
$filename = $result['note_attachment']['filename'];
// Now store the contents in a local file
file_put_contents($filename,$file_contents);
```

The get_note_attachment method is very simple, returning back an array with all the file details. Everything you are looking for is under the `'note_attachment'` key, with two subarray keys, `'file'` and `'filename'`, giving you the actual file content (this is base64 encoded, so you need to decode for your use), as well as the name of the file as it existing in the Sugar instance. You take these two elements and use them with the file_put_contents() method for saving the file on your local filesystem while also using the same name as it was on the server.

Relate Records

One nice part about SugarCRM is the ability to have records from different modules relate to one another. In the same way, the SOAP interface provides the same sort of ability through the set_relationship method call. Listing 4-20 shows you how to do this by relating a Contact to an Account record.

Listing 4-20. Relating a Contact with an Account Using SOAP

```
// Create the SOAP client instance
$soapclient = new nusoapclient('http://sugar_root_url/service/v2/soap.php?wsdl', true);
// Login to the server
$result = $soapclient->call('login',array('user_auth'=>array('user_name'=>$user_name,↵
```

```
'password'=>md5($user_password), 'version'=>'.01'), 'application_name'=>'SoapTest'));
$session = $result['id'];
// Add the new Contact record
$result = $soapclient->call('set_entry',array('session'=>$session,'module_name'=>↵
'Contacts', 'name_value_list'=>array(array('name'=>'last_name' , 'value'=>"Mertic"),↵
 array('name'=>'first_name' , 'value'=>'John'))));
$contact_id = $result['id'];
// Add the new Account record
$result = $soapclient->call('set_entry',array('session'=>$session,↵
'module_name'=>'Accounts', 'name_value_list'=>array(array('name'=>'name' , 'value'=>↵
"John's House of Cards"))));
$account_id = $result['id'];
// Now relate the contact to the account
$result = $soapclient->call('set_relationship',array('session'=>$session,↵
'module_name' => 'Accounts', 'module_id' => $account_id, 'link_field_name' =>↵
 'contacts', 'related_ids' => array($contact_id)));
```

After you create the two new records, you relate them using the set_relationship method. You first specify the parent module name and id in the 'module_name' and 'module_id' parameters. You then indicate which link field you are using to relate with the target module. In the case of the Accounts module, the link field name for the Contact module relationship is 'contacts' (refer to Chapter 2 for information on this field type). Finally, you specify an array list of contact ids that should be marked as being related to the given account_id in the related_ids parameter.

REST

A new addition to the Sugar Web Services framework in the 5.5 release is a REST interface. This has been one of the more requested additions to the service, as it adds a much more lightweight way for developers to gain access to data in a system in comparison to the SOAP interface used in previous versions of SugarCRM. REST is considered the preferable Web Services implementation for higher transactional Web Services implementations (those where lots of calls are made to the Web Service at once), but also when used with browser client-side implementations where all rendering happens in the browser. SugarCRM's implementation of REST makes this even easier, using the Javascript native JSON format as the default return format for all the Web Services calls made with the REST interface, and also using PHP serialized data as an alternate type as well.

You can even define your own data type for input and output of data in the REST interface by simply extending the SugarRest class inside the service/core/REST/ directory. Two methods need to be implemented: serve() decodes the data from the REST method call as it is given, while generateResponse() is used to encode the return data for returning it back to the client. You can mix and match input and output types in the same REST call by specifying the 'input_type' and 'response_type' accordingly, so you could have json data inputted, but serialized data returned.

The examples you'll use in this section will illustrate using the REST interface from Javascript, using the Yahoo Interface Library's connection object.

Logging in Using REST

Logging into the Sugar instance via REST uses the same method calls as you did before when dealing with the SOAP interface, but this time of course you'll need to deal with the data a bit differently due to the different interface used. Listing 4-21 shows you how to do this.

Listing 4-21. Logging into the SugarCRM Using the REST Interface

```
var loginData = [{
        user_name: 'user',
        password: 'password'
},'javascriptTest'];
data = YAHOO.lang.JSON.stringify(loginData);
YAHOO.util.Connect.asyncRequest('POST', 'v2/rest.php' , {success:success},↵
 'method=login&input_type=json&response_type=json&rest_data='+data);

function success(o)
{
    var data = YAHOO.lang.JSON.parse(o.responseText);
    var session = data['id'];
    alert(session);
}
```

You've used the asyncRequest() method of the YUI Connect object to make the REST call. The rest_data argument to the REST service is where you pass the data in. You use the YUI JSON tools for properly preparing this data for use.

Otherwise, all of the previous examples from the SOAP interface equally apply to the REST interface as well.

Custom Web Services

Before the release of 5.5 it was only possible to add new Web Services functionality by modifying out of box core files. Each subsequent upgrade would then require the end Sugar user to check to make sure the newest patch/upgrade being applied did not have any files in conflict. In version 2 of the Web Services interface introduced with SugarCRM 5.5, you now have an extensible framework which allows a developer to add and distribute new Web Services functionality without the need to worry about merging code with each patch/upgrade.

To do this, the following items are needed: create a custom registry, provide an implementation class, and then add the SOAP or REST interface file. You'll create them in a new directory underneath the custom/services/ directory which you'll call v2_1 to help illustrate it as an extension of the existing library.

Create a Custom Registry

First, you'll need to provide your own registry.php file in the new directory previously created. You'll call it customregistry.php, and define it as a child class of the registry class as shown in Listing 4-22.

Listing 4-22. customregisty.php

```php
require_once('service/v2/registry.php');

class customregistry extends registry
{
        public function __construct($serviceClass)
        {
            parent::__construct($serviceClass);
        }

        protected function registerFunction()
        {
            parent::registerFunction();
            $this->serviceClass->registerFunction(
                'get_entry',
                array(
                    'session' => 'xsd:string',
                    'module_name' => 'xsd:string',
                    'id' => 'xsd:string',
                    ),
                array(
                    'return' => 'xsd:string',
                    )
                );
        }
}
```

The main change here is inside the registerFunction() method, where you add the 'get_entry' method to the available list of functions that can be used through this Web Service. In the definition, you specify both the input parameters, as well as the return type for the function. You also call the parent method definition as well, so that you can include all the default functions in the main SOAP interface.

Provide an Implementation Class

Next, you'll extend the SugarWebServiceImpl class to add in the new method which you are exposing the client. Listing 4-23 shows this example.

Listing 4-23. SugarWebServiceImpl_v2_1.php

```php
require_once('service/core/SugarWebServiceImpl.php');

class SugarWebServiceImpl_v2_1 extends SugarWebServiceImpl
{
```

```
    public function get_entry($session, $module_name, $id)
    {
        return $id;
    }
}
```

As you can see, the get_entry method is really simple. It just returns back the passed id.

Add soap.php and rest.php Files

Now you just need to provide the interface file for both SOAP and REST calls. You can see them in Listings 4-24 and 25.

Listing 4-24. Example soap.php to be Accessed at custom/service/v2_1/soap.php

```
Chdir('../..');
$webservice_class = 'SugarSoapService2';
$webservice_path = 'service/v2/SugarSoapService2.php';
$registry_class = 'customregistry';
$registry_path = 'custom/service/v2_1/customregistry.php';
$webservice_impl_class = 'SugarWebServiceImpl_v2_1';
$location = '/custom/service/v2_1/soap.php';
require_once('service/core/webservice.php');
```

Listing 4-25. Example rest.php to be Accessed at http://sugar root url/service/v2_1/rest.php

```
Chdir('../..');
$webservice_class = 'SugarRestService';
$webservice_path = 'service/v2/SugarRestService.php';
$registry_class = 'customregistry';
$registry_path = 'custom/service/v2_1/customregistry.php';
$webservice_impl_class = 'SugarRestServiceImpl_v2_1';
$location = '/custom/service/v2_1/rest.php';
require_once('service/core/webservice.php');
```

You just change the former definitions used to point to the correct locations of the new files you created inside the service/v2_1/ directory.

Summary

In this chapter, you learned about the various Web Service integrations the SugarCRM platform provides. You first looked at Connectors, a feature added in Sugar 5.2 for interfacing directly into remote Web Services from your Sugar instance. You then looked at the Web Services interface, which allows other applications to easily interface into SugarCRM. You saw how easy both the inbound and outbound

Web Services interfaces are to use and how you can easily customize them however you wish.

In the next chapter, you'll finish your dig into the innards of SugarCRM, taking a look at some of the value added features and tools such as User Authentication, Dashlets, and Themes.

■ ■ ■

CHAPTER 5

More Platform Features

In previous chapters, you looked at the large features of the Sugar platform. Chapter 2 focused on the MVC framework, such as how requests are handled, how you can control the output to the user, and how to interact with the database layer. Chapter 3 showed you the metadata framework, which provides a way to build the common views of the application (namely the DetailView, EditView, and ListView) with ease and consistency. Then in Chapter 4, you looked at how you can use Web Services by consuming them within your Sugar instance, as well as how you can expose Web Services from your Sugar instance to be consumed by other applications.

This chapter will focus on the "less major" features of the SugarCRM platform. Think of this chapter as the miscellaneous drawer chapter of the book, where you'll look at several random features that are noteworthy enough to be mentioned in the book, but don't necessarily fit in any of the previous chapters. Things I'll focus on include user and team management, which is essential for any multi-user application. You'll also look at Dashlets, which provides a way to display data from multiple sources on one page. I'll then touch on sugar feeds, record importing and exporting, themes, and the Sugar logger.

Let's start off by looking at user management in SugarCRM.

User Management

A core feature of any multi-user application is user management. It's often one of the first concerns when building a new application, since having this enables security of the application and also enables auditing of user actions. SugarCRM does this for you, providing a very secure default authentication scheme, as well more advanced LDAP authentication. LDAP authentication allows you to hook Sugar into your company's existing LDAP directory server (such as Active Directory) to provide authentication.

By default, Sugar uses its built-in authentication and stores the users information inside the database itself. Users can have many properties and preferences associated with them, as you would expect. In the Admin panel, the User Management option allows you to create, edit, activate, and deactivate users in Sugar. You can create a Sugar user, System Administrator, Group User, or Portal Only User. Table 5-1 describes the different user types.

Table 5-1. User Types in SugarCRM

User Type	Description
Sugar User	Can access and use Sugar modules but does not have administrative privileges.
System Administrator	User who has administrative privileges in Sugar to perform tasks such as creating users. The System Administrator has the rights to access all modules and records.
Group User	A bucket that is used for inbound emails, and does not count toward the number of Sugar licenses that you purchase for your organization. For example, when you create a group mail account for Support, a group user named Support is created to handle customer support issues. Users can then distribute the emails to other users from the group inbox.
Portal Only User	Used by portals created in Sugar to access the system. Portal users do not count toward the number of Sugar licenses that you purchase for your organization.

When you create a user, by default the system creates a Sugar user unless you specify Administrator, Group User, or Portal Only User.

There are many things you can set on a user's account, including preferences on how things should work and look while they use the application. User preferences are stored separately from the user itself as serialize and base64 encoded data. However, it can be easily retrieved and updated using the getPreference() and setPreference() methods of the User bean object. Since the user object for the currently logged on user is always available through the $current_user global, you can get any user preference you need easily. In Listing 5-1, you see how to look up the preference for showing the module's icon as the browser's favicon and act accordingly.

Listing 5-1. Handling the User Preference module_favicon.

```
$user_module_favicon = $GLOBALS['current_user']->getPreference('module_favicon');
if(!isset($user_module_favicon))
if isset($GLOBALS['sugar_config']['default_module_favicon']))
    $user_module_favicon = $GLOBALS['sugar_config']['default_module_favicon'];
else
    $user_module_favicon = false;
```

Here you check the current user's preference for displaying the module's icon as the favicon instead of using the normal application favicon. If you cannot find the preference, you fall back onto looking at the default setting in the $sugar_config, and if it's still not found you simply assume the setting to be false.

Once you have users, you need to control their access to the system. SugarCRM provides an ACL system to do this.

ACL

With a multiuser system, there usually exists many different types of users. Some users may be data entry people, who have little need for the management aspects of the system and don't need a bunch of options they'll never use. Sales folks often have the most restrictions, to keep them from accounting information that wouldn't pertain to them. Very few users need full access to the system (and nor would many system administrators want them to).

ACLs are used to restrict access to Sugar modules, and the data and actions available (e.g., "Delete" and "Save") to users within Sugar modules. ACLs are defined in the roles area of Sugar Admin panel, and can apply to any module in the system and their actions. Sugar Professional and Enterprise Editions take this one step further, allowing administrators to restrict user access down to specific fields, as well as make certain users administrators of certain modules in the system, without having to give them full admin level access to all modules.

You do ACL in SugarCRM by creating user roles. A role defines a set of permissions to perform actions, such as viewing, editing, and deleting information. Then you take these roles and apply them to users, which will affect the modules, actions, and fields that they can see or interact with. Users can have zero or more roles applied to them, which will apply the role rules on them in the order in which they are defined. If a user is not assigned a role, they can, by default, access and take any action in any module. Roles can also be assigned to more than one person, which is handy for managing group and employee-level access permissions. For example, if you want to prevent a group of users in your organization from accessing the Opportunities module, you can create a role that restricts access to this module. When you assign this role to an engineer, the individual will no longer be able to access the Opportunities module. Or, you may want to assign junior sales representatives to a role that allows them to view and edit opportunities, accounts, and contacts but prevents them from deleting these records. The only user exempt from roles is the System Administrator, who always has the right to access all modules and records.

When you create a role, you specify whether access is permitted or not, the modules that the role can access, the access type such as Normal (for regular Sugar users) or administrator, and the actions that can be performed.

Setting up roles for a module involves the following steps:

1. Identify the modules you wish to control access to. It's best to keep ACL rules specific in what their goals are, so you can combine them with other roles to achieve the desired level of access control for the user.

2. Set the Access Level for the module to one of the following options:

3. *Enabled*: This permits the user to see the module.

4. *Disabled*: This hides the module from the user and prevents them from accessing it.

5. *Not Set*: This does not change the existing setting for Access Level.

6. Set the Access Type for the module. The options here are shown in the following list:

7. *Normal*: Gives the user normal rights to the module.

8. *Admin*: Gives the user admin level privilege to the module, such as changing the settings in the Admin panel and being able to view, edit, and delete any record in the module.

9. *Developer*: Allows the user to make changes to the module through Studio, Workflow Manager, and Dropdown Editor.

10. *Admin and Developer*: Combines the previous two privileges.

11. *Not Set*: Does not change the existing setting for Access Type.

12. Set the rights for the Delete, Edit, Export, Import, List, and View permissions to one of the following settings:

13. *All*: Can perform the given action.

14. *Owner*: Only the owner of the record can perform the given action.

15. *None*: Cannot perform the given action.

16. *Not Set*: Does not change the existing setting for the given action.

17. For Professional and Enterprise editions, you can set permission for each field in the module as well to one of the following: Read/Write, Read/Owner Write, Read Only, Owner Read/Owner Write, None, or Not Set.

When a user is assigned multiple roles, the roles definitions are merged and the more restrictive settings prevail. For example, if a user is assigned to two roles pertaining to one module where one role grants administrator access and the other grants end-user access, the user has only end-user access. In this case, the end-user access overrides the role with the administrative access because it is more restrictive.

A special case is the "Not Set" value in a role definition. You can use "Not Set" to ensure that a role does not affect a particular setting. This allows simple roles to be constructed and then combined to achieve the desired security level. For example, if users are assigned to both the following roles:

Role A, where Access Type = Admin and Export (action) = None

Role B, where Access Type = Normal and Export (action) = All

Then, users can only see records that are assigned to them, but they cannot export the data. If you change the Access Type to Not Set:

Role A, where Access Type = Admin and Export (action) = All

Role B, where Access Type = Not Set and Export (action) = None

Then the user can see all records in the module, but cannot export the data.

Password Management

The Password Management feature, which has been added in Sugar 5.5, enables system administrators to create and manage system-generated passwords and password rules for users. It first comes into play when a user is initially created. Here system-generated passwords are automatically sent to new users when system administrators create new user records. System administrators can also send new passwords to users at anytime, giving them the ability to reset the password in case of security issues with the application. You can also provide an expiration date for any password that is automatically generated, forcing the user to reset his password soon after he is issued a new password.

To help with password security, you can set requirements on what kind of password can be used. You can set options for maximum and minimum length, as well as the content of the password itself, such as requiring uppercase or lowercase character, numbers, and symbols. If the default requirements aren't enough, then a regex can be provided that would enforce the rules of what is not allowed in a password. Anytime a password is created, the rules for creating the username must be followed. If not, then the user will be notified and the given password will not be accepted.

A common problem for administrators is when users forget their password. SugarCRM solves this problem by providing the users a Forgot Password link on the Login page, so when the user gives his username and email address (and provided both match an active user in the system) it will send a system-generated link to the page where he can reset his password. You can also require a Captcha on the form, to prevent automated tools from requesting these new password requests. The system-generated links for resetting passwords can be set with an expiration date as well, so that they must be responded to in a short amount of time from when they are sent. You can also custom the email templates used to send users system-generated passwords and links to reset passwords to provide any additional information the user may need. To help further protect your system from those trying to access it without proper credentials, you can also enable the Login Lockout feature to lock users out of the system after a specified number of failed login attempts.

All-in-all, SugarCRM now has a very robust password management scheme, that both help ease the burden on administrators in managing user password, but also helps users solve the common "I forgot my password" problem without IT intervention each time. It also adds another level of security to user passwords, to help avoid accounts being easily cracked into by enforcing configurable password and login failure rules.

Tracking User Actions

Another important feature of any multi-user system is tracking user actions. This has benefits both for users and administrators. While administrators have the ability to track users and access patterns in the system, users also gain the ability to easily get to recent records without having to search for them explicitly. SugarCRM does this all automatically and transparently, giving administrators and developers a very useful addition in managing their application.

Originally, SugarCRM would only track user actions of editing and/or viewing data records. This functionality gave users a list of last viewed records on their screen, which were links to access those records. With SugarCRM 5.1, this was greatly enhanced to also track performance metrics, query metrics, and session information. This kind of information is very useful for system administrators, so they can tweak their systems for the best performance based upon their individual needs. It's also useful for managers, so they can see how much their employees are using the system and what for.

The Tracker Reports dashlet provides a quick and easy way to access this information (we'll talk about Dashlets later in this chapter). Shown in Figure 5-1, it has a simple interface to find the common types of requests for Tracker data

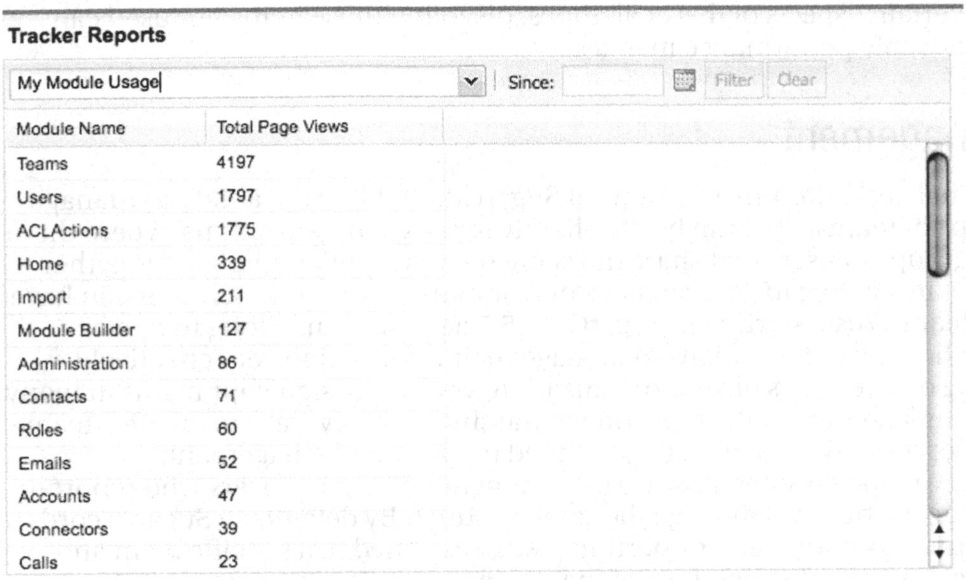

Tracker Reports

| My Module Usage | | Since: | | | Filter | Clear |

Module Name	Total Page Views
Teams	4197
Users	1797
ACLActions	1775
Home	339
Import	211
Module Builder	127
Administration	86
Contacts	71
Roles	60
Emails	52
Accounts	47
Connectors	39
Calls	23

Figure 5-1. Tracker Reports dashlet

There are several reports available in this dashlet, namely:

- Last Ten Modified Records
- Show Active Users
- Active User Count
- Top User
- My Weekly Usage
- My Module Usage
- My Top Three Modules Used
- My Cumulative Login Time (this week)
- Users Cumulative Login Time (this week)

The Tracker backend is also very configurable. The Tracker Settings admin panel allows disabling capturing certain Tracker actions, such as tracking page views, session information, performance metrics, and query logging. You can also adjust the slow query time threshold and the amount of time tracker data is stored. The main reason for doing this would be for performance reasons, since operating the full slate of metric tracking can be quite taxing on the system. Since many admins may not be interested in certain aspects of this at all times, disabling those items not used can result in a noticeable performance increase.

Team Management

The Professional and Enterprise Editions of SugarCRM add on the ability to manage users in groups of teams. This can be very handy for larger organizations, where there are different groups of users that share the same responsibilities and work together on projects. Teams in SugarCRM can have one or more users, and each user can have one or more teams. Also, starting in SugarCRM 5.5 a record can belong to one or more teams, allowing organizations to manage their information very effectively.

Depending on the needs of your organization, you can design your teams in many ways. For example, based on the reporting hierarchy, you may want to create a team of users who report to the same manager. Based on product management requirements, you may want to create a cross-functional team of users who report to different managers, but who manage the same product. By default, all Sugar records such as accounts, contracts, and opportunities are assigned to a specific team and can only be accessed by the members of that team.

As mentioned, a user can belong to one or more teams. When you create a user, the system automatically creates a private team for the person. Any record that the user creates, such as a contract or a quote, is assigned to the user's private team by default. Only the user can access and manage records assigned to this team. But the user can assign a different team to manage the record. Managers can view any record that their subordinates can view, even if the record is not assigned to the same team the manager is a part of.

Users can be both explicitly and implicitly assigned to teams, and will appear as either Member or Member Reports-to. When a user is manually, or explicitly, assigned to a team, the user will appear as a member in the Membership column. For example, Will and Chris both report to Jim. Will is a member of the East team; Chris is a member of the West team. As a result, Jim will be an implicit member of both the East and West teams.

When a user is manually assigned to a team, the user's management reporting hierarchy is implicitly added to the team as well. This ensures that members of the user's management hierarchy also have visibility over the records of the user in question. Implicit members appear as Member Reports-to in the Membership column. However, when a user becomes implicitly part of a team, they cannot be removed manually from the team. Instead, you must remove them from the inherited team. In the preceding example, to delete Jim from the West team either Chris must be removed from the West team, or Chris must no longer report to Jim. You cannot just remove Jim from the West team.

In regard to teams, the new feature added in SugarCRM 5.5 is the ability to have multiple teams for a record. This is handy in larger organizations, where a record might have different parts of it that need to be used by different areas of the company. For example, an Account record may need to be shared by the accounting department, sales team, and the department that does the service work for the account. By having multiple teams for a record, all three teams can share this record between them. An additional fix to the multiple teams feature in Sugar 5.5 is the ability to view records you are assigned to, even if the team you were a member of didn't have access to the record.

The team's functionality in SugarCRM is flexible enough to handle any organizations needs. It also is very easy to use, yet fast and powerful.

Dashlets

Reporting is an important part of any application for keeping on top of the data within it. However, many reporting needs are pretty simple. What are my top ten accounts? What calls need to be made today? Show me a chart of all the kinds of opportunities I have. In a previous life as an in-house application developer for a small company, many of these reports were built by hand, on demand, and would go on for pages and pages. In the end, people would look at the first page and then move on. This wasn't just an inconvenience for the poor application developer, but also the end-user who has to look through so many page to get the information they need.

To solve this problem, the SugarCRM home page is designed to be a dashboard, a place where all kinds of different information is listed in a way that end users can see what's going on in one place. In Sugar 5.0, this has been very much extended by not only enhancing the available Dashlets, but also allowing the user to group their Dashlets into different tabs. Figure 5-2 shows the typical home page with Dashlets.

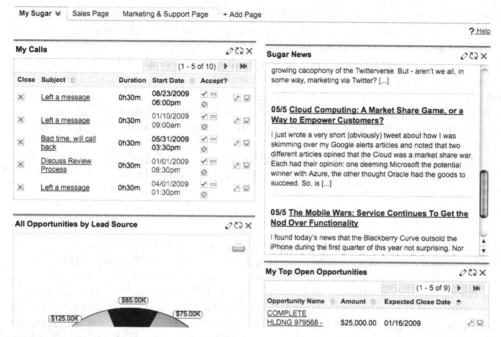

Figure 5-2. Home page with Dashlets

From a developer's perspective, there are many ways to customize here. Dashlets are added at the module level and inside the Dashlets/ directory. Placing a subdirectory underneath with the Dashlet's name, and a PHP script with the child class extended from the base, Dashlet class gets you started.

There are three principal types of Dashlets in Sugar:

- *ListView dashlet*: Displays lists of records like the ListViews or subpanels do.

- *Chart dashlet*: Displays a chart to user using flash.

- *Iframe dashlet*: Displays a web page inside the dashlet.

Let's break these down and see how you can build each one of them.

ListView Dashlet

For this, there is very little actual PHP code required. You require building the subclass from the Dashlet class. Instead of directly inheriting from the Dashlet class, however, you'll instead inherit from the DashletGeneric class, which has all of the common methods for this type of dashlet predefined. This enables you to use metadata to customize the dashlet, instead of having to rely on PHP code. Listing 5-2 shows the child class for the sample ApplicantsDashlet.

Listing 5-2. ApplicantsDashlet Class

```
require_once('include/Dashlets/DashletGeneric.php');
require_once('modules/ApplicantsDashlet/ApplicantsDashlet.php');

class ApplicantsDashlet extends DashletGeneric

{
    public function __construct(
            $id,

            $def = null
            )

    {
        global $current_user, $app_strings;
        require('modules/ApplicantsDashlet/metadata/dashletviewdefs.php');

        parent::DashletGeneric($id, $def);

        if(empty($def['title'])) $this->title = translate('LBL_HOMEPAGE_TITLE', ↵
'test_basic');

        $this->searchFields = $dashletData['ApplicantsDashlet']['searchFields'];
        $this->columns = $dashletData['ApplicantsDashlet']['columns'];

        $this->seedBean = new ApplicantsDashlet();
    }
}
```

All the constructor does here is point everything in the correct direction. You start off by loading the definition file, which contains both the searchfields and the columns for the dashlet. You also set the title and then the bean object for the module.

The next part is defining the search and column fields. For this, you'll have a dashletviewdefs.php file in the module, defined in the metadata directory of the module (see Listing 5-3).

Listing 5-3. ApplicantsDashlet Metadata

```
$dashletData['ApplicantsDashlet']['searchFields'] = array (
  'date_entered' =>
  array (
    'default' => '',
  ),
  'assigned_user_id' =>
  array (
    'type' => 'assigned_user_name',
```

```
        'default' => 'Administrator',
    ),
);
$dashletData['ApplicantsDashlet']['columns'] = array (
  'name' =>
  array (
      'width' => '40%',
      'label' => 'LBL_LIST_NAME',
      'link' => true,
      'default' => true,
      'name' => 'name',
  ),
  'date_entered' =>
  array (
      'width' => '15%',
      'label' => 'LBL_DATE_ENTERED',
      'default' => true,
      'name' => 'date_entered',
  ),
  'assigned_user_name' =>
  array (
      'width' => '8%',
      'label' => 'LBL_LIST_ASSIGNED_USER',
      'name' => 'assigned_user_name',
      'default' => true,
  ),
  'date_modified' =>
  array (
      'width' => '15%',
      'label' => 'LBL_DATE_MODIFIED',
      'name' => 'date_modified',
      'default' => true,
  ),
);
```

You've defined four fields to display: the applicant's name, the date he was entered into the system, to whom the applicant is assigned to, and the date the applicant record was last modified. You've also enabled searching by date entered and assigned user id. The display of this is just like the standard ListView, as you can see in Figure 5-3.

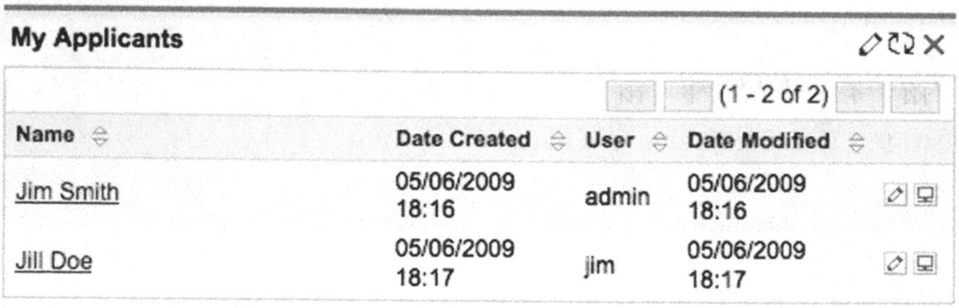

My Applicants				✎ ⟲ ✕
			(1 - 2 of 2)	
Name ⇕	Date Created ⇕	User ⇕	Date Modified ⇕	
Jim Smith	05/06/2009 18:16	admin	05/06/2009 18:16	✎ 💻
Jill Doe	05/06/2009 18:17	jim	05/06/2009 18:17	✎ 💻

Figure 5-3. *ApplicantsDashlet ListView*

You can refresh the dashlet data by clicking the refresh icon in the title bar (the one that has two arrows in a circle), which grabs the updated data in an ajax request. Clicking the X icon will remove the dashlet from the page. You can get to the configuration dialog for the dashlet by clicking the pencil icon, which brings up a window that looks like Figure 5-4.

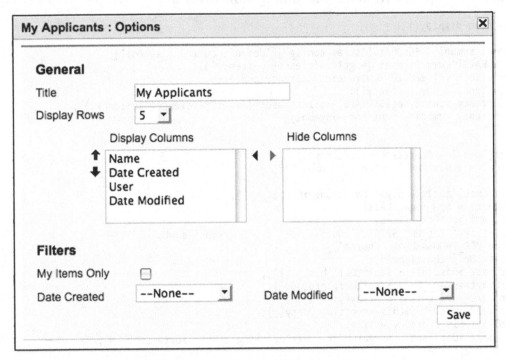

Figure 5-4. ApplicantsDashlet options dialog

The first part of the dialog allows customizing the dashlet itself, such as changing the title, number of rows to display, and the columns to show. The next part incorporates the searchFields you previously defined, allowing you to customize the display dashlet records results. One item that is always added is the 'My Items Only' checkbox, which is handy to filter out other users records in case you are making Dashlets of items just for yourself. These can all be customized via the metadata file shown previously in Listing 2-2.

Chart Dashlets

Chart Dashlets work similarly to the Listview Dashlets, the only difference being in the display of the Dashlet itself. Here you use the display method of the bean to build and display the chart itself. The SugarCharts class can be used for doing this because it has chart templates for many different kinds of charts, such as bar charts, line charts, pie charts, and funnel charts. The display method of the Dashlet child class handles all the building of this, from grabbing the data from the database to displaying it to the end user, as you can see in Listing 5-4.

Listing 5-4. display() method from the OutcomeByMonthDashlet

```php
public function display()
{
    $currency_symbol = $GLOBALS['sugar_config']['default_currency_symbol'];
    if ($GLOBALS['current_user']->getPreference('currency')){
        require_once('modules/Currencies/Currency.php');
        $currency = new Currency();
        $currency->retrieve($GLOBALS['current_user']->getPreference('currency'));
        $currency_symbol = $currency->symbol;
    }

    require("modules/Charts/chartdefs.php");
    $chartDef = $chartDefs['outcome_by_month'];

    require_once('include/SugarCharts/SugarChart.php');
    $sugarChart = new SugarChart();
    $sugarChart->setProperties('',
        translate('LBL_OPP_SIZE', 'Charts') . ' ' . $currency_symbol . '1'
.translate('LBL_OPP_THOUSANDS', 'Charts'),
        $chartDef['chartType']);
    $sugarChart->base_url = $chartDef['base_url'];
    $sugarChart->group_by = $chartDef['groupBy'];
    $sugarChart->url_params = array();
    $sugarChart->getData($this->constructQuery());
    $sugarChart->is_currency = true;
    $sugarChart->data_set = $sugarChart->sortData($sugarChart->data_set, 'm', false,
'sales_stage', true, true);
    $xmlFile = $sugarChart->getXMLFileName($this->id);
    $sugarChart->saveXMLFile($xmlFile, $sugarChart->generateXML());

    return $this->getTitle('<div align="center"></div>') .
        '<div align="center">' . $sugarChart->display($this->id, $xmlFile, '100%',
'480', false) . '</div><br />';
    }

    /**
     * @see DashletGenericChart::constructQuery()
     */
    protected function constructQuery()
    {
        $query = "SELECT sales_stage,".
            db_convert('opportunities.date_closed','date_format',array("'%Y-
%m'"),array("'YYYY-MM'"))." as m, ".
            "sum(amount_usdollar/1000) as total, count(*) as opp_count FROM opportunities ";
        $query .= " WHERE opportunities.date_closed >= ".db_convert("'".$this-
>obm_date_start."'",'datetime') .
```

```
                            " AND opportunities.date_closed <= ".db_convert("'".$this-
>obm_date_end."'",'datetime') .
                            " AND opportunities.deleted=0";
        if (count($this->obm_ids) > 0)
            $query .= " AND opportunities.assigned_user_id IN ('" . implode("','",$this-
>obm_ids) . "')";
        $query .= " GROUP BY sales_stage,".
                            db_convert('opportunities.date_closed','date_format',array("'%Y-
%m'"),array("'YYYY-MM'")) .
                            " ORDER BY m";

    return $query;
    }
```

Here you've refactored out the actual query building into the constructQuery()
method. You feed it directly into the SugarChart::getData() method to handle the
entire chart build process. Displaying the chart you can see is a two-part process. You
first output the xml data used to build the chart into the cache directory, then,
secondly, you feed it back into the SugarChart::display() method, which displays the
chart as an Adobe Flash animation. You can see this in action in Figure 5-5.

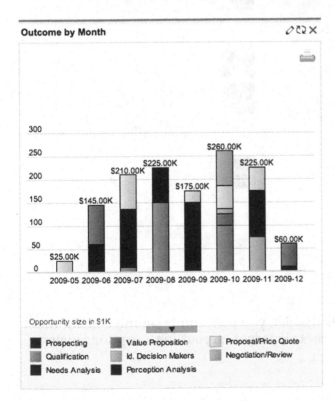

Figure 5-5. *OutcomeByMonth*

Iframe Dashlets

This is a really simple kind of dashlet that just displays a web page to the end user inside an iframe. There's no coding required for this dashlet. You simply add the 'My Portal' dashlet to your Home page then set the URL you want it to point at in the configuration options.

While any web page can be used inside this dashlet, it's really best to suit only certain types of content inside it. One type of content is mobile web pages. They are typically designed for small screens like phones and tablets. Since the proportions of the iframe in this dashlet is in the same situation, it's an excellent choice for iframe dashlets (see Figure 5-6).

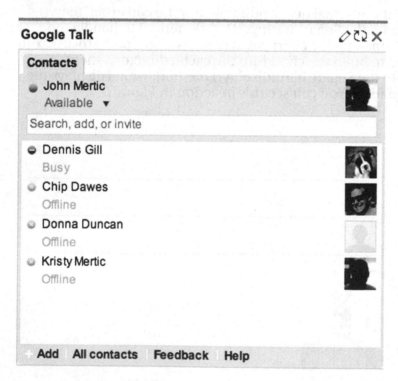

Figure 5-6. Google Talk dashlet

To create the preceding Google Talk dashlet, you can simply set the URL for the dashlet to http://talkgadget.google.com/talkgadget/popout in the options dialog for the dashlet.

Custom Dashlets

You can build any kind of dashlet using the dashlet framework. The only requirement is to extend the Dashlet class and implement the display() method, and optionally the displayOptions() and saveOptions() methods if the dashlet is configurable. You can control if the dashlet is configurable by setting the $isConfigurable property in the child class.

Let's look at an example of a custom dashlet that ships with Sugar, the Team Notices Dashlet, in Listing 5-5.

Listing 5-5. *TeamNoticesDashlet Class*

```
require_once('include/Dashlets/Dashlet.php');

class TeamNoticesDashlet extends Dashlet
{
    public $isRefreshable = false;
    public $hasScript     = true;

    public function __construct(
        $id
        )
    {
        parent::Dashlet($id);
        if(empty($def['title']))
            $this->title = translate('LBL_MODULE_NAME', 'TeamNotices');
    }

    public function displayScript()
    {
    }

    public function display()
    {
        $data = array();

        require_once('include/Sugar_Smarty.php');
        $ss = new Sugar_Smarty();

        require_once('modules/TeamNotices/TeamNotice.php');
        $focus = new TeamNotice();

        $today = db_convert("'".gmdate($GLOBALS['timedate']->dbDayFormat)."'", 'date');
        $query = $focus->create_list_query("date_start",$focus->table_name."↵
.date_start <= $today and ".$focus->table_name.".date_end >= $today and↵
".$focus->table_name.'.status=\'Visible\'');

        if ( $result = $focus->db->query($query) )
            while ( $row = $focus->db->fetchByAssoc($result) )
                $data[] = $row;
```

```
        $ss->assign("data", $data);

        return parent::display() . $ss->fetch↵
  ('modules/TeamNotices/Dashlets/TeamNoticesDashlet/TeamNoticesDashlet.tpl');
    }
}
```

The display method here handles displaying all of the content to the user. Two other properties worth noting are the $isRefreshable property, which controls the display of the refresh button, and the $hasScript property, which is true if javascript is used in the display of the dashlet. This is useful if $hasScript is set to true, then the entire page must be reloaded before the dashlet can be used.

Next, let's look at Sugar Feeds another custom dashlet, which takes interaction in SugarCRM to a whole new level.

Sugar Feeds

Social networking has become the new way of interacting with people. Sites like Facebook, MySpace, and LinkedIn have gone from niche online web applications to primary tools for us to keep in contact with others all over the world. SugarCRM saw this trend, and saw the need to embrace it within the scope of CRM. Many times members of companies and teams may be geographically separated, or may just be out of touch with each other since they are involved in different projects. How can everyone still stay in touch and keep up with what's going on within the organization? For this, the concept of Sugar Feeds was born.

Sugar Feeds is a tool for social networking within SugarCRM. In its simplest form, it acts as an intra-company message board, allowing users to post messages and content for others to see. This content can be a number of different sources: a link to another web page, an image, or even a YouTube video. For those using SugarCRM Professional or Enterprise Edition, you can even direct the content posted to a particular team, which enables intra-team messaging from clogging up the main feed the rest of the enterprise would see. Sugar Feeds are not enabled by default. To enable Sugar Feeds you'll need to go into the Sugar Feeds Settings in the Admin panel and do so. Figure 5-7 shows this.

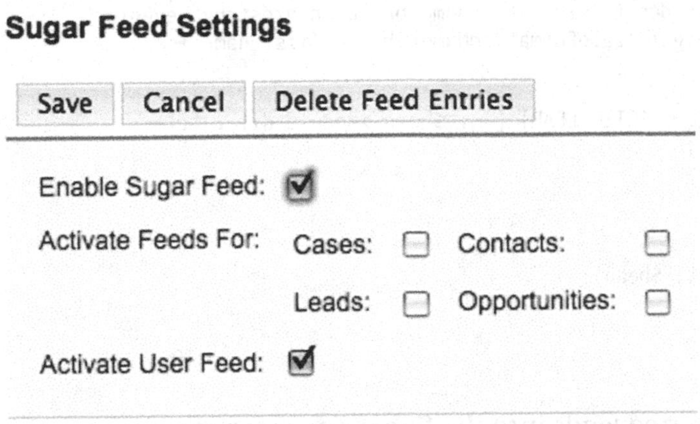

Sugar Feed Settings

Save	Cancel	Delete Feed Entries

Enable Sugar Feed: ☑

Activate Feeds For: Cases: ☐ Contacts: ☐

Leads: ☐ Opportunities: ☐

Activate User Feed: ☑

Figure 5-7. Sugar Feeds Admin panel

There are two different sources for Sugar Feeds. One is the user feeds, which is driven by content and messages posted by users in the Sugar Feeds dashlet. The other source is from logic hooks prior to the save of the module record. Logic hooks are custom code that can be called during certain processes in the application. (You'll learn more about them in Chapter 7.) These logic hooks are automatically added from code that is located in the SugarFeeds/ directory of the module, and are derived from the FeedLogicBase class. They are called during the saving of a modules record, before the actual saving of the data to the database takes place. Only one method is required to be implemented, pushFeed(), which is the code used to push the new feed entry into the feed. Listing 5-6 shows this method for the Leads module.

Listing 5-6. Leads Module SugarFeeds Hook

```
class LeadFeed extends FeedLogicBase

{
    var $module = 'Leads';
    function pushFeed($bean, $event, $arguments)
    {
        global $locale;

        $text = '';
        if(empty($bean->fetched_row)){
            $full_name = $locale->getLocaleFormattedName($bean->first_name,↵
$bean->last_name, '');

            $text = '{SugarFeed.CREATED_LEAD} [' . $bean->module_dir . ':' . $bean->id↵
. ':' . $full_name . ']';
        }else{
            if(!empty($bean->fetched_row['status'] ) && $bean->fetched_row['status']↵
!= $bean->status && $bean->status == 'Converted'){
```

```
                // Repeated here so we don't format the name on "uninteresting" events
                $full_name = $locale->getLocaleFormattedName($bean->first_name,↵
    $bean->last_name, '');

                $text = '{SugarFeed.CONVERTED_LEAD} [' . $bean->module_dir . ':'↵
    . $bean->id . ':' . $full_name . ']';
            }
        }

        if(!empty($text)){
            SugarFeed::pushFeed2($text, $bean);
        }

    }
}
```

Here you push the newly converted leads into the Sugar Feeds for other users to feed. The SugarFeed::pushFeed2() method does this. It grabs the team name from the team of the record and puts it in that team's feed for the Sugar Professional/Enterprise instances. The presence of the preceding class in the SugarFeeds directory is all that's required to make Sugar Feeds work, but you can disable modules which are already 'Sugar Feeds enabled' through the Sugar Feeds admin panel by not checking the boxes for the modules not wanted, as you can see previously in Figure 5-7.

The Sugar Feeds dashlet is the result, and it shows the available feed items to the user in chronological order with the newest items at the top of the list. This is also the interface used by end-users for posting new items to the user feed. Figure 5-8 shows the Sugar Feeds dashlet, which can be added to the Home page or the Dashboard.

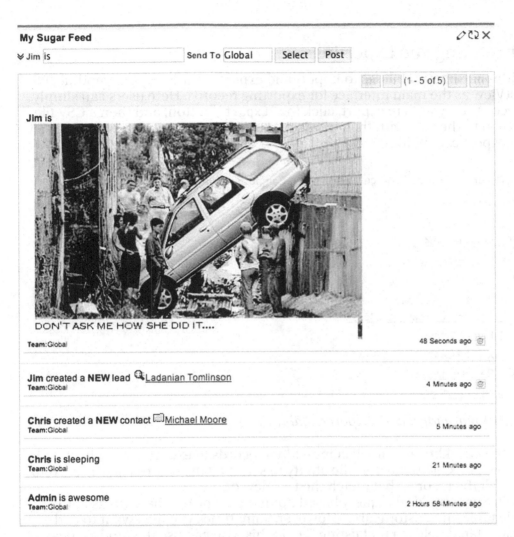

Figure 5-8. Sugar Feeds dashlet

The Sugar Feeds makes interaction between co-workers near and far much easier as well as centralizing communication so that everyone can keep abreast of what's happening in the application. It's also a useful tool for pushing data updates to everyone, keeping end-users aware of additions and changes to records in various modules.

Record Importing and Exporting

Sugar provides automatic abilities to import and export records out of a module. It uses the ListView as the main interface for exporting records. Here users can simply select the records they wish to export, click the 'Export' button, and then a CSV file will be returned to the user with the records requested. Figure 5-9 shows the ListView widget with export capabilities.

Figure 5-9. ListView widget with Export capabilities

Clicking the checkboxes will select individual records to export, while clicking the select dropdown link gives the user the ability to select all the records on the current page, or even all the records that match the ListView query.

By default, Sugar builds the query based upon on all the database fields in the main module table and custom table. However, sometimes you may want to add additional calculated fields to that listing. To do this, you can use the module bean method create_export_query(). It will return back the query to use to build the export list. Listing 5-7 shows an example of this in the Contacts module, by building a query that will also grab some Account information as well.

Listing 5-7. Contacts Module create_export_query() method

```
public function create_export_query(
    &$order_by,

    &$where,

    $relate_link_join=''
```

```
    )
{
    $custom_join = $this->custom_fields->getJOIN(true, true,$where);
    $custom_join['join'] .= $relate_link_join;


    $query = "SELECT
                            contacts.*,email_addresses.email_address email1,
                            accounts.name as account_name,
                            accounts.employees as account_employees,
                            accounts.industry as account_industry,

                            users.user_name as assigned_user_name ";
    if($custom_join){
        $query .= $custom_join['select'];
    }
    $query .= " FROM contacts ";
    $query .= "LEFT JOIN users
                            ON contacts.assigned_user_id=users.id ";
    $query .= "LEFT JOIN accounts_contacts
                            ON ( contacts.id=accounts_contacts.contact_id↵
and (accounts_contacts.deleted is null or accounts_contacts.deleted = 0))
                            LEFT JOIN accounts
                            ON accounts_contacts.account_id=accounts.id ";

    //join email address table too.
    $query .= ' LEFT JOIN  email_addr_bean_rel on contacts.id =↵
email_addr_bean_rel.bean_id and email_addr_bean_rel.bean_module=\'Contacts\'↵
and email_addr_bean_rel.deleted=0 and email_addr_bean_rel.primary_address=1 ';
    $query .= ' LEFT JOIN email_addresses on email_addresses.id =↵
email_addr_bean_rel.email_address_id ' ;

    if($custom_join){
        $query .= $custom_join['join'];
    }

    $where_auto = "( accounts.deleted IS NULL OR accounts.deleted=0 )
                    AND contacts.deleted=0 ";

    if($where != "")
        $query .= "where ($where) AND ".$where_auto;
    else
        $query .= "where ".$where_auto;

    if(!empty($order_by))
        $query .= " ORDER BY ". $this->process_order_by($order_by, null);

    return $query;
}
```

The preceding query will include the account name, employees, and industry field along with the contact data.

The next part of the equation is importing data into your Sugar instance. Sugar 5.1 did a major revamping of the Import process, which greatly enhanced the import user interface and import file capabilities, allowing record imports of more than 100,000 records to occur. It also added a very easy way to add import capabilities to any module in the product—all that is needed is two changes to your existing module. The first change needed is to add the $importable property to the module's bean and set the value to true while the second is discussed after the following code. Listing 2-7 shows the sample module you'll call *Applicants*.

Listing 2-7. *Applicants Module Bean Class with the Importable Property*

```
require_once('include/SugarObjects/templates/person/Person.php');



class Applicants extends Person
{
    // we set importable to true to enable importing in our module
    public $importable = true;



    public function __construct()
    {
        parent::Person();
    }
}
```

The importable property defaults to false if it is not specified otherwise.

The second part is adding the menu option in the left-side shortcuts menu to enter the import process for the current module. The left shortcuts menu is defined in the Menu.php file in the module directory, and all you need to add is an entry for the import option. Listing 2-8 shows this for the *Applicants* sample module you used in the previous example.

Listing 2-8. *Applicants Module Menu.php File*

```
global $mod_strings, $app_strings, $sugar_config;


if(ACLController::checkAccess('Applicants', 'edit', true))

    $module_menu[] = Array("index.php?module=Applicants&action=EditView&return_module=↵
Applicants&return_action=index", $mod_strings['LNK_NEW_APPLICANT'],"CreateApplicants",↵
'Applicants');
if(ACLController::checkAccess('Applicants', 'list', true))
    $module_menu[] =Array("index.php?module=Applicants&action=index&return_module=↵
Applicants&return_action=DetailView",↵
                        $mod_strings['LNK_APPLICANT_LIST'],"Applicants", 'Applicants');
if(ACLController::checkAccess('Applicants', 'import', true))
```

```
$module_menu[] =Array("index.php?module=Import&action=Step1&import_module=↵
Applicants&return_module=Applicants&return_action=index", $app_strings['LBL_IMPORT'],"Import",
'Applicants');
```

The typical left shortcut menu for a module will have two links: one to create a new record and another to access the ListView for the module. What you've done is add a link after that to start the import process. With those two changes, you have made a module available to be imported into. Pretty simple, all things considered.

There are other customizations available for the import process as well. One common one is to exclude fields from being imported into. The reasons for doing this are normally due to a field being calculated in some way in the module, so you wouldn't want the given imported setting to overwrite that calculation. To have a field be excluded, you simply need to add the importable attribute to the field definition in the vardefs.php file, as shown in Listing 2-9. You also can handle the situation where a certain field must be imported into. Again, you can use the importable attribute of the field definition here, setting it to the value 'required'. When the field is set to required, then it must be mapped during the mapping step of the import process.

Listing 2-10. Examples of Field Definitions Using the 'importable' attribute

```
$dictionary['Applicants']['fields']['applied_position'] => array (
    'name' => 'applied_position',
    'vname' => 'LBL_APPLIED_POSITION',
    'type' => 'varchar',
    'source' => 'non-db',
    'len' => '32',
    'importable' => 'required',
);
$dictionary['Applicants']['fields']['applied_department'] => array (
    'name' => 'applied_department',
    'vname' => 'LBL_APPLIED_DEPARTMENT',
    'type' => 'varchar',
    'source' => 'non-db',
    'len' => '32',
    'group'=>'portal',
    'reportable' => false,
    'importable' => 'false',
);
```

The previous is a very typical example of a field you wouldn't want to import. The applied_department field in the case is a calculated field based upon the position code, which is given in the applied_position field, so you wouldn't want to allow importing a value into this since you would not use it in the record. Additionally, the applied_position field is a required field, since you want every applicant to be connected to a position he is applying for.

101

As you can see, adding importing to a module is a very simple thing to do. Customizing the import process for a module, where we can control the fields available to import into and what fields must be mapped, is also just as simple.

Let's now look at how you can customize the look and feel of Sugar with themes.

Themes

Theming a web application is one of the most important aspects of any application. It's important for end-user acceptance, because if the application is not aesthetically pleasing or has poor usability, people will not feel very favorable to your application (even if it does make their life much easier). In enterprise deployments, theming that includes corporate branding is an often important requirement to those stakeholders.

A huge step forward for theme development has been made with Sugar 5.5. The biggest hurdle previously to theme development was in creation. You would normally start by copying an existing theme into a new directory then change the items you wish to change. The biggest problem with this approach is it was very difficult to apply styles from new UI elements, often requiring the developer to do lots of work to bring their theme to be current with the new version. It's especially inconvenient if there are very few changes needing made to customize the theme to your liking. Another issue is that the out-of-the-box themes were not customizable at all, which meant any change you would make to those themes would need to be reapplied on every upgrade.

With the advent of Sugar 5.5, the theme framework has been dramatically improved. To begin with, themes now only contain images, css files, smarty templates, and javascript code but no PHP code as there was previously. Doing so greatly simplifies the directory layout, as shown in Figure 5-10.

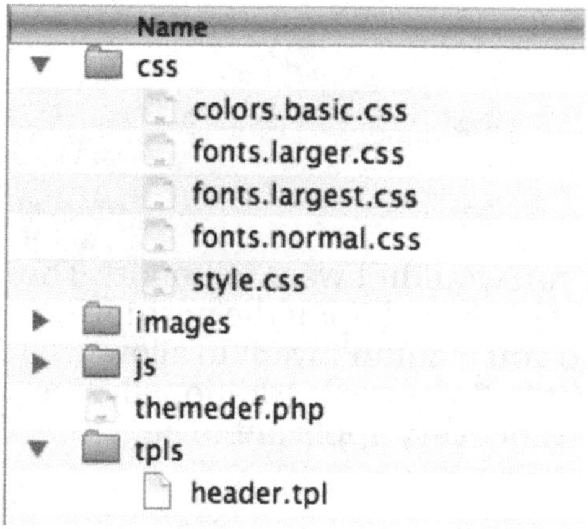

Figure 5-10. Theme directory layout

You've probably noticed I've told a small fib, there is one PHP file that is a part of the theme. It is a theme definition file, created in the same way as many of the other definition files in the application as an associative array. Listing 5-8 shows the structure of that file.

Listing 5-8. themedefs.php file

```
$themedef = array(
 'name' => "Sugar", // theme name
 'description' => "Sugar", // short description of the theme
 'colors' => array("sugar","red","green","blue","purple","gray"), ↵
// list of color.*.css files provided
 'fonts' => array("normal", "larger", "largest"), // list of font.*.css files provided
 'maxTabs' => $max_tabs, // maximum number of tabs shown in the bar
 'pngSupport' => true, // true if png image files are used in this theme, false if gifs
 'parentTheme' => "ParentTheme", // name of the theme this theme inherits from, ↵
if something other than the default theme.
 'barChartColors' => array(....),
 'pieChartColors' => array(....),
);
```

One thing to note is the `'parentTheme'` attribute because this is where the magic happens. Let's say you like the out-of-the-box Sugar theme, but need to make a few adjustments to it. Before, you would have copied them to a new directory and start hacking away. But with the new framework in Sugar 5.5, you can simply create a new theme, and specify `'Sugar'` as the parent theme. From there, the new theme will only contain changes to the parent theme needed to get the desired result, so if you wanted to use different images you would put images with the same name as the original in the images/ directory of the new theme, and put any css changes in the style.css file in the css/ directory. Javascript files and Smarty templates can also be overidden. In the case of CSS and javascript files, the given files will be added to the existing files, while smarty templates and images override the existing files.

You also now have opened the possibility of making custom modifications to themes. These customizations use the same inheritance framework as you have with building new themes on top of existing themes, but do so by adding a directory custom/themes/*themename*/ with the same structure as the original theme, only specifying the parts that you wish to change.

Pulling together the ability to customize any existing theme in an upgrade-safe way or build a new theme upon an existing theme, you can drastically change the user interface with very few lines of code. Let's say you want to add a more dramatic header background to the default Sugar theme. You would begin by creating the custom/themes/Sugar/images/ and custom/themes/Sugar/css/ directories, which will hold your changes. Then, you'll add a style.css file in the custom/themes/Sugar/css/ directory, which will contain the changes you wish to make to the theme. Listing 5-9 shows the style.css file, which has a rule for adding a background to the #header div (this div contains the entire top section of the theme template).

Listing 5-9. Custom style.css file for Changes to the Sugar Theme

```
#header
{
    background: url(../../../../custom/themes/Sugar/images/header.jpg);
}
#globalLinks, #welcome, #search, #sitemapLink,
#globalLinks a, #welcome a, #search a, #sitemapLink a
{
    color: white !important;
}
```

You'll add the new image to the custom/themes/Sugar/images/header.jpg directory. Since the image you picked has some darker colors in it, I've decided to make the text white so it stands out more. The finished product is shown in Figure 5-11.

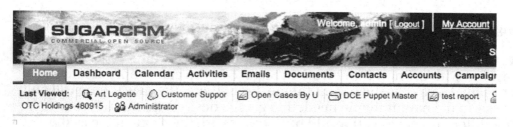

Figure 5-11. Sugar theme with custom modifications

You can see here that making a few small changes to a theme can result in a big difference. That's the power of the Theme Framework in Sugar 5.5. It enables the user to do small things that can result in huge differences to the product as a whole. This kind of ease for the developer helps sell the Sugar user experience to your end-users, which in turn makes your life as a developer a bit easier, too.

Logger

As a developer, one of the most difficult tasks is debugging problems. Tracking down where your customizations go awry can be a daunting task, one that even the most experienced developer can struggle with at times. While PHP does have rich debugging and tracing tools, such as apd or XDebug (one of my personal favorites), these kinds of tools do slow down your code a considerable amount, making their use in a production environment less than ideal.

Fortunately, SugarCRM comes with its own logger known internally as the SugarLogger. It's a very simple tool that is configurable to be as quiet or as verbose as needed, which makes it ideal for all kinds of logging needs. Much of the code that comes with SugarCRM uses the logger extensively to aid the developer in helping to diagnose problems without impacting the end-user at all (except, of course, for the slight performance hit the extra calls will have).

There are two parts to the using the logger. The first part is enabling the logger, which can be done from the config.php file in the root directory or in the 'System Settings' section of the Admin panel. To set the logger up manually, you can simply edit the config.php and change the setting for the 'logger' key, as shown in Listing 5-10. The way to change it in the UI is shown in Figure 5-12.

Listing 5-10. config.php 'logger' key

```
'logger' =>
  array (
    'level' => 'fatal', // options here can be one of: 'debug', 'info', 'warn',↵
'error', 'fatal', 'security', or 'off'
    'file' => array (
      'ext' => '.log', // log file name extension
      'name' => 'sugarcrm', // log file base name
      'dateFormat' => '%c', // date format used in the log file for the entries;↵
uses the settings from the PHP strftime() function
      'maxSize' => '10MB', // max size of a single log file before it rolls over
      'maxLogs' => 10, // max number of log files before it deletes the oldest one
    ),
  ),
```

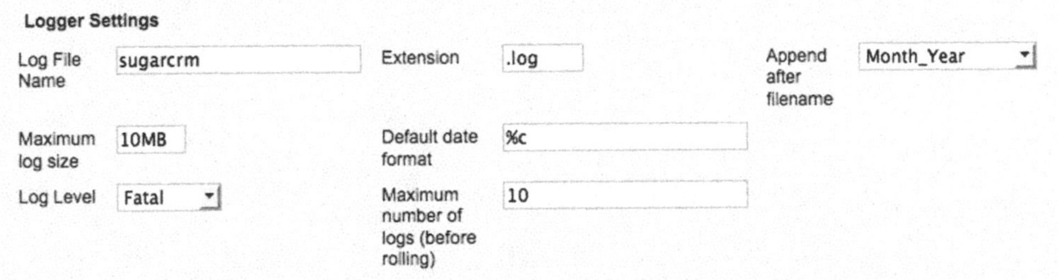

Figure 5-12. Changing the logger settings in the System Settings UI

The choice of log level is important since you can filter the amount of logging you do by changing the level. The order of the logging levels is 'debug', 'info', 'warn', 'error', 'fatal', 'security', then 'off', with 'debug' being the most verbose logging, and 'off' having no logging at all. Now in your code, you can easily trigger the logger by making calls to it, as shown in Listing 5-11.

Listing 5-11. Making Calls to the Logger

```
$GLOBALS['log']->info( "Write me to the info log"); // write to the log at the info level

$GLOBALS['log']->debug( "Variable set to $x"); // write to the log at the debug level,↵
 with the current value of $x

$GLOBALS['log']->security( "Illegal access by user {$current_user->username}");↵
 // write to the log at the security level, with the current user's username
```

With the preceding, you can easily watch for problems in your application that are major (such as security level issues) as well as troubleshoot problems with your code using the 'debug' level logging, or use one of the settings in the middle to give the appropriate amount of logging needed.

Summary

You can see now that SugarCRM provides several tools that most applications will use, like User Management, Dashboard items, Import and Export, Themes, and Logging, automatically and fully integrated into the product. They are also very controllable from a GUI perspective, allowing developers to truly put the day-to-day operations of the system into the user's hands.

You have now seen the main parts of the SugarCRM platform. In the next section of the book, you'll look into the tools available to customize it to fit your organization's needs.

PART 2

Customizing SugarCRM Out of the Box

With the knowledge of how SugarCRM works internal behind you, you'll next dive into customizing SugarCRM to meet your need. You'll see how to do simple customizations using the easy to use GUI developer tool Studio, see how to interject business logic into your applications with Logic Hooks and Workflows, and see how to customize every last little bit of Sugar with custom PHP code

CHAPTER 6

■ ■ ■

Easy Customizations Using Studio

In Part 1 of the book, you saw all the guts of SugarCRM and how they work together. I didn't leave any stone unturned, showing how the MVC processes each request meticulously, how the database structure is built using vardef files, how the metadata framework removes the need for manually coding common views, and where to look for the various components of a module. Although I hinted at ways to customize this as you went along, in this section of the book you'll dedicate your time to actually looking at customizing the application from how it ships to how you need to use it. The customizations you'll look at are just extensions of the already existing modules. In Part 3 of the book, you will focus on actually building new functionality on top of SugarCRM.

I'll show the easiest ways to customize Sugar in this chapter, using the Studio. You'll see how simple yet powerful this tool is, because it enables most customizations of SugarCRM to take place without having to touch any PHP code. This tool is also a big factor in the approachability of SugarCRM to those with little to no programming experience, empowering them to easily extend their instance.

Starting with Studio

Studio, one of the several developer tools SugarCRM ships out of the box, is designed to be used from within the application itself. It's a unique tool for a web application (or any business application) because it allows you to make upgrade-safe customizations to your instance using a simple GUI tool. Figure 6-1 shows how Studio looks when you first enter it, from the Admin ➤ Studio link.

Figure 6-1. *Main screen for Studio*

The interface for Studio has three distinct parts: the left-most column is a tree view of all of the customizable modules in your instance. You can expand the tree to access the customizations available for any particular part of a module. The center section is the main content view for Studio, containing the primary information you are concerned with when doing customizations. The right-most column is used to display help as you work through Studio, to help guide on how to use Studio effectively and show the impact of your changes.

I mentioned previously that the only modules that are shown here are modules that are customizable. When I say customizable, I mean Studio customizable. Not all modules are customized in such a way, mainly because some have a lot of legacy code in them or very customized views. For these, you cannot use Studio, but instead will need to customize them using code which you'll see in Chapter 8. For those that are customizable using Studio, you just need to add a studio.php file inside the modules/*modulename*/metadata/ directory. The file doesn't need to have anything inside—it's mere presence let's studio know the module is ready for customizing.

Studio is designed to enable the user to do the following kinds of customizations:

- Add new fields to a module.

- Change the display names (the name of the field as the user sees it) of existing fields in a module.

- Edit the various label strings used in a module.

- Customize the layouts of the Edit, Detail, and List views, as well as the Search box at the top of the Listviews and the Quickcreate form used in the left column on the page.

- Add new relationships from the given module into another module (or even the same module).

- Customize the display of Subpanels in the DetailView record for the given module.

I'll break apart the previous topics into sections to show how each of them work.

Adding New Fields to a Module

Adding fields is one of the most common customizations people do to SugarCRM. The biggest reason for this is that everyone has those one or two extra fields that they need for their own purposes, whether a checkbox to indicate a status for something or perhaps a field to specify an internal identification number of an account. This is one thing that SugarCRM understands about its user base. CRM is not a one-size-fits-all type of application, so it's silly to force people into that kind of thinking. In that respect, the first and foremost use for Studio is to be able to add new custom fields to a module.

Adding new custom fields is a very simple exercise. From the main screen of Studio, click on the module you wish to edit, and then click on the 'Fields' link. From there, a list of all the fields in the module will show, as you can see in Figure 6-2.

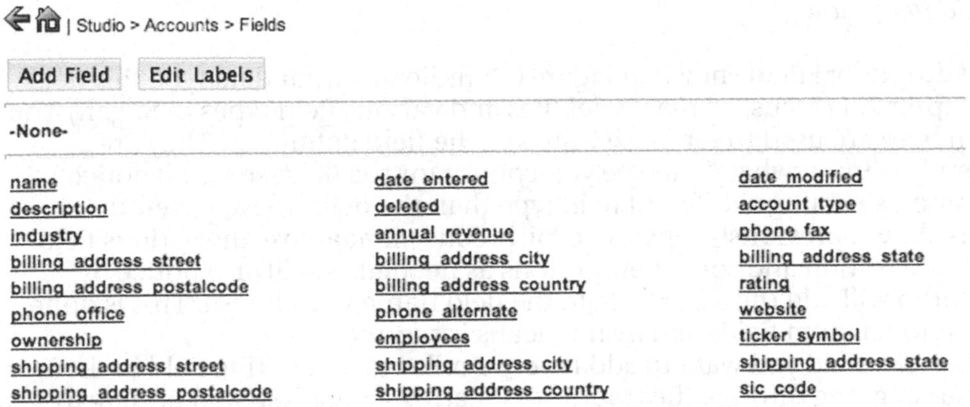

⬅ 🏠 | Studio > Accounts > Fields

| Add Field | Edit Labels |

-None-

name	date entered	date modified
description	deleted	account type
industry	annual revenue	phone fax
billing address street	billing address city	billing address state
billing address postalcode	billing address country	rating
phone office	phone alternate	website
ownership	employees	ticker symbol
shipping address street	shipping address city	shipping address state
shipping address postalcode	shipping address country	sic code

Figure 6-2. View of fields for the Accounts module

Notice the fields list is divided up into separate sections. The top section (which currently has no fields so you see the '-None-' label) is where all the custom fields for a module will be listed. Below the horizontal line is where the normal fields for the module are listed. This is handy since custom fields allow lots of customization to them through Studio, while normal fields only allow their display label to be changed.

From here, you can add new custom fields to your module. To do this, you simply click the 'Add Field' button, which will bring up a new dialog window for giving the details of the new field to add (see Figure 6-3).

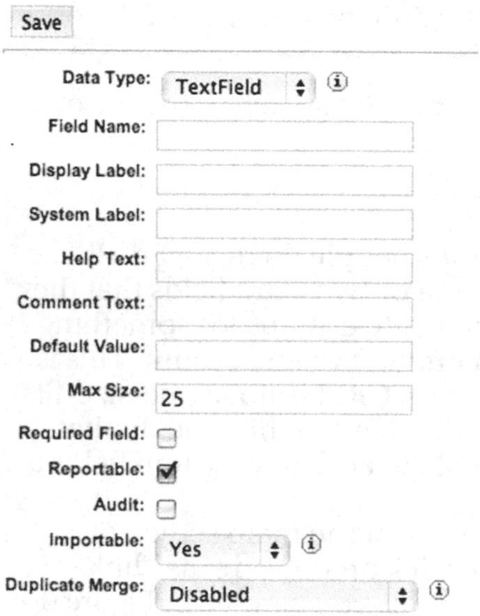

Save

Data Type:	TextField
Field Name:	
Display Label:	
System Label:	
Help Text:	
Comment Text:	
Default Value:	
Max Size:	25
Required Field:	☐
Reportable:	☑
Audit:	☐
Importable:	Yes
Duplicate Merge:	Disabled

Figure 6-3. *Add field dialog*

The initial dropdown field shown in Figure 6-3 indicates what data type this field will be. (In Chapter 2, I discussed the vardef files and various field types in Sugar.) The options shown here are used to set those values in the field definition. They are different depending upon what data type you choose for the field, so you'll notice them change upon selecting a different field type than the default. However, the typical options shown previously tend to be fairly consistent across the various field types, with a few addition and some new options as needed. You'll also notice by default that Studio will add the suffix '_c' to the field name you choose. This is done as a convention for custom fields and by no means is required.

Let's say the new field you want to add is very similar to an existing field in the module. Instead of going through the trouble of creating a new field and hoping to get all the settings right, you can simply just clone the field you wish to copy from to make the new field. To do this, click on the field you wish to clone your new custom field from, which brings up the edit dialog. Next to the Save button will be a Clone button, which when clicked will open a new field edit view with the settings from the current field already filled in. From here you can change anything you wish (especially the field name) and then click Save to save the field.

Looking at how fields are added into SugarCRM from a behind-the-scenes perspective, the new fields added through Studio are actually added separately from the default fields for a module. For each primary module table, a secondary table with the suffix '_cstm' is added when you create custom fields, and this table holds the custom fields for a module. During the save and retrieve process, you join the fields in the primary table and the custom table in order to get all the fields needed for the record. This is important to know for performance reasons, because if you have custom fields that you are going to be heavily searching against, you may want to consider adding indexes for them as well. This is something you'll need to do in the database itself using some form of the SQL CREATE INDEX command. Be sure that when you do this, you include the record id field ('id_c') to ensure that this index is chosen by the database's query optimizer.

Once you have added the fields you need to the module, the next step is to add the fields to the views so that users can interact with them.

Customizing View Templates

Each of the metadata views are customizable through Studio. Doing it through Studio offers numerous advantages compared to editing them by hand. As you saw in Chapter 3, it can be tedious to get everything correct and avoid errors in the metadata files. The Studio method allows you to edit through drag and drop, making the customization of the forms a snap.

Customizing Edit and Detail Views

Let's begin by looking at the Detail and Edit views. You can get to these by going to the Layouts section after selecting the module you wish to customize. From there, you can select either the EditView or DetailView links to customize the given view. When the view loads, you'll see a screen similar to Figure 6-4.

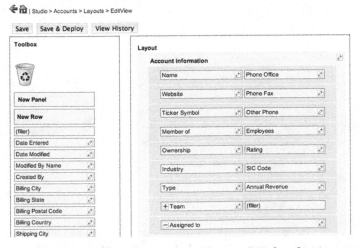

Figure 6-4. *Studio EditView editing for the the Accounts module*

The main section of this form shows the layout of the EditView. If you recall from Chapter 3 when I talked about the metadata framework, the forms are laid out in a table form, and you can group sets of fields into different panels to help ease the data entry and viewing of records. The left side has a list of fields available to add to the form as well as an element to add a new panel to the form and add a new row to an existing panel. Panels are more for organizing fields into groups of related fields, like putting all the address fields into one section. Each panel contains one or more rows, where you can put in a field for each column cell. The view is very interactive. You can add and remove elements from the form by simply clicking and dragging the various form elements around to get the resulting view you wish to have. When you are content with your changes, you can click Save to save them, or Save & Deploy to save your changes and then push them out for all your users to see immediately.

There are a few other views that use this style of editing as well. For example, the QuickCreate view forms are used for creating or edit records from the subpanel inline using ajax instead of loading the full edit view. They use this same editing form for customizing their views. Those using the Professional and Enterprise versions of Sugar also have the ability to use their mobile device, such as an iPhone or BlackBerry, with a specially formulated view of the application that can be easily used on the go. Starting with Sugar 5.5, these views can be edited through Studio as well through the same interface previously shown. The main issue people may run into with the mobile version of Sugar is that only a few of the modules are enabled to be used with mobile devices by default, and thus are missing from Studio to be customizable there. Fortunately, another Sugar 5.5 addition was a UI for adding and removing modules available from the mobile version of Sugar, as shown in Figure 6-5.

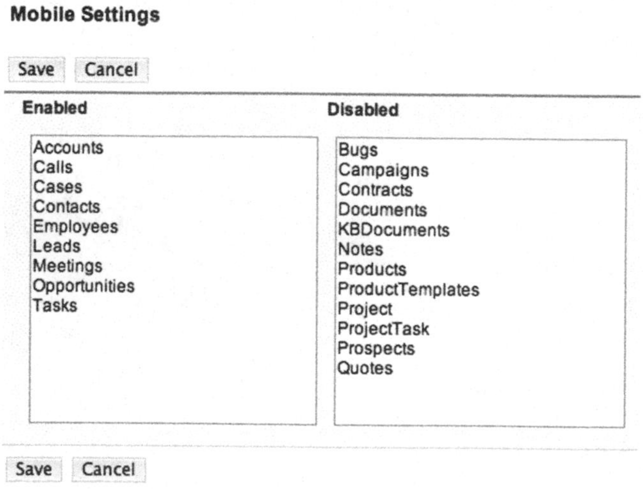

Mobile Settings

Save   Cancel

Enabled	Disabled
Accounts	Bugs
Calls	Campaigns
Cases	Contracts
Contacts	Documents
Employees	KBDocuments
Leads	Notes
Meetings	Products
Opportunities	ProductTemplates
Tasks	Project
	ProjectTask
	Prospects
	Quotes

Save   Cancel

Figure 6-5. *Dialog to add and remove modules from the mobile version of Sugar*

This can also be done in Sugar 5.1 or 5.2 by creating the custom/include/MVC/Controller/wireless_module_registry.php file and adding an entry $wireless_module_registry['modulename'] = array(); to it.

Customizing ListViews

ListViews are a bit different than their Edit and Detail view counterparts. For one, the physical layout is different, as it focuses more on column data rather than a large form. But one other big difference is that ListViews can also be customizable by the user. They can both change around the order of columns, but also remove and add columns to the display. Because of these facts, you need to have Studio act differently.

To begin with, ListViews can be customized with Studio by selecting ListView after choosing the module you wish to customize. Figure 6-6 shows you the editing view for the ListView by default.

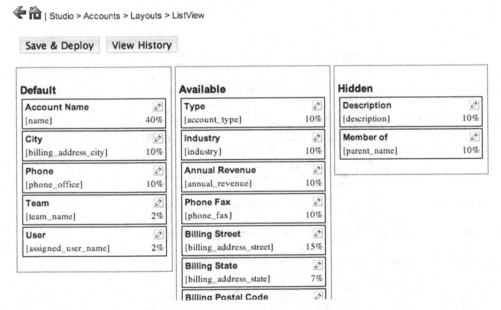

Figure 6-6. Customizing the ListView for the Accounts module in Studio

The ListView editor has three columns of fields. The first column is a list of fields that will show by default when you are on the ListView for the module. If you would look at the listviewdefs.php file for the module, you see these fields listed with the 'default' attribute set to true. The middle column is a list of fields that are available to the user to be included in the ListView, but aren't shown by default. Finally, the last column is a list of all columns that are hidden from display to the user. This column should include only the field that under no circumstance an end user could have included in the ListView.

The form is itself is very interactive, just as the Edit and Detail view editors were. You can freely reorder any of the fields in the columns shown, as well click, drag, and drop fields between the columns as needed. Clicking the ✎ icon allows you to change the display label and widths of each column, which is handy as it can help your ListView fit much better and display the data much clearer if it doesn't do so by default. When you have the fields the way you want them, clicking Save & Deploy will push the changes out to everyone to begin using immediately.

For customizing the subpanels and search panels using Studio, a modified version of the ListView editing screen is used. Since the users cannot customize what fields appear in the search or for a subpanel, you can remove the Available column from the editing view, as shown in Figure 6-7.

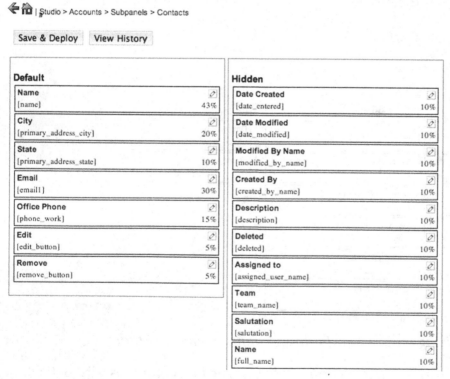

Figure 6-7. Customizing the Contacts subpanel in the Accounts module using Studio

The editing view works exactly the same as the editing for the ListView worked: by allowing drag and drop field placement and ordering in the view. Working with the search panels is identical to this, except you'll want to be cognizant of the number of columns used in the search panel if you are trying to group or line up fields since the editor in Studio doesn't make that very clear. The mobile counterparts to the search panels and ListView will work just the same as the normal search panels and ListView, respectively.

Editing Labels

As you have seen, SugarCRM separates out strings into language files to enable the application to be easily translated into different languages. This has been quite successful for Sugar, as it has been translated into over 75 different languages since its inception, making it a truly global aware product. But this abstraction layer also enables users to change the display verbiage used in various parts of the application to match the terms that make the most sense to their company or workflow.

There are two primary ways to do this. The most straightforward way to make the change is though the Labels option under the module in Studio. Figure 6-8 lists out all of the strings for the current language in the given module, allowing you to edit them right then and there.

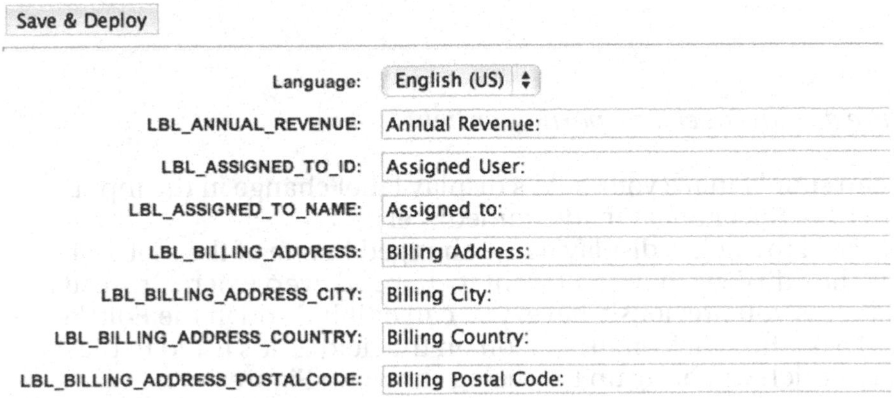

Save & Deploy	
Language:	English (US) ⬍
LBL_ANNUAL_REVENUE:	Annual Revenue:
LBL_ASSIGNED_TO_ID:	Assigned User:
LBL_ASSIGNED_TO_NAME:	Assigned to:
LBL_BILLING_ADDRESS:	Billing Address:
LBL_BILLING_ADDRESS_CITY:	Billing City:
LBL_BILLING_ADDRESS_COUNTRY:	Billing Country:
LBL_BILLING_ADDRESS_POSTALCODE:	Billing Postal Code:

Figure 6-8. Editing labels for a module

The editing screen is very simple, providing the current values for the various strings and an input box for changing them. If you have multiple language packs installed on your Sugar instance, you can select the language you wish to edit in the Language dropdown at the top of the form to change the string used in the other languages. Once you have made your changes, clicking Save & Deploy saves the changes and applies them immediately to the current instance.

The second way is that you can also make changes to a field directly. This approach may be preferred since it allows you to know exactly which display string will be used with each field, removing any ambiguities in deciding what label to edit in the Labels option under the module in Studio. To access this, you just click on the field name listed in the Fields option under the module, and are returned a form similar to Figure 6-9.

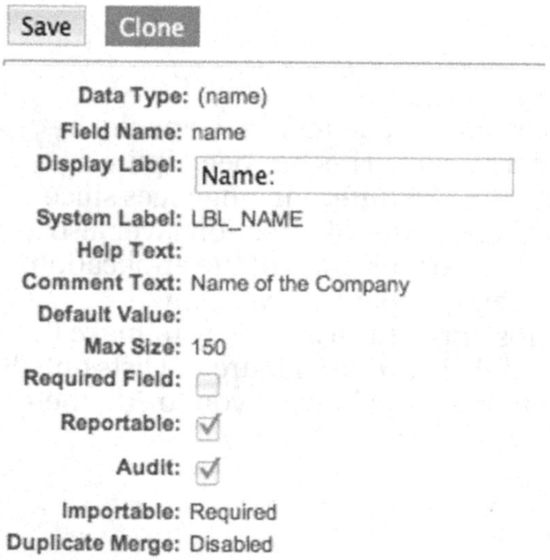

Figure 6-9. *Editing the display label for a particular field*

From here, you can simply make your field's display label change in the input box, and click save to have the changes made immediately.

Let's say you just need the field's display name changed in one of the metadata driven views, such as the EditView, but don't want it changed everywhere. Instead of editing the display label as you previously have, you can edit it through the EditView customization view. To do this, click on the ⧉ icon on the field as it's listed in the view template display, which will bring up the dialog shown in Figure 6-10.

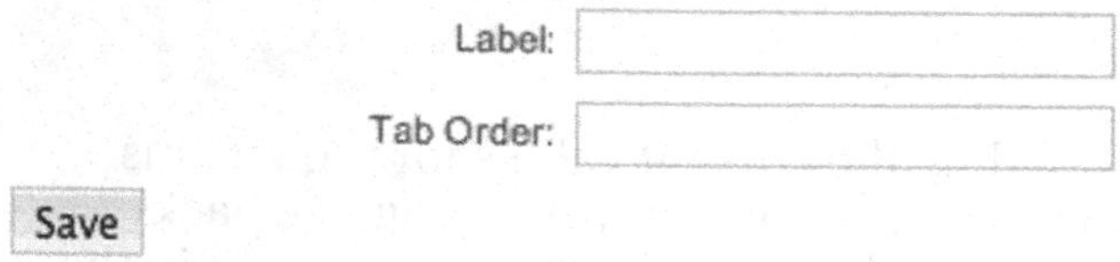

Figure 6-10. *Edit field name through the view template customization screen*

Here you can specify the exact label you wish to use for this field for this metadata view. Saving your change will commit you to using the given string for this field in the view. If you leave it blank then the default string for the field will be used instead.

Relationships, Relationships, Relationships

One of the most useful tools in Studio is the ability to add new relationships to other modules in the product. If you remember from Chapter 2, you can define many different types of inter-module relationships to handle the specific needs you have in your Sugar instance. Doing this by hand can become a very tedious multistep process, requiring you to correct add the needed pieces to the vardefs for both modules, create subpanels to display the data, and even add extra fields to the EditView and DetailViews of the module to display this extra data. Fortunately, Studio's ability to create relationships handles this all automatically and gets it ready to go in an instance.

To begin to create new relationships, go to the Relationships link under the module you wish to customize. Once you've done that, you see a screen similar to Figure 6-11.

⇐ 🏠 | Studio > Accounts > Relationships

Add Relationship			
Name	Primary Module	Type	Related Module
member_accounts	Accounts	one-to-many	Accounts
account_cases	Accounts	one-to-many	Cases
account_tasks	Accounts	one-to-many	Tasks
account_notes	Accounts	one-to-many	Notes
account_meetings	Accounts	one-to-many	Meetings
account_calls	Accounts	one-to-many	Calls
account_leads	Accounts	one-to-many	Leads
campaign_accounts	Campaigns	one-to-many	Accounts

Figure 6-11. Relationship listing for the Accounts module in Studio

The relationships list for the module shows all the relationships that currently exist for the module. You can see the name of the relationship, the Primary module of the relationship (often referred to as the parent module), the type of relationship, and the module it's related to (also known as the child module). Any modules that you have added through Studio will also be shown here with an asterisk next to the relationship name.

Once you've made it here, you can simply click on Add Relationship to add a new relationship. When you do so, the new relationship screen will be shown, as you can see in Figure 6-12.

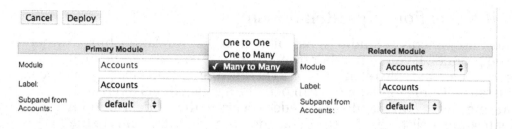

Figure 6-12. Creating a new relationship with the Accounts module using Studio

The new relationship form allows you to select the primary and related modules for the relationship. There are three options for this type of relationship that you can create through this form:

- *One to One*: The primary module has one record which relates to only one record in the related module.

- *One to Many*: The primary module has one record which relates to one or more records in the related module.

- *Many to Many*: The primary module can have one or more records which relates to one or more records in the related module.

The new relationship form is very dynamic, so when you change the relationship type in the middle column of the form, the relationship details on each side of the column will change accordingly. If the side of the relationship contains the Many part (which would mean that module has more than one record relating to the other side of the relationship), then the options to provide a label for the subpanel in the opposite side of the relationship is available, along with an option to choose the subpanel layout to use.

After clicking Deploy, the relationship becomes permanent and immediately available to all users. This is where the "magic" happens. One of many different things occur, depending upon the relationship type you choose:

- *One to One*: The primary module and the related module will have relate fields added to the Edit and Detail views to enable the end users to build the relationship between the records.

- *One to Many*: The primary module will have a subpanel listing all the related records in the related modules, which includes the ability to add existing records related to that record or add a new record which is related to that record from there. In the related module, relate field will be added to the Edit and Detail views to enable end users to relate the record to a record in the primary module

- *Many to Many*: Both the primary and the related modules will have a subpanel listing all the related records in the opposite module, which includes the ability to add existing records related to that record or add a new record which is related to that record from there. Adding a record to be related to the other module will make it show up in the subpanels for both that record and the record in the opposite module.

You can see Studio really does everything you need here to add relationships to any Studio customizable module in Sugar. One thing that Studio doesn't allow is the ability to delete relationships you've added, but I will give you a solution to that problem in the next section.

Help! My Customizations Have Gone Awry

Let's say you've played around with Studio as you have gone through this chapter. You added a bunch of new fields, customized the module views, and added a relationship or two. After going through the journey of learning the ins and outs of customizing your Sugar instance with Studio, you realize that you went too far, and now wish to go back. Have no fear, as everything you've done can be undone fairly easily.

All of the metadata customizations (customizations to any of the detail/edit/list views and subpanels) done are stored in the /custom directory. By simply removing the associated metadata file (editviewdefs.php, detailviewdefs.php, listviewdefs.php, etc.) from the /custom/modules/*modulename*/metadata/ directory, the customized view is undone and you can resume using the out-of-the-box view layouts. Studio also stores the history your view changes inside the custom/history/modules/*modulename*/metadata/ directory, so you can step back through the changes you've made to the view of the form. Figure 6-13 illustrates this in action and you can access it by clicking the View History button.

Figure 6-13. Historical view of changes made by Module Builder for a view

Clicking the Preview gives you a look at what the view looked like at that point in time. When you find the one you want, just click Restore and it comes back to life.

Removing custom fields is very simple from the Studio UI, just simply click the field you wish to delete from the Fields view, and then click the Delete button on the field's edit view. You can also remove them by hand, but it is bit more tedious of a task. If you remember, custom field definitions are actually stored in the database rather than in the file system itself. Therefore, the process to remove the field actually involves looking into the field_meta_data table, and removing the custom field definition from the table. To look for the field, check for the id of the field to be set to the module name plus the field name. If your custom field name in the Accounts module is foobar_c, look for the record with the id field set to `Accountsfoobar_c`. From there, you can set the deleted field value in that row to 1, or simply delete the row from the table. You'll then need to rebuild the vardef files. You can do this in Sugar by going to Admin ➤ Repair ➤ Repair Database, so simply by removing the cache/modules/*modulename*/*modulename*vardefs.php file.

Relationships are also dealt with entirely inside the custom/ directory, but they don't come with the pretty UI to remove them (recall the giant warning message about the inability to remove any created relationships). Have no fear though, as you can dig through the custom/ directory to undo these changes as well. There are three different files that need removed:

- custom/metadata/*relationship_name*MetaData.php

- custom/Extension/modules/*firstrelatedmodulename*/Ext/Vardefs/
custom*relationship_name*.php

- custom/Extension/modules/*secondrelatedmodulename*/Ext/Varde
fs/custom*relationship_name*.php

Substitute the name of the relationship (usually *firstrelatedmodulename_secondrelatedmodulename*) in the previous examples. If the relationship relates back to the same module, then you'll only have two files to delete. Once those files are removed, you'll need to go to Admin ➤ Repair ➤ Rebuild Relationships followed by an Admin ➤ Repair ➤ Repair Database to clean up all the remaining references to the previous module in the cached vardefs. If you have any related fields to the parent module from the child module, then you'll also want to remove those manually from the metadata viewdef files or using Studio.

Please remember that undoing any customization is just as hazardous as doing customizations, so I greatly recommend trying this on a test instance before doing so on your production instance. Undoing can be especially dangerous, since you may lose any customizations you didn't mean to remove.

Summary

In this chapter, you have learned all about Studio, a very powerful and unique tool that enables end-users to customize their Sugar instance with little or no programming experience required. Studio allows you to add new custom fields to a module, customize the string used in a module, and add additional relationships between the given module and another module, or even back to the current module. You explored each of these topics in detail, showing the ease of use that Studio provides to make these customizations. You also saw how to back out the changes made while using Studio, either by using the Studio UI itself, removing the files from the custom/ directory and/, or removing the entries from the field_meta_data table.

In the next chapter, you'll look at customizations designed to modify the data in the application based upon the actions the users take. Much like Studio, these hooks will have user friendly front ends to them, but also allow more powerful changes through custom PHP code.

CHAPTER 7

■ ■ ■

Workflows and Logic Hooks

Think about business processes for a second. They usually involve various steps with decisions to make at each step on how to continue. They involve all sorts of logic, asking questions on the results of a step or the status of process, and how to use that to make the transition to the next step in the process. These processes can get very complicated. I remember from old projects that sometimes the end diagram looks like a giant maze of circles and arrows that makes you dizzy from just looking at it. But, the reality is that most businesses depend upon these kinds of processes (even if they are confusing), and need the ability to model them in their software applications as well. Fortunately, SugarCRM comes with a safe way to do this.

In this chapter, you'll take a look at logic hooks, which provides a tool to add these processes into your Sugar instance. You'll also look at workflows, which is a way to create many common logic hooks using a point and click interface.

What Are Logic Hooks?

Logic hooks provide ways to extend SugarCRM with PHP code. What makes it different than most customizations is that you aren't changing or overriding existing code with the customization. Instead, you are adding code that is designed to be called in certain circumstances during the application execution. Think of logic hooks as your playground, where you can add any sort of code to have the application perform the actions needed.

There are a number of places in the app where you can add logic hooks. Table 7-1 outlines them.

Table 7-1. Types of Logic Hooks

Type	Description
after_ui_frame	Fired after the frame has been invoked and before the footer has been invoked. This hook does not have access to the current bean object (meaning you cannot view or change a record's values).
after_ui_footer	Fired after the footer has been invoked. This hook does not have access to the current bean object.
server_round_trip	Fired at the end of every SugarCRM page. It is called in the in the sugar_cleanup() method, which is called as the shutdown function for Sugar. This hook does not have access to the current bean object.
before_delete	Fired before a record is deleted using the SugarBean::mark_deleted().
after_delete	Fired after a record is deleted using the SugarBean::mark_deleted().
before_restore	Fired before a record is undeleted using the SugarBean::mark_undeleted() method.
after_restore	Fired after a record is undeleted using the SugarBean::mark_undeleted() method.
before_retrieve	Fired before a record has been retrieved from the database using the SugarBean::retrieve() method. This hook does not fire when you create a new record.
after_retrieve	Fired after a record has been retrieved from the database using the SugarBean::retrieve() method. This hook does not fire when you create a new record.
before_save	Fired before a record is saved using the SugarBean::save() method. One thing to note is that with certain modules, such as Cases and Bugs, the human-readable ID of the record (like the case_number field in the Case module), is not available within a before_save call since the business logic that calculates this value simply hasn't been executed yet.
after_save	Fired after a record is saved using the SugarBean::save() method. One thing to note is that with certain modules, such as Cases and Bugs, the human-readable ID of the record (like the case_number field in the Case module), is not available within an after_save call since the business logic that calculates this value simply hasn't been executed yet.
process_record	Fired immediately prior to the database query resulting in a record being made current. This gives developers an opportunity to examine and tailor the underlying queries. This is also a perfect place to set values in a record's fields prior to display in the DetailView or ListView. This event is not fired in the EditView.
before_logout	Fired before a user logs out of the system.

Type	Description
after_logout	Fired after a user logs out of the system. This hook does not have access to the current bean object.
after_login	Fired after a user successfully logs into the system.
before_login	Fired before a user logs into the system. This hook does not have access to the current bean object.
login_failed	Fired on a failed login attempt. This hook does not have access to the current bean object.

You can see from Table 7-1 there are many logic hooks available to use. You'll notice many of these are application level hooks and some are module level hooks—all of the application level hooks (after_ui_frame, after_ui_footer, server_round_trip) are designed to handle application level actions, so no bean object information will be available to them. All other logic hooks will have the current bean information available to them (with the exception of the after_logout, before_login, and login_failed hooks, since no User bean object will be available).

Now that you know what's available to use as logic hook writers, let's dive right into creating your very first logic hook.

Creating Your First Logic Hook

Now that you've seen all the logic hook options, let's actually build one. The hooks themselves are PHP classes while the methods in them are the actual hooks that will be executed. There are two parts to any logic hook: the hook definition file and the hook itself.

The hook definition file will install the logic hook into the running instance, making it instantly available. This is done automatically during the early parts of the request. It looks inside the custom/modules/*modulename*/logic_hooks.php file and the custom/modules/logic_hooks.php file for these definitions. The definition file has an array structure, a sample of which appears in Listing 7-1.

Listing 7-1. Sample logic_hooks.php File

```
$hook_version = 1;
$hook_array = Array();
$hook_array[after_save] = Array();
$hook_array[after_save][] = Array(1, AccountHooks,↵
 custom/Accounts/AccountHooks.php,AccountHooks, checkForLead);
$hook_array[before_save] = Array();
$hook_array[before_save][] = Array(1, AccountHooks, ↵
custom/Accounts/AccountHooks.php,AccountHooks, getParentAccountIndustry);
```

There are two essential elements to the logic hook definition files. The first part is specifying the $hook_version value, which should be set to the integer value '1.' (This is designed to be used in case SugarCRM updates the API for building logic hooks.) Next, you build the array of logic hook definitions as an associative array. The first level of the multidimensional array indicates the type of hook you are defining. From there, each element in the array points to the individual hooks to call. That array has five elements with the following specifications:

- *Parameter 1*: Sorting index used to sort the arrays of logic hook definitions before they are processed.

- *Parameter 2*: A string value to identify the hook.

- *Parameter 3*: Path to the PHP file to include which contains your logic hook code.

- *Parameter 4*: Name of the PHP class the logic hook method is in.

- *Parameter 5*: Name of the PHP method to call.

With the logic hook definition file defined, you can actually begin to write a logic hook for your application. To do this, you'll continue with the example you started in Listing 7-1. You'll have two logic hooks for execution before and after the save of an account record. The after_save hook will do a quick check to make sure you haven't defined the account given already as a Lead, using the name and address information. If you have, then you'll link the Lead record to this record. Then in the before_save hook, you'll check the parent account record (if one is given) for a value for the industry field if it is not currently set in the current record. Listing 7-2 shows this all in action.

Listing 7-2. Sample Account Module Logic Hooks File AccountHooks.php

```php
require_once(modules/Leads/Lead.php);
require_once(modules/Accounts/Account.php);


class AccountHooks
{
    public function checkForLead(
        SugarBean $bean,
        $event,
        $arguments
        )
    {
        $leadFocus = new Lead;
        $leadFocus->retrieve_by_string_fields(
            array(
                name => $bean->name,
                primary_address_street => $bean->billing_address_street,
                primary_address_city => $bean->billing_address_city,
```

```
                    primary_address_state => $bean->billing_address_state,
                    primary_address_postalcode => $bean->billing_address_postalcode,
                    primary_address_country => $bean->billing_address_country,
                    account_id => ,

                    ),
                false);
        if ( !empty($leadFocus->id) ) {
            $bean->load_relationship(leads);
            $bean->leads->add($leadFocus->id);
        }
    }
}

    public function getParentAccountIndustry(
        SugarBean $bean,
        $event,
        $arguments
        )
    {
        if ( empty($bean->industry) && !empty($bean->parent_id) ) {
            $parentAccountFocus = new Account();
            $parentAccountFocus->retrieve($bean->parent_id);
            if ( !empty($parentAccountFocus->id) )
                $bean->industry = $parentAccountFocus->industry;
        }
    }
}
```

You've successfully created the logic hooks. Now on every save of an Account record, the application will check for Leads that are of the same name and address of the current one and relate them, as well as backfill the industry field from the parent account record into the current one. Next, you'll add a few more logic hooks to your module as well.

Let's say you have added some custom fields that are calculated from other fields in the application. For example, perhaps you group your accounts into regions based upon the state they are located in. Assuming you've created an app_strings_list array of the options for the region field name account_region_dom, you can add a simple logic hook as shown in Listing 7-3 to handle this case.

Listing 7-3. getRegion after_retrieve logic Hooks for the Accounts Module

```
public function getRegion(
    SugarBean $bean,
    $event,
    $arguments
    )
{
    switch ( strtoupper($bean->billing_address_state) ) {
      case "AL":
case "AK":
case "AZ":
```

```
case "AR":
case "CA":
case "CO":
case "CT":
            $bean->region_c = $app_list_strings[account_region_dom][Region1];

            break;

case "DE":
case "FL":
case "GA":
case "HI":
case "ID":
case "IL":
case "IN":
case "IA":
case "KS":
case "KY":
            $bean->region_c = $app_list_strings[account_region_dom][Region2];

            break;
case "LA":
case "ME":
case "MD":
case "MA":
case "MI":
case "MN":
case "MS":
case "MO":
case "MT":
case "NE":
case "NV":
case "NH":
case "NJ":
case "NM":
            $bean->region_c = $app_list_strings[account_region_dom][Region3];

            break;
case "NY":
case "NC":
case "ND":
case "OH":
case "OK":
case "OR":
case "PA":
case "RI":
case "SC":
case "SD":
case "TN":
case "TX":
case "UT":
case "VT":
case "VA":
```

```
            $bean->region_c = $app_list_strings[account_region_dom][Region4];

            break;
case "WA":
case "WV":
case "WI":
            $bean->region_c = $app_list_strings[account_region_dom][Region5];

            break;
    }

}
```

The previous code checks the billing address state of the Account to determine this field value. This provides the advantage of having this field always accurately displayed to the client easily. The nice part is this case can be customized easily when business needs change to accurately reflect the correct region.

Another common change would be to add some logic to the login_failed logic hook. For example, maybe you want to email the system admin when someone has trouble logging into the admin accounts. Listing 7-4 provides a solution for that.

Listing 7-4. Login_failed Logic Hook for Alerting on Failed admin Logins

```
class LoginHooks
{
    public function alertSystemAdminOfBadAdminLogin(
        $event,
        $arguments
        )
    {
        if ( $_REQUEST[user_name] == admin ) {
            mail("admin@localhost","BAD ADMIN LOGIN","Someone tried to login to the↵
 admin account and failed. Better check it out!");
        }
    }

}
```

You just check the username given and if it matches the admin account, you'll shoot an email out to the system admin about it. You may want to even include the user's mobile phone too with an SMS if you get quite a few in a row.

Now that you've seen how to write our own logic hooks, let's look at how you can use the Workflows tool to do many of these with a point and click interface.

Point and Click Logic Hooks with Workflows

You've seen how to build logic hooks using PHP code that is interjected into various points of the application. The downside is that logic hooks require PHP coding skills to create them, which can make it difficult for the average person to build them. To help those poor souls out, SugarCRM comes with a tool to help them build the most common logic hooks called Workflows. (Workflows are available only in the Professional and Enterprise versions of SugarCRM.)

Workflows enable you to create logic hooks using an easy-to-use user interface instead of having to write PHP code. This is especially useful for those with little or no programming experience. They can simply go through the dialogs to create the logic they wish to add. Because you are using a GUI, the tradeoff to using the Workflows interface to create custom logic is not as extensive as can be done with logic hooks, so if you have very complicated needs then you may be better served by writing the logic hooks by hand. You'll see the limitations as you walk through creating a workflow from start to finish, which will help you judge which approach is the best for you.

Creating the Workflow

The Workflow module is tucked away in the Admin panel under the title, Workflow Definitions. To create your workflow definition, you'll start by clicking the Create Workflow Definition link, which brings up Figure 7-1.

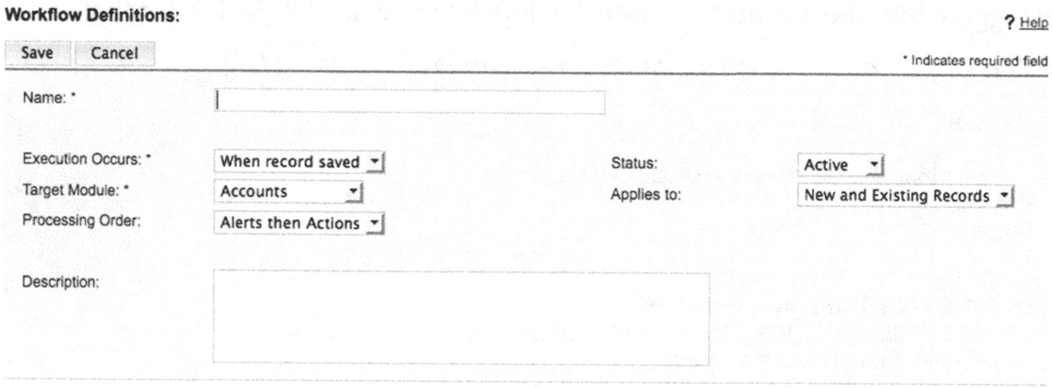

Figure 7-1. Create Workflow Definition dialog

After giving your workflow a name, you then need to choose when you wish the workflow to be executed. The choices here are when a record is saved or after time elapses (this option basically adds your workflow to be a scheduled event rather than triggered by data changes, provided you have the SugarCRM cron scheduler tool running at that time). You then choose which module this workflow applies to, whether you want it to trigger off creation of a new record, saving an existing record, or both—and whether you want the alerts or actions to be processed first. You can also add a description to the workflow, which is a good idea so everyone knows what it does without having to dig through the whole definition to figure it out. I would be sure to mark the Workflow as Inactive here for the status until you have it all set up, so it doesn't partially execute beforehand.

Once you have all the options set the way you want, click Save and the workflow will be added. You will then be at the DetailView screen for the workflow, as shown in Figure 7-2.

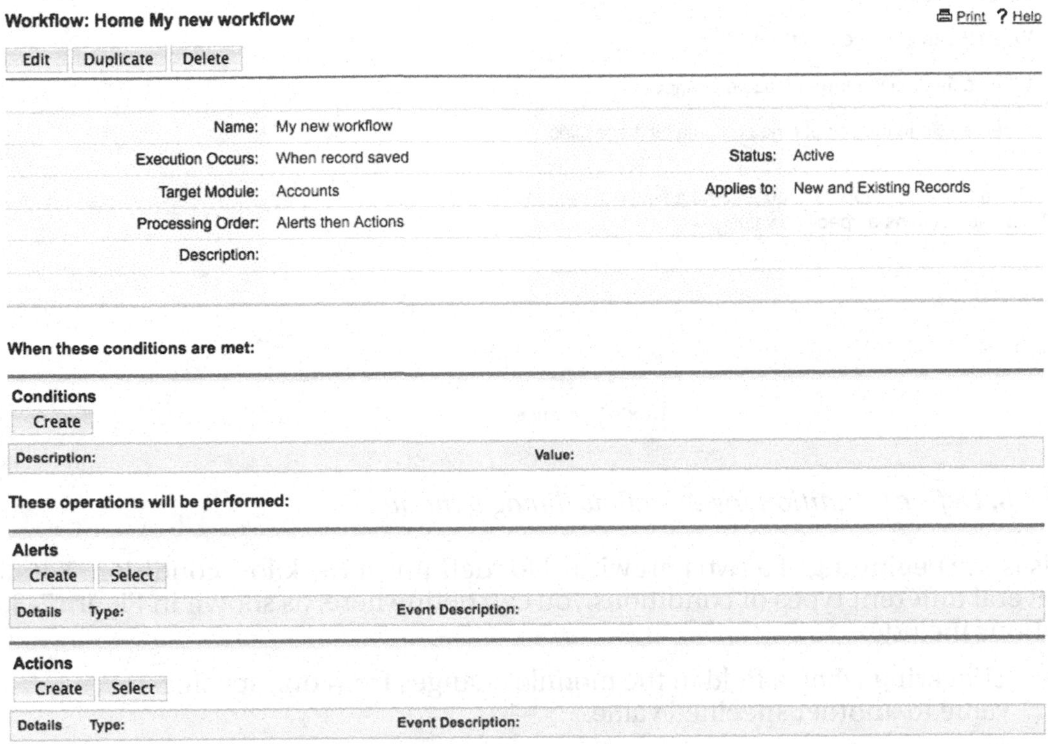

Workflow: Home My new workflow   🖶 Print ❓ Help

| Edit | Duplicate | Delete |

Name:	My new workflow		
Execution Occurs:	When record saved	Status:	Active
Target Module:	Accounts	Applies to:	New and Existing Records
Processing Order:	Alerts then Actions		
Description:			

When these conditions are met:

Conditions

| Create |

| Description: | Value: |

These operations will be performed:

Alerts

| Create | Select |

| Details | Type: | Event Description: |

Actions

| Create | Select |

| Details | Type: | Event Description: |

Figure 7-2. Workflow Detail View

You can now begin to build the guts of the workflow from here. Workflows have three basic parts: The first part of the workflow is the conditions, which define what needs to be done in order for the workflow to be executed. The other two parts are the Alerts, which specify emails or messages that will be sent to specific users on a condition being true, and Actions, which define the data changes that are to occur when the conditions are met. You'll look at those last two parts in a minute, but first let's walk through creating a condition for your workflow.

To create a new condition for a workflow, begin by clicking the Create button underneath the Conditions subpanel. After doing so, you'll see a popup window like the one in Figure 7-3.

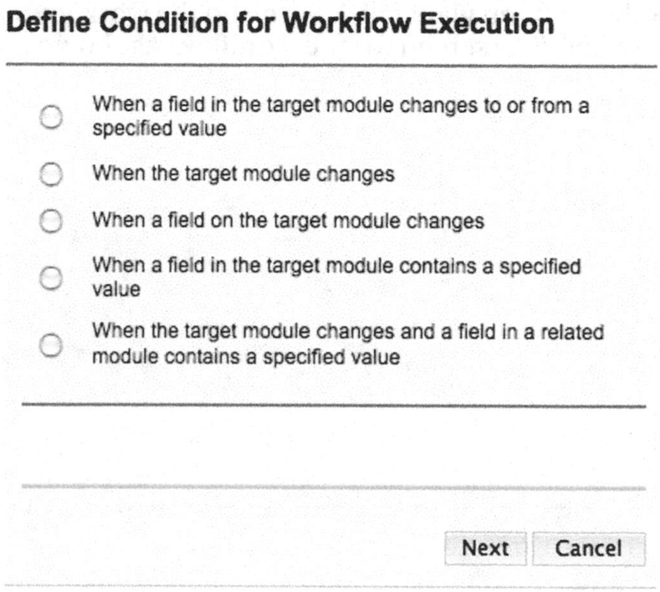

Define Condition for Workflow Execution

○ When a field in the target module changes to or from a specified value

○ When the target module changes

○ When a field on the target module changes

○ When a field in the target module contains a specified value

○ When the target module changes and a field in a related module contains a specified value

Next   Cancel

Figure 7-3. Define Condition for Workflow dialog window

This is the beginning of a two part wizard for defining a workflow condition. You have several different types of conditions you can define here, as shown in Figure 7-3. The options include:

- Triggering when a field in the module changes from one specific value to another specified value.

- Triggering when anything in the module changes.

- Triggering when a specific field in the target module changes.

- Triggering when a field in the module contains a specific value.

- Triggering when anything the module changes AND a field in the module contains a specific value.

When you click on the radio button for your choice, the white box section of the dialog changes to text that indicates what the condition will do. An example of this is shown in Figure 7-4.

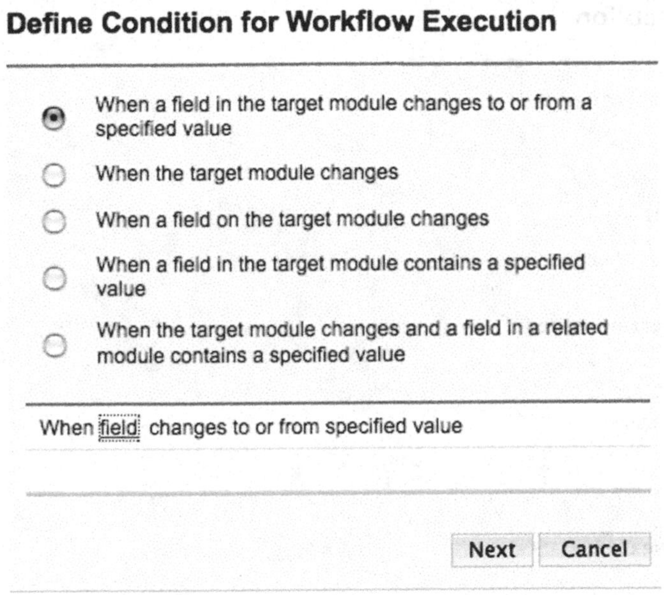

Define Condition for Workflow Execution

⦿ When a field in the target module changes to or from a specified value

○ When the target module changes

○ When a field on the target module changes

○ When a field in the target module contains a specified value

○ When the target module changes and a field in a related module contains a specified value

When field changes to or from specified value

Next   Cancel

Figure 7-4. Define Condition for Workflow dialog window after choosing an option

The highlighted link portion is where you can click to choose the field you will be dealing with in this workflow condition. Clicking that link will bring up a dialog, like the one in Figure 7-5.

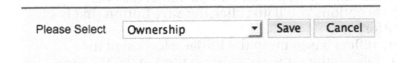
Please Select   Ownership   ▼   Save   Cancel

Figure 7-5. Field selection popup during Define Condition for Workflow dialog

Here you just select the field you want to use and then click Save, or click Cancel if you don't want to save your selection. If you would click Save here, then the original dialog window would be updated as follows in Figure 7-6.

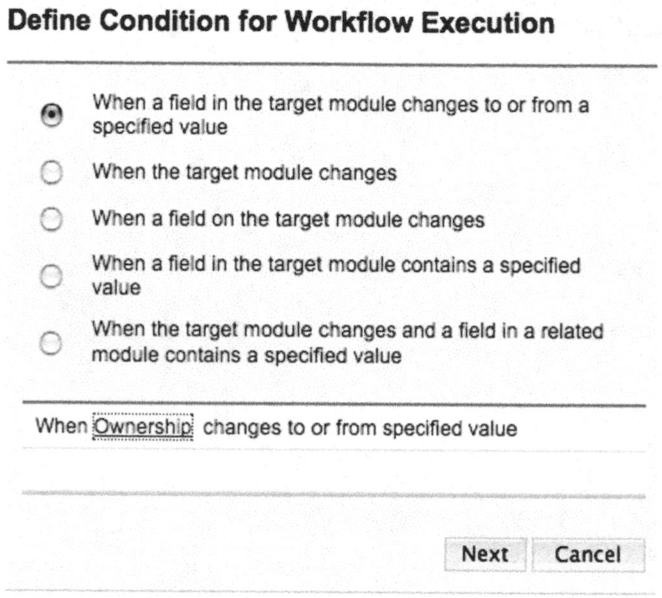

Define Condition for Workflow Execution

◉ When a field in the target module changes to or from a specified value

○ When the target module changes

○ When a field on the target module changes

○ When a field in the target module contains a specified value

○ When the target module changes and a field in a related module contains a specified value

When Ownership changes to or from specified value

[Next] [Cancel]

Figure 7-6. *Define Condition for Workflow dialog window after choosing an option and field*

From here, you can click next to apply further the rest of the specification to the condition. Note that some of the condition types do not have a second step (namely "When the target module changes" and "When a field on the target module changes"), so if you choose those options you'll just click the Save button that is present instead of the Next button.

The second part of the form differs based upon the initial selection of the condition type, but it generally follows the same convention used in the previous dialog. For the previous example of changing the Ownership field from one value to another, you'll see a form similar to Figure 7-7.

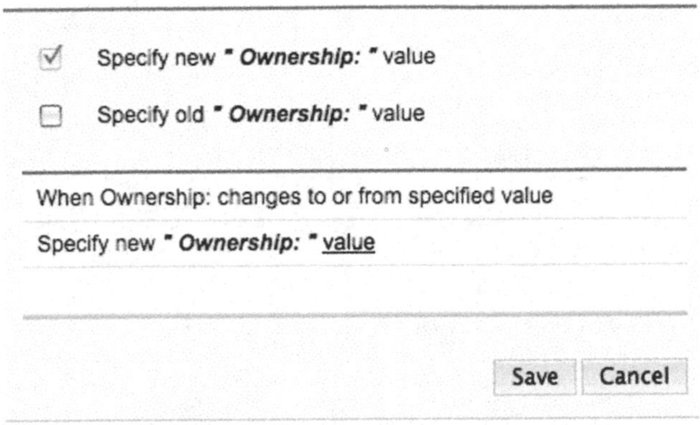

Figure 7-7. Define Condition for Workflow dialog window for specifying the changed field information.

Again, here you'll have the same sort of editing capabilities that you had in the previous dialog, where you can click a link to edit that portion of the condition definition. Upon clicking the value link, you'll again have a pop-up form where you can specify the value the field should or should not be, as shown in Figure 7-8.

Figure 7-8. Specifying the condition field value

You'll go ahead and make your condition to be when the Ownership value changes from Bar to Foo. To do this we'll checkbox both the Specify new Ownership: value and Specify old Ownership: value checkboxes, which puts both rules into your condition. You'll then click the field link to make the field value specifications accordingly for the before and after values you wish to have. Figure 7-9 shows the ending results.

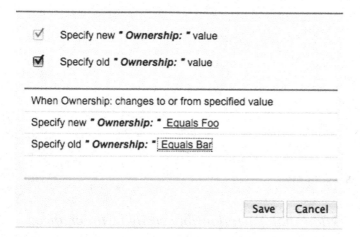

Figure 7-9. Define Condition for Workflow dialog window for specifying the changed field information all completed

Now all you need to do is click save and your condition is now saved. You can add as many conditions as you wish to a workflow to be sure that the workflow is executed under the correct conditions.

Now let's move on to building alerts for when a workflow takes place.

Defining Workflow Alerts

Many times all that needs done when fields change or a module changes is that someone needs to know about it. For example, using the previous example, maybe you need to notify a certain person when the Ownership field changes, so that they can perhaps call the customer to verify or update accounting to change their pricing structures. This is a trivial option with workflows, and one you can also add a bit of customization in as well.

To begin creating new alerts, just click on the Create button in the Alerts subpanel, and you'll see the Alerts EditView, as shown in Figure 7-10.

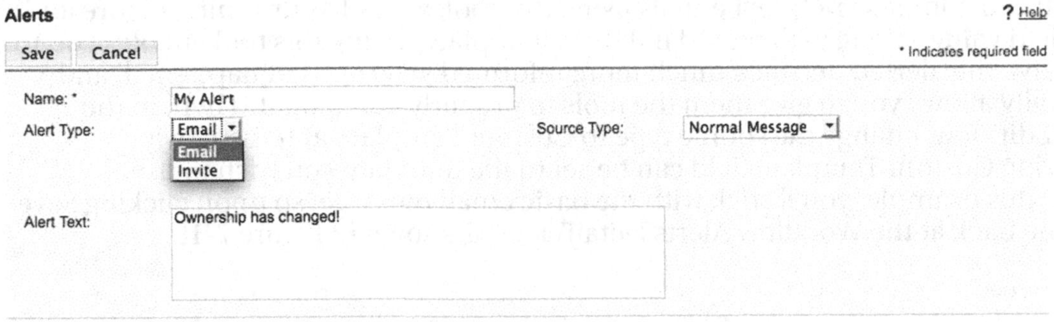

Figure 7-10. Workflow alerts EditView.

Alerts can be as simple as an email message, which just sends the specified text to the alerted person. But you also have the option of creating an alert email template, so that you can provide the alerted person with much more detailed information. First, you need to first create that alert template. You can do this by clicking the Alert Email Templates in the sidebar and on the resulting screen choose the module you wish to create a template for and click Create. You'll then be presented with the Alert Templates EditView, as shown in Figure 7-11.

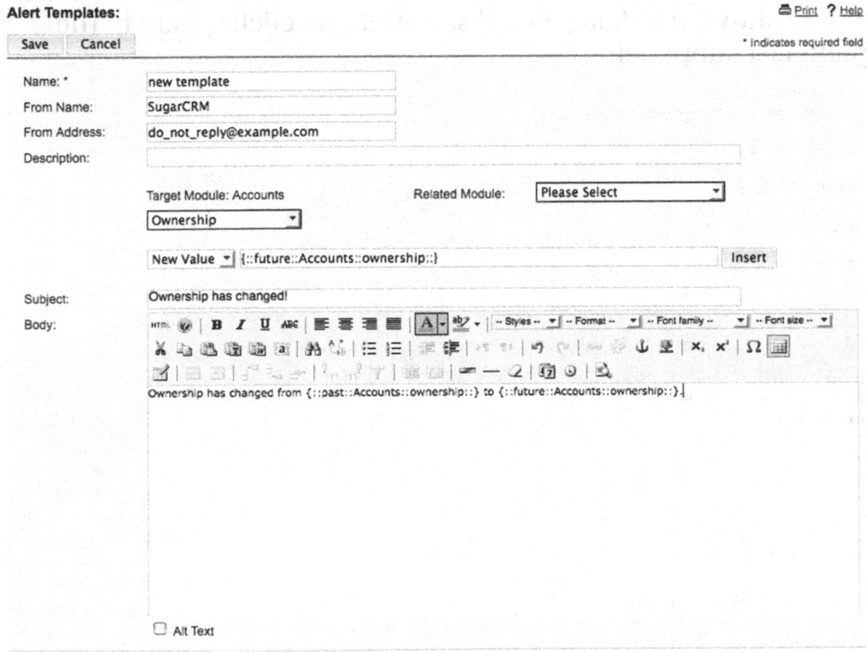

Figure 7-11. Alert Templates EditView

You can compose rich-text emails using this tool, as well as dropping before and after field values along with record links into template. Using this tool enables you to really give the alerted person a much more informed view of what happened, and optionally allows you to give them the tools to properly act upon it. Then, in the Alerts EditView, change the source type to Custom Template and the newly appearing Custom Template field can be set to the template you wish to use.

For this example, you'll stick with the basic email message, so upon clicking Save you'll be back at the Workflow Alerts DetailView, as shown in Figure 7-12.

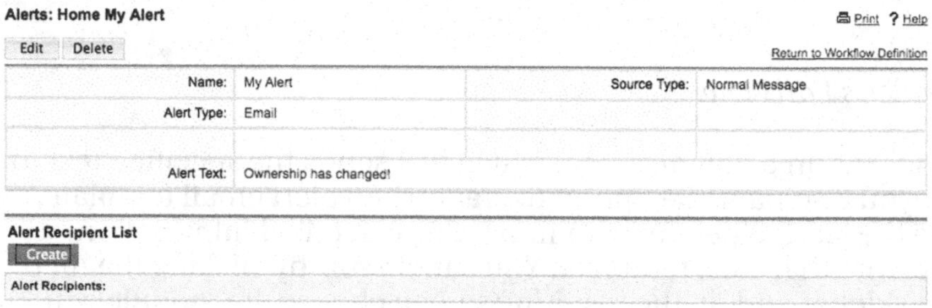

Figure 7-12. *Workflow alerts DetailView*

Now you just need to add recipients to your email. This is another trivial task with lots of options. Figure 7-13 shows the dialog you'll see after you click Create in the Alert preceding Recipient List subpanel.

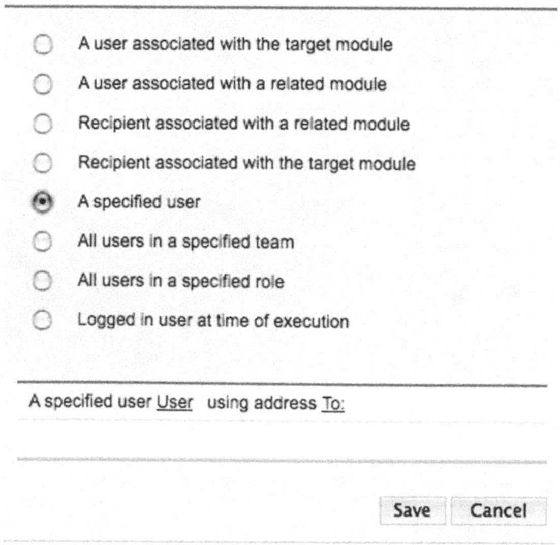

Figure 7-13. *Alert Recipient List popup dialog*

Again, you have many options here, from notifying the assigned user to the record to notifying all related team and role members, or just notifying a certain person each time. The dialog box works exactly the same as the workflow conditions one, where clicking on the links allow us to "fill in the blanks" so to speak. You'll also notice you have the option to indicate which address field should be used in the mail for the user's email address, whether it be To:, CC:, or Bcc:, so, again, there are many options. To do any email notifications triggered from a workflow, you must have emails enabled in Email Settings in the Admin panel.

Like the workflow conditions, you can add as many alerts and recipients to alerts as you wish for the given condition. Let's now move on to look at how create actions for your workflow.

Workflow Actions

The last piece of the workflow puzzle (and often the most important part) is what data actions should take place when the conditions are met. Again, you have an easy-to-use dialog to define this. You'll start by clicking Create under the Actions subpanel in your workflow to get the popup dialog shown in Figure 7-14.

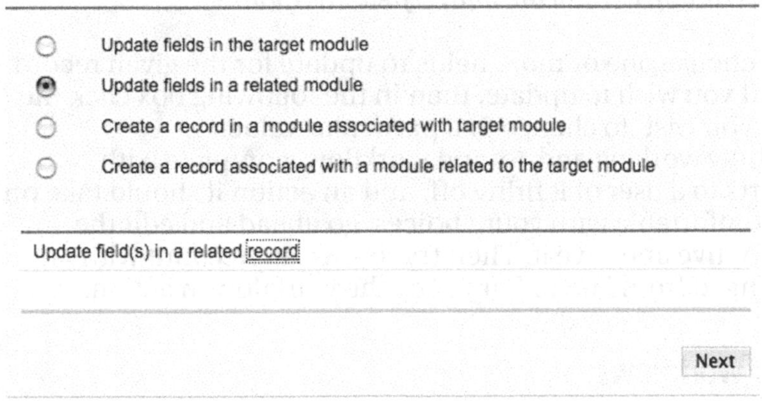

○ Update fields in the target module

◉ Update fields in a related module

○ Create a record in a module associated with target module

○ Create a record associated with a module related to the target module

Update field(s) in a related record

Next

Figure 7-14. Workflow Actions dialog

Here you have a few choices on what to do: You can update fields in the given record or a related record to the record, or even create new records in the current module or a related one. Similar to how the workflow conditions dialog worked, clicking one of the radio buttons begins building the rules, allowing customization if you see linked fields during it. For this example, let's choose to update fields in the current record, so when you click Next you can see the dialog shown in Figure 7-15 and choose which fields to update.

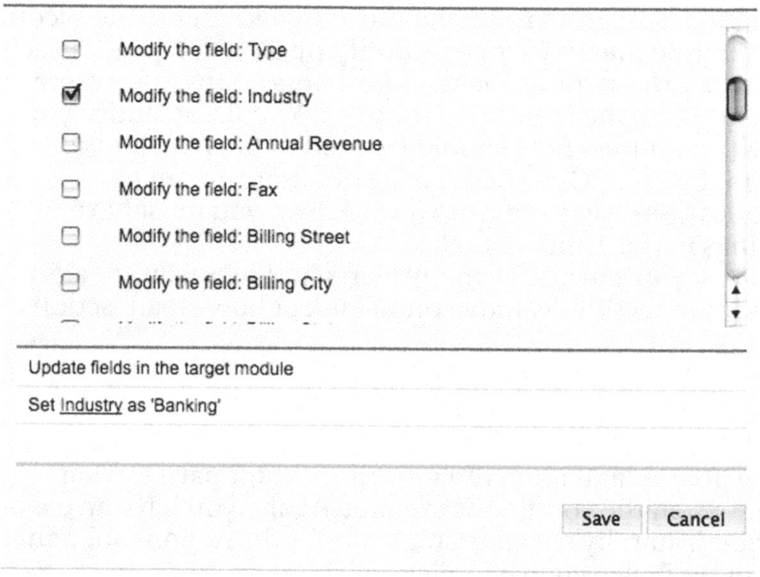

Figure 7-15. Workflow Actions dialog to indicate which field to update.

This dialog allows you to choose one or more fields to update for the given record. You simply checkbox the field you wish to update, then in the following box click the field link to specify the value you wish to change to a particular value.

Now you have created a fully working end-to-end workflow, complete with conditions for execution, alerts to a user of it firing off, and an action it should take on the given record. If you are comfortable with your choices, go ahead and edit the workflow to make the status Active and save it. Then try to save an Account with an Ownership field that has changed from Foo to Bar to see the workflow in action.

Managing the Sequence of Workflows

Sometimes workflows can interfere with each other (as can logic hooks, which I'll talk more about in the "Logic Hooks Pitfalls" section to follow) or it's important for the workflows to be processed in a certain order to get the desired effect. For example, one workflow may set a one field's value and another may set a second field's value based upon the initial field's value used in the other workflow. For these and other reasons, the option to order your workflows in a certain order may be very important, so Sugar has the ability to customize this as well. Selecting the Workflow Execution Order link in the sidebar and then choosing the module you wish to view will give you the list of current workflows for it, similar to Figure 7-16.

Workflow Sequence   🖶 Print ? Help

Please select a module: Accounts ▾   Select

Workflow Sequence: Accounts

			(1 - 2 of 2)
Name	Execution Occurs:	Status	Process Order:
My new workflow	When record saved	Active	↑ up ↓ dn
Another workflow	When record saved	Active	↑ up ↓ dn

Figure 7-16. Workflow Execution Order screen

In this screen, you can click the up and down arrows to change the position of the workflow in the workflow sequence for the given module. The first one listed is the first to execute, followed by the next one in the list.

As you have seen, workflows are a very useful tool for creating logic hooks that deal with very common tasks. When workflows can't handle it, then the logic hooks that you learned to build in the first part of this chapter can step in to provide the extra needed support you need to perform the actions you need to happen. Sometimes the tools can also create a world of trouble if you aren't careful. In the following section, you'll explore some of these potential issues and what you can do about them.

Logic Hooks Pitfalls

If you go to the Sugar Forums and search for logic hooks, you'll probably get a ton of results with people who have mysterious things going on with their logic hooks. Logic hooks are far from trivial, and often time can be lead to quite confusing results if you don't pay attention to what the code is doing. In this section, I'll point out a few areas where you can quickly get into trouble with logic hooks and discuss the best way to get out of them.

Modifying the Bean Object

One thing that is very important to remember is that the bean object passed to you is a live object. While this opens up the ability for your logic hook to do some powerful things, it can also create issues. Let's look at one example in Listing 7-5.

Listing 7-5. *Sample AccountsHooks.php file containing logic hooks for the Accounts module*

```
class AccountHooks
{
    public function reassignNewRecordTeamBasedOnIndustry(
        SugarBean $bean,
        $event,
        $arguments
        )
    {
        $teamBean = new Team;

        // Set the team based upon the given industry.
        switch ( $bean->industry ) {

        case "Banking":

            $teamBean->retrieve("Banking");
            $bean->team_id = $teamBean->id;

            break;

        case "Energy":
            $teamBean->retrieve("Banking");
            $bean->team_id = $teamBean->id;

            break;
        }

    }
}
```

This logic is designed to be called a before_save event. When you call this after you initially save a new record, everything works as expected and saves the newly created record. But you'll notice further saves of the record seem to cause problems. This is because the code is indiscriminate of whether the record has been saved or not. Therefore, you will keep reassigning the record to the team indicated in the logic hook, keeping you from changing it down the road. To correct this, you need to add a check to be sure the record does not already exist. Listing 7-6 shows the modified example to correct this problem.

Listing 7-6. *Sample AccountsHooks.php file containing logic hooks for the Accounts module with a fix to not trigger it on creation of new records.*

```
class AccountHooks
{
    public function reassignNewRecordTeamBasedOnIndustry(
        SugarBean $bean,
        $event,
```

```
        $arguments
        )
    {
        // Don't execute if the we aren't creating a new record
        if ( !empty($bean->fetched_row) && !empty($bean->fetched_row['id']) )

            return;

        $teamBean = new Team;
        // Set the team based upon the given industry.
        switch ( $bean->industry ) {

        case "Banking":

            $teamBean->retrieve_by_string_fields (array('name' =>"Banking"),false);
            $bean->team_id = $teamBean->id;

            break;

        case "Energy":
            $teamBean-> retrieve_by_string_fields (array('name' =>"Energy"),false);
            $bean->team_id = $teamBean->id;

            break;
        }

    }
}
```

You've added a simple check to see if the record's id field has been set previously. You checked it in the fetched_row array since the actual id record will already have been set by the time the logic hook call regardless of whether it is a newly created record or not. However, the fetched_row array will not be set on new records, so it's safe to check it to determine if this is a new record or not.

It's also important to be aware of when a hook is called during the application execution. Let's take a look at the logic hook in Listing 7-7.

Listing 7-7. Cases Logic Hook to Check for Certain Thresholds of Case Numbers

```
class CaseHooks
{
    public function alertSystemAdminOfCaseNumbers(
        SugarBean $bean,
        $event,
        $arguments
        )
    {
        // Don't execute if the we aren't creating a new record
        if ( !empty($bean->fetched_row) && !empty($bean->fetched_row['id']) )

            return;
```

```
        if ( $bean->case_number % 1000 == 0 ) {
            $GLOBALS['log']->info("Reached case number " . $bean->case_number . "!");
        }
    }
}
```

The biggest problem here is that your info level on the sugarcrm.log file will now be filled with Reached case number 0! for every save. This isn't what you want at all.

The problem is that the case_number field is an auto_increment field, which like all auto_increment fields relies on the database to handle getting the correct value. Because of this, the value generated is not available in either the before_save or after_save event. However, you can look it up in the database from the after_save event with the following modifications to the original logic hook, as shown in Listing 7-8.

Listing 7-8. *Fixed Cases Logic Hook to Check for Certain Thresholds of Case Numbers*

```
class CaseHooks
{
    public function alertSystemAdminOfCaseNumbers(
        SugarBean $bean,
        $event,
        $arguments
        )
    {
        // Don't execute if the we  aren't creating a new record
        if ( !empty($this->fetched_row) && !empty($bean->fetched_row['id']) )

            return;


        $casesBean = new Case;

        $casesBean->retrieve($bean->id);


        if ( !empty($casesBean->id) && $casesBean->case_number % 1000 == 0 ) {
            $GLOBALS['log']->info("Reached case number " . $casesBean->case_number . "!");
        }

    }
}
```

Now the info sugarcrm log messages will be much more sensible, and only report when you've reached every 1,000 new cases in the system.

Conflicting Logic Hooks

Another trap you can get yourself in is having logic hooks that are doing actions which conflict with each other. This often leads to unpredictable results. Let's look at an example of this in Listing 7-9.

Listing 7-9. Bugs Logic Hooks to Check fixed_in_release and Found_in_release Fields

```php
require_once('modules/Releases/Release.php');


class BugHooks
{
    public function autoSetFixedInRelease(
        SugarBean $bean,
        $event,
        $arguments
        )
    {
        if ( empty($bean->fixed_in_release) )
            $bean->fixed_in_release = $bean->found_in_release;
    }

    public function adjustInvalidFoundInRelease(
        SugarBean $bean,
        $event,
        $arguments
        )
    {
        if ( !empty($bean->fetched_row) && !empty($bean->fetched_row['found_in_release'])
            && ( $bean->fetched_row['found_in_release'] != $bean->found_in_release ) ) {
            $releaseBean = new Release;
            $releaseBean->retrieve($bean->found_in_release);
            if ( !empty($releaseBean->id) && $releaseBean->status == 'Inactive' )
                $bean->found_in_release = '';
        }
    }
}
```

Let's say you have a SOAP client that is modifying Bugs records (I say this since Inactive releases are not visible in the normal UI) and your client accidentally sets the found_in_release field to an invalid release. Ideally, the adjustInvalidFoundInRelease() hook would kick in and clear that up for you, removing the invalid release specification from that field. However, what if the autoSetFixedInRelease() hook runs first? The inactive release specification finds its way to the fixed_in_release field first, then the found_in_release field gets cleared out right afterward. The best way to fix this is to make sure the hooks get executed in the correct order by specifying them as in the logic hooks definition file for the module, as shown in Listing 7-10.

Listing 7-10. Sample Bugs Logic Hook File

```
$hook_version = 1;
$hook_array = Array();
$hook_array['before_save'] = Array();
$hook_array['before_save'][] = Array(1, 'BugHooks',↵
 'custom/Accounts/BugHooks.php','BugHooks', 'adjustInvalidFoundInRelease');
$hook_array['before_save'][] = Array(1, 'BugHooks',↵
 'custom/Accounts/BugHooks.php','BugHooks', 'autoSetFixedInRelease');
```

By specifying them in the order you wish them to be executed as you have in the previous listing, you've fixed the problem of fields being mysteriously updated.

Logic Hook Being Nullified by the Existing Code

As much as logic hooks allows you to interject your own behaviors into an object, sometimes things are just out of your hands. Let's look at the following code in Listing 7-11 as an example.

Listing 7-11. Before_save logic Hook to Specify Your Own Record Ids

```
class AllHooks
{
    public function setGUID(
        SugarBean $bean,
        $event,
        $arguments
        )
    {
        // Only execute if the we are creating a new record
        if ( empty($bean->id) )

            $bean->id = myRecordIDGenerator();
    }
}
```

This is a logic hook. Your goal in the preceding logic hook is the use of the assumed myRecordIDGenerator() function (you assume this to be some sort of id generator that won't give duplicate IDs) to give the record ID to use for this newly created record. But if you push the logic hook function into the before_save method of any given module, you'll find it will never get called. Why is this? Because the record ID is generated prior to this record being created, so your attempt here to change it is just nullified. You can correct this by changing your detection code, as shown in Listing 7-12.

Listing 7-12. Corrected before_save Logic Hook to Specify Your Own Record Ids

```
class AllHooks
{
    public function setGUID(
        SugarBean $bean,
        $event,
        $arguments
        )
    {
        // Only execute if the we  are creating a new record
        if ( empty($bean->fetched_row) && !$bean->new_with_id )

            $bean->id = myRecordIDGenerator();
    }
}
```

You simply adjust the code to check for there not being a fetched row (meaning there is a new record, since it doesn't exist in the database), so if the `new_with_id` property is being set to `false` you know which you should interject to your record id generator logic.

Logic Hook Weaknesses

In addition to all of the previous issues that I've illustrated, there are a number of other possible issues you should be aware of when dealing with logic hooks. Following is a list of a few of those items:

- Logic hooks are tied to the low-level application functions (such as record retrieval, record save, etc.) and not to the specific user interface actions in the EditViews and DetailViews. This means that you cannot write a logic hook that is only destined to be fired on DetailViews. However, any functions of the user interface actions that use the low-level application functions, such as saving a record or retrieving a record, will fire the corresponding logic hook.

- If the user action makes a direct query against the database (i.e., not using the SugarBean methods) then the corresponding logic hooks will not be called. In other words, if you add a before_save() logic hooks, if code does a direct SQL INSERT to the underlying table, then the logic hook won't be called. It's best for portability reasons to always use the SugarBean save() and retrieve() methods unless there is a specific need those methods cannot address, but also since not doing so bypasses any logic hooks.

- One of the most simple causes for logic hooks not to work are permissions problems. The logic hook files (just like any customized file in the instance) need to be readable by the web server. It's best to simply keep the custom/ directory readable at all times, just to avoid any possible issues here.

Logic hooks are one of the most powerful features of SugarCRM, but also one of the ones which cause the most problems in the application for developers. It's important to be aware of what you are getting yourself into when designing logic hooks, and be sure to fully test many different use cases in which your logic hooks are designed to handle before deploying it to any production environment.

Summary

In this chapter, you learned all about logic hooks in SugarCRM, which are a powerful tool for customizing how many different behaviors in the application occur. You first looked at the various types of logic hooks offered, then saw some examples of how to use them in action, including examples of adding additional logic before and after saves and when loading a record in particular. Next, you saw the point and click way to do logic hooks, which is called Workflows. Workflows are a very powerful tool for those without much programming knowledge to set up the most common logic hooks easily using a very easy-to-follow interface. You then ended the chapter looking at all the "gotchas" of logic hooks—things that cause end users grief when writing them and things to be aware of that could cause problems down the road.

Module builder and Logic hooks and workflows are mechanisms that are designed in mind for developers and end-users to help customize their instances. But sometimes they aren't enough, and you need to make more detailed changes that these tools can't handle. In the next chapter, you'll do a deep dive into many of the other customizations that are available to developers, and how to write them in an upgrade-safe way to avoid problems with future releases and updates.

CHAPTER 8

■■■

Overriding Existing Code

Up to this point, you've looked at ways to customize SugarCRM using the standard developments tools, such as Studio, Workflows, and Logic Hooks. These tools are generally considered the easiest way to customize SugarCRM, since it is the most supported and most common way to customize your instance. Sometimes SugarCRM doesn't achieve the level of customization you may need. Perhaps you need to alter some of the default behaviors of the application or maybe the GUI tools you looked at in Chapter 6 just don't do exactly what you need. At this point, code level customization is truly the only option.

SugarCRM has been built and designed with the anticipation of users needing to customize their instances. Because of this, SugarCRM has taken the approach of giving developers this ability, but without compromising their installation as a whole. In this chapter, you'll look at this ability, and in turn take a look at many common code customizations that you can do in the product with ease.

Safety Lies in the Custom Directory

The biggest pain to the customization of any product is supporting it in the future. While the version you have today may meet your needs perfectly, what if compelling updates and new features become available and you wish to integrate them back into your version? Or what if the publisher has bug fixes, security patches, and performance improvements? Surely you would want to integrate them back into your local application. But when you have customized your instance, at what cost does this come? In many cases, the costs outweigh the benefits, which is why legions of legacy applications exist all over the world (many in mission critical environments) that keep chugging along in versions no longer supported by their vendors, causing never-ending headaches for those tasked with them. (This especially rings true for me, as I supported several DOS based Foxpro applications in a past company until they could justify their replacement.)

SugarCRM has taken the approach of allowing upgrade-safe customizations to the application, which means providing a mechanism to customize your instance in such a way that any future upgrades or maintenance fixes will not override your customizations. To do this, you have a custom/ directory in the root of the Sugar instance directory, where these customizations can be made. For the most part, any Sugar upgrade or install changes anything in this directory. It is completely the developer's playground and it is reserved for their use. The only thing is, Sugar uses this directory yet the GUI developer tools (Studio, Module Builder, etc.) also store their customizations here as well, and because of this during an upgrade you may fix some of the files created by those tools.

The layout of this directory generally matches that of the main application tree, with the addition of a few more directories to handle Studio/Module Builder customizations and some that are built automatically in the metadata and vardef building processes. Table 8-1 details those directories.

Table 8-1. *Subdirectories "{ XE "Custom directory:subdirectories" }in the Custom/ Directory and Their Uses*

Subdirectory	Description
history/	Contains the history of all EditViews, DetailViews, ListViews, and searches that are customized through Studio.
modulebuilder/	Contains the module code as built by Module Builder (more on Module Builder is in Chapter 9).
modules/	Customizations made to the modules. This is where much of the MVC and metadata frameworks will look for customizations. Some customizations here are autogenerated from those made in the custom/Extension/modules/ directory, such as language string changes, subpanel customizations, menu changes (the one typically on the left sidebar), and Vardef changes.
Extension/	This is where the source of many customizations are made. They will be rebuilt into the custom/modules/ directory and be cached there.
include/	Customizations to files in the include/ directory.
themes/	Custom themes or customizations made to themes that came with Sugar. Custom themes are considered individual themes in their own right, but of course can be extended from any other theme that can be selected by a user, while customizations to existing themes will actually change that theme.
workflow/	Contains any application-level workflows.
working/	Legacy, used by Studio pre 5.0.
backup/	Legacy, used by Studio pre 5.0.

Anything outside of the predefined directory structure here is also fair game. Let's say you have some home-brewed libraries that are used to interface into a legacy system. You could add them here in a subdirectory, so that they can be easily included into any further modifications you make. Since all customizations are stored entirely within the custom/ directory, you could even manage all of your customizations through a source control system such as Subversion or Git. This method guarantees that none of your changes will be overridden by a SugarCRM version upgrade or maintenance patch.

Customizations You Can Make

The freedoms of the custom directory allow us to customize the out-of-the-box actions in SugarCRM with ease through many different means. Some customizations are done by simply providing alternative files for what exists already in the system, where the replacement files take the place of what already is there. Other customizations are additive, which means they take the existing definition and apply the changes you specify to it. Finally, some customizations provide a new function to a module where it didn't exist before. The biggest example of this is adding an entirely new view to a module.

Since not all customizations are made the same way, it's best to be aware of what you're getting yourself into. The rest of this chapter will go through several common customizations you may make in code in Sugar and how to do each one of them. Let's jump right in with alter view actions, whether they are existing view actions or new ones.

Altering View Actions

View actions are some of the simplest things to override through the custom directory. You learned about these in Chapter 2, when you saw how the Sugar MVC framework functions. By simply dropping the view class file in the custom/*modulename*/views/ directory, the ViewFactory will know to use that custom view file instead of the default one specified by the module or by the application. By default, any view action file defined in the custom/ directory will be used instead of a view action file being defined in the module directory or the base view definition defined in the include/MVC/View/views/ directory.

The easiest view customization to make is to add a new view. If you want to have the customization apply only to one module then you can drop the new view files inside the custom/*modulename*/views/. Listing 8-1 shows how to add a new view to the Accounts module.

Listing 8-1. *Accounts Module Custom view.quickinfo.php*

```php
require_once('include/MVC/View/SugarView.php');

class CustomAccountsViewQuickinfo extends SugarView
{
    public function __construct()
    {
        parent::SugarView();
    }


    public function preDisplay()
    {
        if ( empty($_REQUEST['record']) )
            sugar_die($GLOBALS['app_strings']['ERROR_NO_RECORD']);

        if ( !$this->bean->ACLAccess('view') ) {
            ACLController::displayNoAccess(true);
            sugar_cleanup(true);
        }
    }

    public function display()
    {
        echo <<<EOHTML
<h2>{$this->bean->name}</h2>
<p>{$this->bean->description}</p>
EOHTML;
    }
}
```

The Quickinfo view you've defined is a read-only view that just shows the Account's name and the description. This is useful if you just need to see the notes about an account. You've done quite a few things here. First, you defined the preDisplay() method to check for the existence of the record id being passed in the URL. You'll call sugar_die() if it isn't. You also went through the trouble of checking the ACL to see if the user has access to the record or not. Finally, in the display() method you do the actual outputting of data to the user. For the sake of brevity, I just outputted straight HTML from here, but you could have also called a Smarty template to do this as well. You can access the Smarty object from the view in the SugarView::$ss member variable.

You need to do one other thing to make sure your view is accessible, which is to register it with the SugarController class. You saw two different ways to handle this in Chapter 2. The more elaborate way is to subclass the SugarController and add the view from there. However, the much easier way (and the recommended way unless you need to interject logic into the controller) is to initiate a new action view map by dropping it in the action_view_map.php file inside the custom/*modulename*/ directory. Listing 8-2 shows what that file would look like for the preceding example.

Listing 8-2. action_view_map.php file for the custom Accounts View Quickinfo

```php
<?php
$action_view_map['quickinfo'] = 'quickinfo';
```

Once this (or the aforementioned controller subclass) is in place, you can access the previous view directly from the browser using the URL http://*instancename*/index.php?module=Accounts&action=quickinfo&record=*record id*.

The other form of view customization is overriding the base view action with your own actions. For this example, you'll use the Bugs module, overriding the Bugs edit view. You'll be extending the ViewEdit class since the Bugs module doesn't define its own specific ViewEdit subclass (if it did, you would extend from that instead). You'll use this to help set a default value for the found in release field, to the main active release (as determined by the list_order field setting in the releases table). The records for the releases table are setting in the Admin panel under Releases (see Listing 8-3).

Listing 8-3. Bugs Module EditView

```php
require_once('include/MVC/View/views/view.edit.php');

class CustomBugsViewEdit extends ViewEdit
{
    public function __construct()
    {
        parent::ViewEdit();
    }

    public function display()
    {
        if ( empty($this->bean->id) ) {
            $releaseFocus = new Release();
            $releases = $releaseFocus->get_releases(TRUE, "Active");
            $this->bean->found_in_release = array_shift(array_keys($releases));
        }
        parent::display();
    }
}
```

The preceding example is pretty simple. You just modify the bean value to whatever the first active release name is provided you are creating a new Bug (you know this by checking to see if the id field has been set or not). The return value from $releaseFocus->get_releases() is an associative array of release id, release name pairs, so you used the array_keys() function to just get the keys as an array and the array_shift() method to get the first item array item, which is the first active release id.

One problem you may run into with view customizations is if there are changes to Sugar from a new release. Sometimes a new view may be added to help fix a bug in the product, where your new custom view might ignore that. Therefore, before creating any new custom view that will extend or replace an existing one, you should check to be sure you are not missing something that has been added since you made your initial customization.

Changing the Metadata-Driven Views

For the Edit and Detail views, it's not completely necessary to change the view code to make modifications. Many customizations can be made within the metadata definition files themselves. You learned about the structure of these files in Chapter 3, and what options are available to you as a module writer for customizing these views. You can use all those features that are available to customize the display as you need it.

To customize the view you'll need to copy the metadata file that you wish to change to the custom/modules/*modulename*/metadata/ directory. This metadata file will then be called instead of the original one. Also, be sure to turn Developer Mode on in the System Settings in the Admin panel before doing any customizations to these files, so your changes will be picked up automatically. A simple example would be to remove the date_modified and date_created fields from the DetailView of the Notes modules module. The resulting detailviewdefs.php file would look like the code in Listing 8-4.

Listing 8-4. Customized detailviewdefs.php Metadata File for the Notes Module

```
$viewdefs['Notes']['DetailView'] = array(
    'templateMeta' => array('maxColumns' => '2',
        'widths' => array(
            array('label' => '10', 'field' => '30'),
            array('label' => '10', 'field' => '30')
            ),
        ),
    'panels' => array(
        array (
            'contact_name',
            array (
                'name' => 'parent_name',
                'customLabel' => '{sugar_translate label=\'LBL_MODULE_NAME\'↵
module=$fields.parent_type.value}',
                ),
            ),
        array (
            array('name' => 'contact_phone', 'type'=>'phone', 'label' => 'LBL_PHONE'),
            ),
        array (
            array('name' => 'contact_email', 'label' => 'LBL_EMAIL_ADDRESS'),
```

```
        ),
    array (
        array('name' => 'name', 'label' => 'LBL_SUBJECT'),
        ),
    array(
        array('name'=>'filename', 'type'=>'file', 'displayParams'=>array('id'=>'id',↵
'link'=>'filename')),
        ),
    array (
        array('name' => 'description', 'label' => 'LBL_NOTE_STATUS'),
        ),
    ),
);
```

By default the DetailView will show three buttons at the top and bottom of the form (Edit, Duplicate, and Delete) and the EditViews will show two buttons (Save and Cancel), and may also show the View Change Log button if the module has auditing enabled. Let's say you want to add the ability to search for duplicate records from the EditView. You'll update your metadata to list the buttons you wish to have in Listing 8-5.

Listing 8-5. *Customized editviewdefs.php File for the Contacts Module with the Added Find Duplicates Button*

```
$viewdefs['Contacts']['EditView'] = array(
    'templateMeta' => array(
        'form'=>array(
            'hidden'=>array(
                '<input type="hidden" name="opportunity_id"↵
value="{$smarty.request.opportunity_id}">',
                '<input type="hidden" name="case_id" value="{$smarty.request.case_id}">',
                '<input type="hidden" name="bug_id" value="{$smarty.request.bug_id}">',
                '<input type="hidden" name="email_id" value="{$smarty.request.email_id}">',
                '<input type="hidden" name="inbound_email_id"↵
value="{$smarty.request.inbound_email_id}">'
                ),
            'buttons'=>array('SAVE', 'CANCEL', 'FIND_DUPLICATES'),
            ),
                'maxColumns' => '2',
        'widths' => array(
            array('label' => '10', 'field' => '30'),
            array('label' => '10', 'field' => '30'),
            ),
        ),
    'panels' =>array (
        'lbl_contact_information' => array (
            array (
                array (
                    'name' => 'first_name',
                    'customCode' => '{html_options name="salutation"↵
options=$fields.salutation.options selected=$fields.salutation.value} <input↵
```

```
name="first_name" size="25" maxlength="25" type="text"↵
value="{$fields.first_name.value}">',
                ),
                'phone_work',
                ),
        array (
                array('name'=>'last_name','displayParams'=>array('required'=>true),),
                'phone_mobile',
                ),
        array (
                array('name'=>'account_name', 'displayParams'=>array('key'=>'billing',↵
'copy'=>'primary', 'billingKey'=>'primary',↵
'additionalFields'=>array('phone_office'=>'phone_work'))),
                'phone_home',
                ),
        array (
                'lead_source',
                'phone_other',
                ),
        array (
                'campaign_name',
                'phone_fax',
                ),
        array (
                'title',
                'birthdate',
                ),
        array (
                'department',
                ),
        array (
                'report_to_name',
                'assistant',
                ),
        array (
                'sync_contact',
                'assistant_phone',
                ),
        array (
                'do_not_call',
                ),
        array (
                'assigned_user_name',
                ),
                ),
        'lbl_email_addresses'=>array(
                array('email1')
                ),
        'lbl_address_information' => array (
                array (
                        array (
                                'name' => 'primary_address_street',
                                'hideLabel' => true,
```

```
                    'type' => 'address',
                    'displayParams'=>array('key'=>'primary', 'rows'=>2, 'cols'=>30,↵
'maxlength'=>150),
                        ),
                array (
                    'name' => 'alt_address_street',
                    'hideLabel'=>true,
                    'type' => 'address',
                    'displayParams'=>array('key'=>'alt', 'copy'=>'primary', 'rows'=>2,↵
'cols'=>30, 'maxlength'=>150),
                        ),
                    ),
                ),
        'lbl_description_information' => array (
            array (
                array(
                    'name'=>'description',
                    'displayParams'=>array('rows'=>6, 'cols'=>80),
                    'label'=>'LBL_DESCRIPTION'
                    ),
                ),
            ),
        )
);
```

All of the search boxes in SugarCRM are three columns wide by default. Let's say most of your end users are on small screens or really have a desire to keep their screens at 800×600 (I had the exact same situation when I wrote a small business app for a previous company). You can make a simple adjustment searchdefs.php file to handle this situation by changing the maxColumns attribute in the templateMeta section of that file. Listing 8-6 shows an example of how this would look if you modified the Contacts module.

Listing 8-6. Customized searchdefs.php File for the Contacts Module

```
$searchdefs['Contacts'] = array(
    'templateMeta' => array(
        'maxColumns' => '2',
        'widths' => array('label' => '15', 'field' => '35'),
        ),
    'layout' => array(
        'basic_search' => array(
            'first_name',
            'last_name',
            'account_name',
            array('name'=>'current_user_only', 'label'=>'LBL_CURRENT_USER_FILTER',↵
'type'=>'bool'),
            ),
        'advanced_search' => array(
            'first_name',
            array('name' => 'address_street', 'label' =>'LBL_ANY_ADDRESS', 'type' =>↵
'name'),
```

```
            array('name' => 'phone', 'label' =>'LBL_ANY_PHONE', 'type' => 'name'),
            'last_name',
            array('name' => 'address_city', 'label' =>'LBL_CITY', 'type' => 'name'),
            array('name' => 'email', 'label' =>'LBL_ANY_EMAIL', 'type' => 'name'),
            'account_name',
            array('name' => 'address_state', 'label' =>'LBL_STATE', 'type' => 'name'),
            'do_not_call',
            'assistant',
            array('name' => 'address_postalcode', 'label' =>'LBL_POSTAL_CODE', 'type' =>↵
'name'),
            array('name' => 'primary_address_country', 'label' =>'LBL_COUNTRY', 'type' =>↵
'name', 'options' => 'countries_dom', ),
            'lead_source',
            array('name' => 'assigned_user_id', 'type' => 'enum', 'label' =>↵
'LBL_ASSIGNED_TO', 'function' => array('name' => 'get_user_array', 'params' =>↵
array(false))),
          ),
      ),
  );
```

Another modification you may want to make is to disable sorting for a module. Some fields are impossible fields to sort with the ListViews (any nondatabase fields, such as calculated fields or fields that come from other modules), so you definitely want to make sure those can't be sorted. You may also want to block sorting by a particular field for performance reasons since it may be too resource intensive for the database so you cannot add an index on that field in the database. For this, you just need to add the sortable attribute set to false for that field. Listing 8-7 shows an example of this which disables sorting by priority in the Bugs ListView.

Listing 8-7. Customized listviewdefs.php Template File for the Bugs ListView

```
$listViewDefs['Bugs'] = array(
    'BUG_NUMBER' => array(
        'width' => '5',
        'label' => 'LBL_LIST_NUMBER',
        'link' => true,
        'default' => true),
    'NAME' => array(
        'width' => '32',
        'label' => 'LBL_LIST_SUBJECT',
        'default' => true,
        'link' => true),
    'STATUS' => array(
        'width' => '10',
        'label' => 'LBL_LIST_STATUS',
        'default' => true),
    'TYPE' => array(
        'width' => '10',
        'label' => 'LBL_LIST_TYPE',
        'default' => true),
    'PRIORITY' => array(
```

```
            'width' => '10',
            'label' => 'LBL_LIST_PRIORITY',
            'sortable' => false,

            'default' => true),
    'RELEASE_NAME' => array(
            'width' => '10',
            'label' => 'LBL_FOUND_IN_RELEASE',
            'default' => false,
            'related_fields' => array('found_in_release'),
            'module' => 'Releases',
            'id' => 'FOUND_IN_RELEASE',),
    'FIXED_IN_RELEASE_NAME' => array(
            'width' => '10',
            'label' => 'LBL_LIST_FIXED_IN_RELEASE',
            'default' => true,
            'related_fields' => array('fixed_in_release'),
            'module' => 'Releases',
            'id' => 'FIXED_IN_RELEASE',),
    'RESOLUTION' => array(
            'width' => '10',
            'label' => 'LBL_LIST_RESOLUTION',
            'default' => false),
    'ASSIGNED_USER_NAME' => array(
            'width' => '9',
            'label' => 'LBL_LIST_ASSIGNED_USER',
            'default' => true)
);
```

There are many more customizations possible as well by tweaking the metadata file to do whatever you need it to do. The most common customization done through the metadata files is to customize the field display, which can be done through the 'customCode' attribute of each field. Also in the ListViews, you can overwrite the get_list_view_data() method of the module's bean class to change how the value of a field displays in the ListView. Sometimes you want the same changes done every time a field type is used. You can do this by modifying that field as you see fit, which you'll look at next.

Adding New Custom Field Types

Sugar comes with many different field types by default that handle just about all the different types of fields you may want, from standard input boxes to multiple selection lists. This doesn't mean that there may be a different type of field you may want to be available to use throughout the Sugar instance. Or maybe you need to tweak an existing field specification to either handle some other kind of parameter or display it differently to the user. The SugarFields are customizable in both ways, giving you as a developer quite a bit of leverage in customizing how fields look and work in your Sugar instance.

The easiest thing to do is to customize how a field displays. You may do this for many different reasons. For example, you may not like the way you display fields, so you may wish to change it to display what you want it to. For example, the file field (which represents an uploaded file) simply presents a file input box ready for you to select the file you are uploading. It doesn't indicate if a file has already been uploaded, so you know not to replace it. To do so, you can make a few changes to the field definition. First, you'll display the name of the file uploaded right underneath the file, so you'll copy the include/SugarFields/Fields/File/EditView.tpl to custom/include/SugarFields/Fields/File/EditView.tpl and make your modifications to the template as shown in Listing 8-8.

Listing 8-8. Custom File EditView Template File

```
<input id="{{sugarvar key='name'}}" name="{{sugarvar key='name'}}" type="file"↵
 title='{{$vardef.help}}' size="{{$displayParams.size|default:30}}" {{if↵
 !empty($vardef.len)}}maxlength='{{$vardef.len}}'{{elseif↵
 !empty($displayParams.maxlength)}}maxlength="{{$displayParams.maxlength}}"↵
{{else}}maxlength="255"{{/if}} value="{$fields[{{sugarvar key='name'↵
 stringFormat=true}}].value}" {{$displayParams.field}}>
<br />{$fields[{{sugarvar key='name' stringFormat=true}}].value}
```

You'll notice in some places in Listing 8-8 you use double brackets ({{) versus single brackets ({). This is because most of the metadata-driven Smarty templates are built in two passes. Pass one pulls all the field templates into the main templates and then saves it in the cache directory, so it doesn't need rebuilt every time. Pass two fills in the actual data values that will be shown to the user in the final built template. This pass is done on every request.

In the preceding, you've just simply added to the existing template a line break and then the string value of the given field. From now on, when you use a file SugarField in any EditView, the above widget definition will be used instead of the default one.

Let's say you want to take this a step forward and have a File field type that only allows you to initially upload the file, but not ever change it. This behavior is similar to how the Documents module works with the File SugarField type. To do this, you'll extend the File field type into a new field type you'll call Filereadonly. You'll create this field in the custom directory under custom/include/SugarFields/Fields/Filereadonly/. Next, you'll start defining the field type. The first part of this field type is to create the SugarField child class for the widget, so you know to inherit all the File SugarField type actions (see Listing 8-9).

Listing 8-9. Custom Filereadonly SugarField child class

```
require_once('include/SugarFields/Fields/File/SugarFieldFile.php');


class SugarFieldFilereadonly extends SugarFieldFile
{
```

```
public function save(&$bean, $params, $field, $properties)
{

    if ( !empty($bean->id) && isset($_REQUEST[$field]) )

        unset($_REQUEST[$field]);

    return parent::save(bean, $params, $field, $properties);
}

}
```

In Listing 8-9, you see the use of the save() method in a SugarField subclass. This is called during the pre_action() part of the save view call in the SugarController on each field to apply any needed field transformation before actually saving the data. In this case, you'll use it for clearing out any passed value for this field if you are not creating a new record, thus preserving your original intent of not allowing the specified uploaded file to be changed.

The next part of this customization involves reworking the EditView template to display the correct widget to the user, as shown in Listing 8-10.

Listing 8-10. Custom Filereadonly EditView Template File

```
{if $id == ''}
<input id="{{sugarvar key='name'}}" name="{{sugarvar key='name'}}" type="file"↵
 title='{{$vardef.help}}' size="{{$displayParams.size|default:30}}" {{if↵
 !empty($vardef.len)}}maxlength='{{$vardef.len}}'{{elseif↵
 !empty($displayParams.maxlength)}}maxlength="{{$displayParams.maxlength}}"↵
{{else}}maxlength="255"{{/if}} value="{$fields[{{sugarvar key='name'↵
 stringFormat=true}}].value}" {{$displayParams.field}}>
{else}
{$fields[{{sugarvar key='name' stringFormat=true}}].value}
{/if}
```

The $id variable is set by default for all EditViews. It specified the record id for the current record. You use this variable to trigger what to do when you reach this field widget. If no id is defined, then you assume this to be a new record, so you display a file input box to the user for them to locate and upload the file from their local filesystem. If there is a record id, you can then not allow a file to be uploaded, so you will just display the name of the file which has already been uploaded, allowing no changes from the user. To use this widget instead of the normal file one, change the field's vardef 'type' attribute to 'filereadonly'.

One issue you may run into with custom classes is in the few remaining sections of the product, such as ListViews and Reports, that use the older type of widget known as the SugarWidget to display data instead of the more common SugarField object, which is used just about everywhere else. For these cases, you'll want to set the 'dbType' attribute of the field definition to one of the more built-in types, such as varchar, so a valid SugarWidget can be used if the field is used in these areas of the product. This is one area which should be cleaned up in a future version of SugarCRM, so you won't require adding this to the vardefs.php file for the module.

Changing Language Strings

A very common customization you see (and as it turns out, a very simple one to do) is to customize the language strings that are used throughout the product. You saw in Chapter 6 that you can do some of these customizations within Studio itself, but sometimes they are much simpler to customize right in the code itself.

There are three types of language strings in SugarCRM:

- *app_strings*: These are strings the can be used anywhere in the application.

- *mod_strings*: These are strings that are particular to a certain section of the application.

- *app_list_strings*: These are associative arrays, which are often used for fields such as enums or multienums.

Each type of language string is customized differently. For app_strings and app_list_strings, you can either add the string changes to the custom/include/language/en_us.lang.php or the custom/application/Ext/Language/en_us.lang.ext.php. Either location will be parsed for string changes. For example, you want to change the Bug status options to have some more options and change the wording on a few of them. You'll add a new option Reopened, as well as changing the display string for New to Newly Created. Listing 8-11 shows what you would need to add to the file to make this happen.

Listing 8-11. Customized en_us.lang.php file Updating the bug_status_dom key in the app_list_strings

```
$app_list_strings['bug_status_dom']['New'] = 'Newly Created'; // was 'New'
$app_list_strings['bug_status_dom']['Reopened'] = 'Reopened'; // new entry
```

The other main application-level string file can be updated in the same way by adding the strings you wish to update in that same file. It's best to keep your changes inside the custom/include/language/en_us.lang.php file since the custom/application/Ext/Language/en_us.lang.ext.php file is typically used for Studio string changes. Also note that any changes you make in the custom/include/language/en_us.lang.php file are made after those in the custom/application/Ext/Language/en_us.lang.ext.php file, so check in the former file if your Studio changes aren't making it to the user.

Strings specific to the module (referred to above as mod_strings) are kept inside each module and are only available within that module. To customize them, you can drop the en_us.lang.php file in the custom/modules/*modulename*/language/ directory. Customizations for the mod_strings work the same as those for the the the app_strings and app_list_strings, as seen in Listing 8-12, which shows how to override a few strings in t the Bugs module.

Listing 8-12. Customized en_us.lang.php File Updating Some mod_strings for the Bugs Module

```
$mod_strings['LBL_SOURCE'] = 'Defect Source:'; // was 'Source'
$mod_strings['LBL_PRODUCT_CATEGORY'] = 'Product Category:'; // was 'Category'
```

You've been directing your language fixes to the standard US English language pack. By using the other IETF language tags in place of en_us, you can adjust the strings of any language pack you are using with your Sugar instance. Let's say you've installed the French language pack from SugarForge and you need to adjust a few strings in the Calls module. Just drop the fr_FR.lang.php file shown in Listing 8-13 in the custom/modules/Calls/language/ directory and you'll be good to go.

Listing 8-13. Customized fr_FR.lang.php file Updating Some mod_strings for the Calls Module

```
$mod_strings['LBL_SUBJECT'] = 'Appel Sujet:'; // was 'Sujet:'
$mod_strings['LBL_CONTACT_NAME'] = 'Appel Contact:'; // was 'Contact:'
```

You can see that changing language strings around is also a very pain-free exercise. Let's now try your hand at modifying a few of the vardef.php files.

Tweak vardef Definitions

As you learned in Chapter 2, vardef files define the structure and specifications of the fields used inside any given module in the application. Most of the time, the given defaults work as expected—a common way to work around when they don't is to add a custom field to replace the offending field. If you aren't scared to get a bit "down and dirty" with the code itself, getting away from the safe confines of Studio, you can adjust the fields to work the way you wish. Let's look at a few common scenarios which are easy to change through vardef customizations. Each of these customizations should be saved in a file ending with the .php extension in the custom/Extension/modules/*modulename*/ directory.

Let's say you want to be sure that everyone when importing Bugs actually indicates which release the bug occurred in and which release it should be fixed in. Listing 8-14 shows the way here by setting the importable attribute for the field to required.

Listing 8-14. Setting the Importable Attribute for the Given Bugs Fields to Required

```
$dictionary['Bug']['fields']['fixed_in_release']['importable'] = 'required';
$dictionary['Bug']['fields']['found_in_release']['importable'] = 'required';
```

Another situation is that you may want to enable searching by an extra field in the global search. This search is the one that is typically in the header of the application and is designed to be a tool to easily look for records based upon the given string across one or more modules at a time. Modules can be included in this search by adding the 'unified_search' attribute set to true in the root of the $vardef array for a module, and an individual field can then be added by also setting the same 'unified_search' attribute to true in the field definition. Listing 8-15 shows an example of how you can add enabled searching in the contact_name field when you include the Calls module in your global search.

Listing 8-15. Setting the unified_search Attribute for the Given Calls Module Field to True

```
$dictionary['Call']['fields']['contact_name']['unified_search'] = true;
```

You can also define new indices as well. It's useful to define them here instead of just adding them to the database, so that they can easily repair the database later on if you need to without losing the added indices in the process. To do this, you can just add the index definition as an array to the vardef definition for the module An example is shown in Listing 8-16 where you add an index on id + name + reference_code to the Contracts module.

Listing 8-16. Adding a New Index to the Contacts Module

```
$dictionary['Contract']['indices'][] = array(
    'name' => 'idx_contract_id_name_refcode',
    'type' => 'index',
    'fields' => array('id', 'name', 'reference_code')
);
```

To add this change to your module, you can add them inside the custom/Extension/modules/*modulename*/Ext/Vardefs/ directory, with any filename of your choosing. You can add as many files as you like here as well, which is handy since it allows you as a developer to group your vardef customizations into different files for better organization of your code.

Custom Themes and Theme Customizations (Yes, They Are Different)

In Chapter 5, the new Themes Framework that has been added in Sugar 5.5 was mentioned. One very handy and long-awaited feature of this is to utilize the custom directory for theme customizations. Theme customizations are very useful, because they allow developers to alter the look and feel of their Sugar instance to match what their users like or expect the application to look like. Up until Sugar 5.5, this has been a non-upgrade safe modification, as well as very difficult since it required basically copying one of the out-of-the-box themes, changing the elements you wish to change, and then maintaining it throughout any upgrades or patches to Sugar since they may require you to change your customizations by hand to get the new bug and security fixes in them. With Sugar 5.5, you've created a default theme that has all of the elements you need for any theme ready to go, and now allow developers to base any new themes off of existing themes in the product. In addition, you can also make simple and easy customizations to the included themes in case you don't like what has been chosen by default.

Let's start with the easiest type of customization. In case, you don't like the image used for a particular part of the application you can , just dump an image of the same name into the custom directory for that theme> If you wanted to override the Accounts.gif image you would drop your version of it in the custom/themes/*themename*/images/Accounts.gif file. The new file will then be picked up with no code changes required: The only thing you may have to do is clear out the themes cache through the Admin ➤ Repair ➤ Clear Theme Cache option. You can also specify this to override the default image used in all themes for this image by dropping it in the custom/themes/default/images/Accounts.gif file instead.

One other thing to make sure of is that the file name is the same type as the original. Let's say you are a big fan of png images and want to use a png instead of gif file here. No problem, just name the file custom/themes/*themename*/images/Accounts.png and it will replace the original themes/*themename*/images/Accounts.gif or themes/default/images/Accounts.gif file as well. You can also substitute in files ending in .jpg, .bmp, or .tif as well, giving you more options in providing image types; the order checked for files is gif, png, jpg, tif, and bmp.

The other type of customization you can make is to the CSS used in displaying the content to the user. These are specified in the custom/themes/*themename*/css/style.css file, and will be appended after the original style files of the theme. Javascript customizations can be made in a similar way as well by dropping the style.js file inside the custom/themes/*themename*/js/ directory, which will allow it to be added to any existing javascript code provided by the theme. With these tools available, customizing a theme for use on your instance is a snap.

But let's say you want to not override one of the existing themes, but actually make a new theme based upon it. To do so is a simple task; just make a new directory in the named custom/themes/*newthemename*/ and add a themedef.php file to it similar to the one in Listing 8-17.

Listing 8-17. themedef.php file for a new custom theme SugarCustom

```
$themedef = array(
 'name' => "SugarCustom", // theme name
 'description' => "Sugar Custom Theme", // short description of the theme
 'parentTheme' => "Sugar", // name of the theme this theme inherits from, if something⏎
 other than the default theme.
);
```

You've specified the name of your new theme will be SugarCustom, so this file will be located in the custom/themes/SugarCustom/ directory, which will also contain all images, css files, and javascript that will custom define this theme. The key attribute in the theme definition file is the parentTheme item. This indicates which theme you wish to inherit from. If you don't specify an existing theme in the product here, then you'll just receive the default theme css, javascript, and images, which may be a good start if no other theme is close to what you wish to build.

Summary

In this chapter you learned about all the other type of customizations, you can make to your Sugar instance through code. You learned about the custom directory, which holds all the customizations you can do in the product, and saw where you would make different types of customizations. You then took a look at a few common customization examples, such as customizing views, metadata, vardefs, language packs, and themes.

At this point in the book, you now know how to take a Sugar instance and customize it to work and look at how you would like it. Coming up in the next section of the book you'll learn how to build new modules on top of Sugar to handle different kinds of data you may wish to manage with it.

■ ■ ■

PART 3

Building New Functionality on Top of SugarCRM

This part of the book focuses on building new modules on top of Sugar. You'll learn to do this using both the built in GUI developer tool Module Builder, as well as building a module piece by piece using custom PHP code. You then see how you can put all the concepts learned in this book together to build a complete typical business application.

CHAPTER 9

∎ ∎ ∎

Using Module Builder to Build Custom Modules

At this point in the book, you now know about the guts of what makes SugarCRM tick, from the big stuff like the MVC framework, the Metadata layer, and Web Services to the smaller items like User Authentication and Dashlets. After that thorough study of Sugar, you then looked at how to customize Sugar right out of the box. I started by showing the easy-to-use Studio tool that enables customizing the metadata views through an easy point and click interface. You then saw how to interject business logic into your application through the use of logic hooks and how to interject common logic into your application using workflows, which provide a point and click way for the non-programmers among us to add business logic as well. If neither of those options for customizing does the job, you then saw how to customize several other areas of the application from views and metadata to field types and themes.

What if that level of customization isn't enough for your needs? CRM is a not "one-size-fits-all" solution, so the exact pieces to include and exclude are not concrete. CRM is meant to be a tool to enhance your business productivity, so whatever you need to make that so is of paramount importance, whether adding new pieces or altering or removing existing ones. This is the main reason behind the strong customization tools I discussed in Part 1 as well as what you'll see here in Part 3 on adding new modules to Sugar.

In this chapter, you'll look at Module Builder. Module Builder is a GUI tool for building a module that can be used within your Sugar instance or exported to be installed in other Sugar instances. It has a very similar look and feel to Studio, with which Module Builder shares a lot of code. Let's go ahead and jump right into learning how it all works.

Getting Started

As mentioned, Module Builder is a GUI tool that shares the same look and feel of Studio, which you saw previously in Chapter 6. You can get to it from the Admin panel by clicking the Module Builder link in the developer tools section. Once you click that link, you'll see the screen shown in Figure 9-1.

Figure 9-1. Default Module Builder screen

Module Builder organizes things into units called Packages, each of which can contain one or more modules. The reason for this approach is because most times you are designing a complete solution, which involves many modules that work in conjunction with each other to fill a need, rather than just a simple module. In order to create a new module, you first need to create the package that will contain it, so you'll click on the New Package link shown in Figure 9-1 which will bring up the New Package form shown in Figure 9-2.

Figure 9-2. *Module Builder New Package dialog*

This form is used to enter the details of the package you are building. You'll set the name of your package to MyNewPackage (it must be alphanumeric with no spaces), and put in my name (John) for the author of the package. The Key value is used to prefix each of the module's object names to help ensure that the module names don't interfere with another module, as well as give an easy way to identify in the directory structure of which modules go with the package. If you would build a new module called dog then it would appear as pack_dog in the directory structure (that would be the module name as well). You can also add a description to the package optionally, as well as a readme file, which is displayed to the user when it is installed through Module Loader. You'll see that when you actually install the custom module using Module Loader.

Upon clicking Save in the form in Figure 9-2, the new package will be created and you'll be left at the main page of the package, as shown in Figure 9-3.

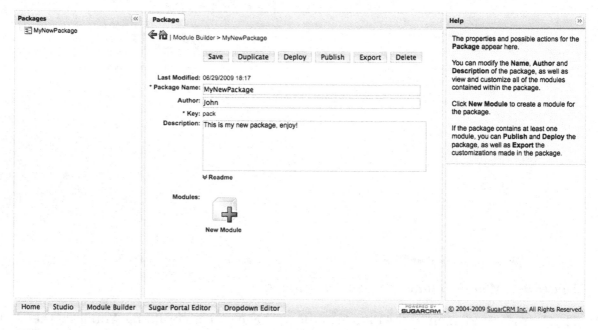

Figure 9-3. *Main screen in Module Builder of a package*

You'll notice the leftmost column in Figure 9-3 now shows your package in the listing of packages. This is where you'll base all your new actions in the package, and where you can begin to create a new package, which you'll see how to do in the next section.

Designing a New Module

Once you have a package created, you can then add a new module to it. To do this, you'll click the New Module link in the main screen of your package (shown in Figure 9-3), which will bring up the form shown in Figure 9-4.

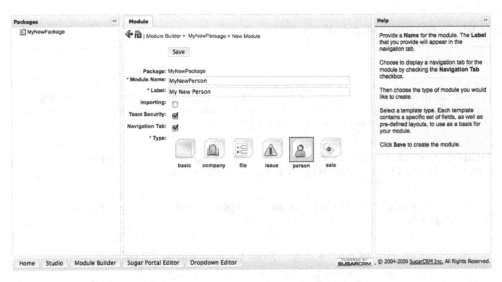

Figure 9-4. *Create new module screen in Module Builder*

You start off by naming your new module, giving it both an internal name in the Module Name field, which is used when referring to your module in the code, as well as a display name for your module, which is how your end-users will refer to your module. At this point, you have a few more options to use for this module:

- *Importing*: This enables the Sugar import tool for importing data into your module.

- *Team security*: Check this item if you want team security in your module, which means that you can assign this module's records to one or more teams and restrict access to records that are based upon which team the user is part of.

- *Navigation tab*: Check this item if you want the module displayed in the navigation tab that is usually along the top of the screen with all the other available modules. The main reason you would not want this option checked is if the module is a submodule of another module, where you wouldn't want people to typically have direct access to it.

Now you can select the type of module you wish to create. These are the same choices you saw for SugarObject templates in Chapter 2, but I'll outline them once again for your reference in Table 9-1.

Table 9-1. *Module Types and Descriptions*

Module Type	Description
basic	A basic template with only fields for a name and description, plus those "behind the scenes" fields like id, the deleted flag, and created/modified timestamps. This template is intended to be the base of all the following templates listed.
company	Fields that would normally be used with a company, such as name, address, phone, web site, or industry. It also contains the fields in the basic template.
file	Used when the object stores files that the user uploads. It also contains the fields in the basic template.
issue	For modeling an issue or job tracking system. It also contains the fields in the basic template.
person	Fields that represent a person, such as name, address, phone, or email. A new feature of Sugar 5.5 is that this module will automatically give users the ability to import and export vCards in the module. It also contains the fields in the basic template.
sale	Used when the object is for sales transactions or forecasting. It also contains the fields in the basic template.

Once you have everything the way you want it, click Save and your module will be created. You'll be directed to the newly created module's main screen, as shown in Figure 9-5.

Figure 9-5. *Main screen for a module with a package in Module Builder*

With that, you have created a new module. But your module is rather boring at this point, because just the defaults are set for it. Let's begin by adding new fields, which you'll learn about in the next section.

Fields

The first thing most people want to do when designing a module is to add the fields they need to the module. This is an easy task to handle. You just need to click on the View Fields button on the main screen for the module (shown in Figure 9-5) and you'll be at the fields screen for the module, shown in Figure 9-6.

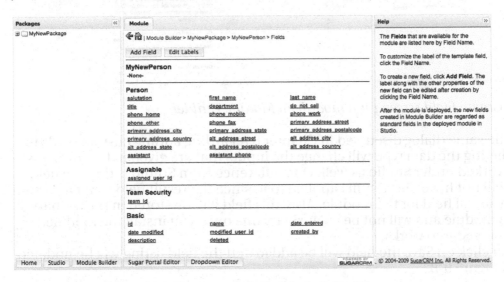

Figure 9-6. Fields screen for a module in Module Builder

The fields screen breaks the fields into sections. The topmost section lists the fields that are specific to the module you have created. Each section represents fields that are inherited from other SugarObjects, so for the previous Person module which has Team Security enabled you'll inherit fields from the Person, Assignable, Team Security, and Basic templates. If you choose a different module type back when you created the module in the previous section (or chose to disable Team Security), you would have a different list of fields inherited.

In Figure 9-6, you have no fields currently defined specifically for this module. To change this, click the Add Field button and you'll be able to add a new field using the screen that is shown in Figure 9-7.

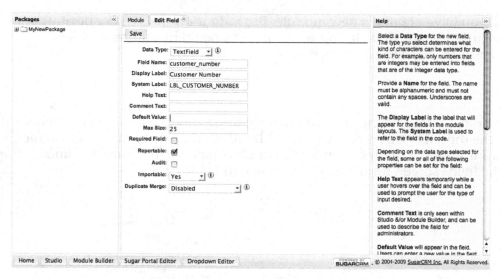

Figure 9-7. *Create Field screen for a module in Module Builder*

This is the same dialog discussed in Chapter 6 regarding adding custom fields in Studio. Changing the data type will change the inputs that are given in the form, just like how it worked under Studio as well. One difference from Studio is that the field you create will not have the _c suffix applied to it, since the result field is not a custom field, but an actual field for the module. Also, this field will be stored in the primary table for the module and will not be an auxiliary one once you install the module, contrary to how Studio works.

Once you click on Save the field will be added and the field listing will be updated, as shown in Figure 9-8.

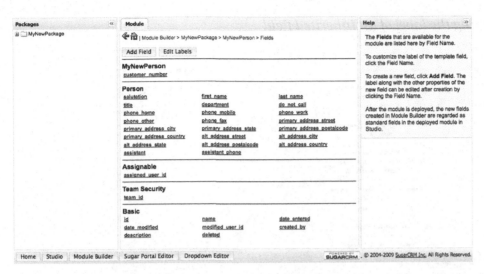

Figure 9-8. *Create Field screen for a module in Module Builder once you've added a field*

While you can't change any of the field properties of the fields inherited from the other SugarObjects, you can customize labels of the fields that are displayed to the end-user. This could be handy if you wanted to repurpose those fields for your own needs, or even if the given description is not the same terminology that the end-user would be familiar with. In either case, you can change the field labels in one of two ways: You can edit an individual field by clicking on the field name in the main module menu (shown in Figure 9-9) or by clicking the Edit Labels buttons and changing the labels in question, as shown in Figure 9-10.

Figure 9-9. Editing the label of an inherited field

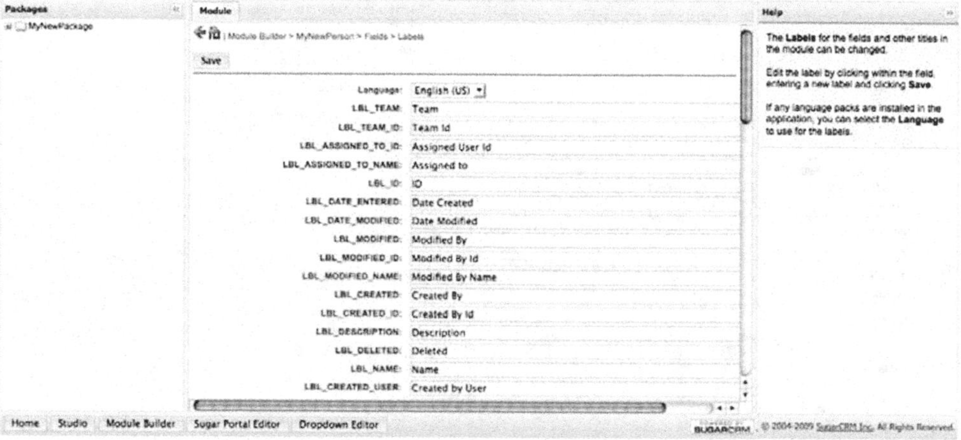

Figure 9-10. Editing all the labels of a module

The benefits of using the latter option (editing all fields at once) is that you can also edit the labels used in other language packs as well at the same time, just like you could in Studio. This is because using the latter option edits the definition for the default strings while editing the field title on the Fields screen changes what string definition is used for the field.

Now that you have your fields set in stone for your module, you can customize the layouts for the various metadata forms used.

Metadata

You learned back in Chapter 3 about the virtues of metadata and how they make it easy to build up the primary data interaction views of your module in a very standardized way. Just like Studio, you can also edit these views from Module Builder as well. To do so, just click on the View Layouts link on the main screen for the module, which will launch the module's layouts screen, as shown in Figure 9-11.

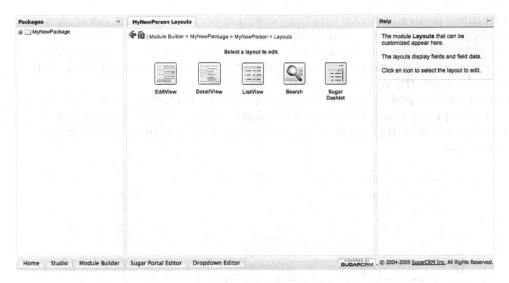

Figure 9-11. Module layout screen in Module Builder

You can click on any of the links in the screen shown in Figure 9-11 to customize the view in question. In Module Builder, just like in Studio, you can add or remove any of the fields on the form and adjust the position and grouping on the screen. You cannot change any of the buttons at the top of the screen (that must be done manually). To customize the EditView for your module, you can click the EditView link, which launches the screen shown in Figure 9-12.

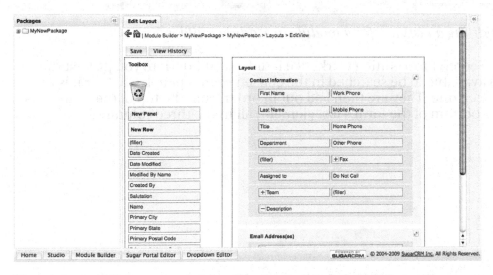

Figure 9-12. Editing a module's edit view in Module Builder

You'll remember from Chapter 6 that this screen is very easy to use, because you can drag and drop the fields you are looking to add or remove from the form easily by using the rich AJAX interface. The form works identically to how it works in Studio. You can add new rows or panels to the form and add and remove fields as you wish. When you have the form the way you want it, just click Save.

You can edit the ListView as well, just as you did in Studio (see Figure 9-13). This form allows you to specify both default fields to show in the ListView in addition to the fields that are available in general, as well as giving a default field order for the fields in the ListView.

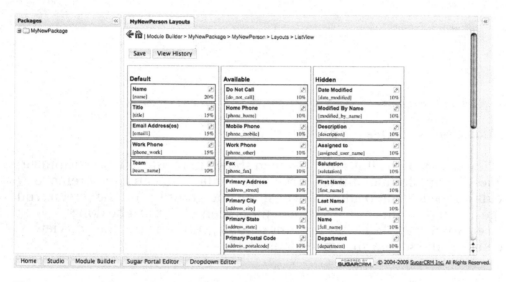

Figure 9-13. Editing a ListView for a module in Module Builder

Again, the Search form editing works like it did in Studio. Here you just list the fields that are available to be searched in the chosen search panel, whether it is the basic or advanced one. They are then laid out in order from the top of the form's first element to the bottom of the form's last element, all in the three columns.

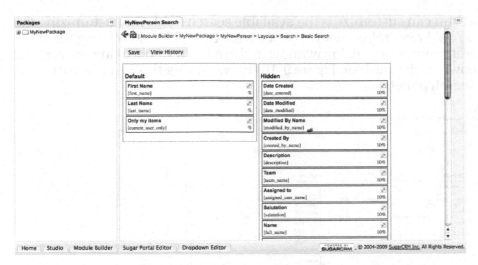

Figure 9-14. Basic search panel editing for a module in Module Builder

One additional thing to edit is the dashlet created automatically for your module. Dashlets are the tool you learned about in Chapter 5 that allow you to display information about a module or any other part of Sugar on the homepage for quick and easy reference. The dashlet that gets created by Module Builder is the ListView type, so you have two parts of it available for customization. The first part is the fields that show up in the ListView itself. You'll have a ListView editor available, as shown in Figure 9-15.

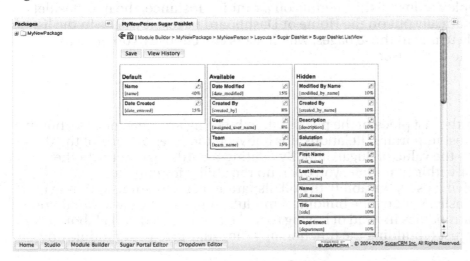

Figure 9-15. Dashlet ListView editor for a module in Module Builder

The other part you can customize is the available search fields for customizing the dashlet's display. You'll remember that these fields are available when going into the dashlet's configurations options dialog window and are a way of tweaking the records that would get shown in this dashlet. Figure 9-16 shows editing this just like you would a normal search panel.

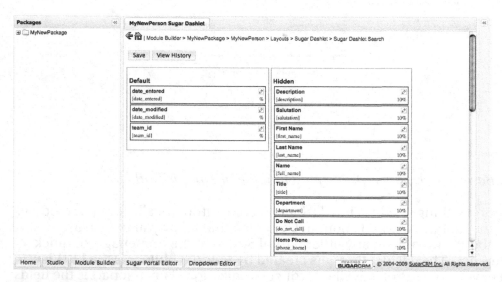

Figure 9-16. Editing the dashlet search fields for a module in Module Builder

When you deploy or install this module on a running instance, the new dashlet will not be automatically put on the Home or Dashboard pages. It will be in the list of Dashlets available to add to those pages, which users can choose to do once the module is available to the user.

Relationships

Relationships are the last piece of the puzzle when building any new module, but in many ways the most important. Relationships between modules are one of the things that truly enhance the value of SugarCRM. By relating records together, whether across modules or within a module, you open up the ability for enhanced productivity by giving users the ability to pull disparate pieces of information in a system together easily. For anyone building a module, it makes it easy to build upon the existing Sugar modules instead of having to make complicated and elaborate hooks to them or just rebuilding the functionality they may give your module on your own.

To get started, click View Relationships from the module's main screen, which will bring up the dialog shown below in Figure 9-17.

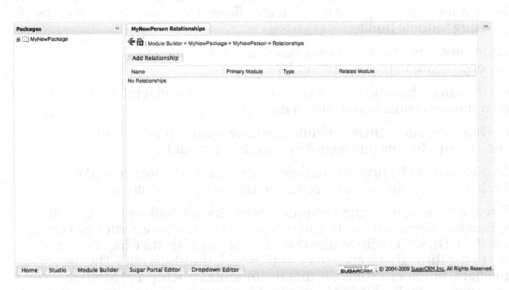

Figure 9-17. Relationship listing for a module in Module Builder

By default no relationships exists for a module, so if you want to add one you'll need to click on the Add Relationship button on the form to add it. When you do, you'll be at the create relationship screen, as shown in Figure 9-18.

Figure 9-18. Create Relationship screen in Module Builder.

This screen (much like most of Module Builder) works the same as its counterpart in Studio. Remember from Chapter 3 that you are allowed to create different types of relationships using Module Builder:

- *One to One*: The primary module has one record which relates to only one record in the related module.

- *One to Many*: The primary module has one record which relates to one or more records in the related module.

- *Many to One*: The primary module can have one or more records which relates to only one record in the related module.

- *Many to Many*: The primary module can have one or more records which relates to one or more records in the related module.

One difference here with editing relationships in Module Builder versus Studio is that Module Builder allows you to edit and delete your relationships after you create them through the GUI, while with Studio this was not possible. (In Chapter 6, you learned a way to dig through the code to clear these relationships out.) The big reason it can be done here, but not in Studio, is that the module structures in Module Builder are much more malleable in Module Builder than Studio. Studio is writing out the customizations immediately while Module Builder only does this on a publish or deploy.

Once you have created the many-to-many relationship, click Save and the relationship will be built. You'll be back at the relationships screen with the new relationship added, as shown in Figure 9-19.

Figure 9-19. Create Relationship screen in Module Builder after adding a relationship

A consideration you should make when adding relationships to modules that you don't ship with your package is that you should make sure that you aren't adding relationships to modules that don't exist on the target system. For example, let's say you have a relationship to the Contracts module, but someone wants to install your package on the CE version of Sugar. They'll run into all sorts of problems since that module is not available. Things like this should be clearly documented in the README file if they exist, so that administrators can be aware of them and avoid potential problems.

What Do I Do with This Package?

Now you have your module just the way you want it: all the fields you need are present, the metadata views property customized, and the labels correct. It's time to show it off to the world! To accomplish this, Sugar provides three approaches:

- Publish the module package as a loadable package that can be installed into an instance using Module Loader. This is a common approach if you are developing a module for deployment on many different Sugar instances, since the administrator can just load the package into their instance and install it easily.

- Deploy the module package into the current running instance.

- Export the module package as a loadable package that will only be installed back into Module Loader for further customization on the target system. This approach is most commonly used when multiple developers are working on a package, so they can share changes back and forth between them, or if the package may need some additional configuration once it is installed on the individual Sugar instance.

You'll take a look at each of the options available and how each of them work.

Deploy to the Current Instance

You'll first look at the easiest and common solution, which is to deploy the module into the current running instance. To do this, all you need to do is click the Deploy button on the main package screen and the package will be deployed into the current instance.

Figure 9-20 shows Deploy dialog when deploying a package using Module Builder onto the current instance.

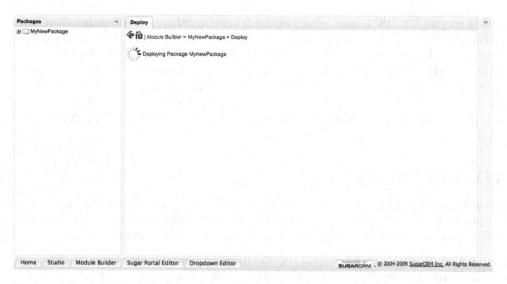

Figure 9-20. Create Relationship screen in Module Builder after adding a relationship

When it is done, the module is then immediately available to the end-users in the current running instance. As you make changes to your module, you can continue to deploy your module again and again, and your changes will override the current ones in the module.

Publishing Your Changes and Installing Them with Module Loader

If you are looking to distribute your module to the world, you'll want to click the Publish icon instead, which will download the built module as a zip file into your local computer. Then, you can take this zip package and install it in any other Sugar instance very easily using Module Loader. To do this, you'll go to the main Module Loader screen by clicking the Module Loader link in the Admin panel in the Developer Tools section, which shows the dialog shown in Figure 9-21.

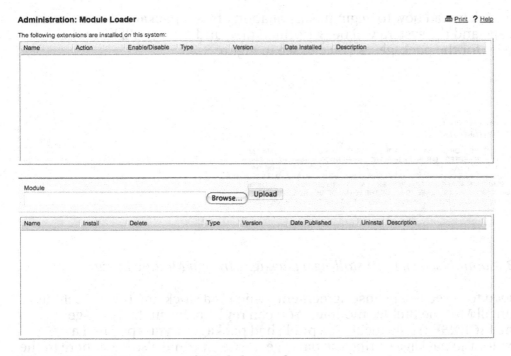

Figure 9-21. *Main screen of Module Loader*

To begin to install your package, you first need to upload it. The second section of the screen in Figure 9-21 is where you do this. Just browse to select the zip package you downloaded on your local computer and then click Upload to upload it to the Sugar instance. When you do so, it will appear in the list of modules shown in Module Loader, as you can see in Figure 9-22.

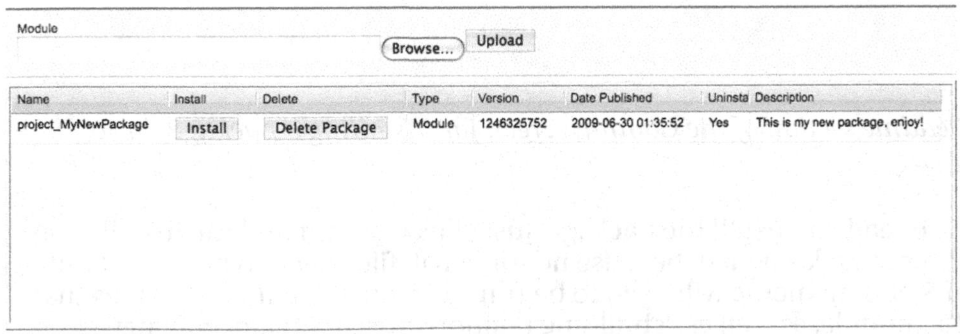

Figure 9-22. *Module Loader after you upload a package*

You can click Install now to begin the installation of your package. A few checks on the package and the system will be performed first, and then you'll be at the commit screen for the package, as you can see in Figure 9-23.

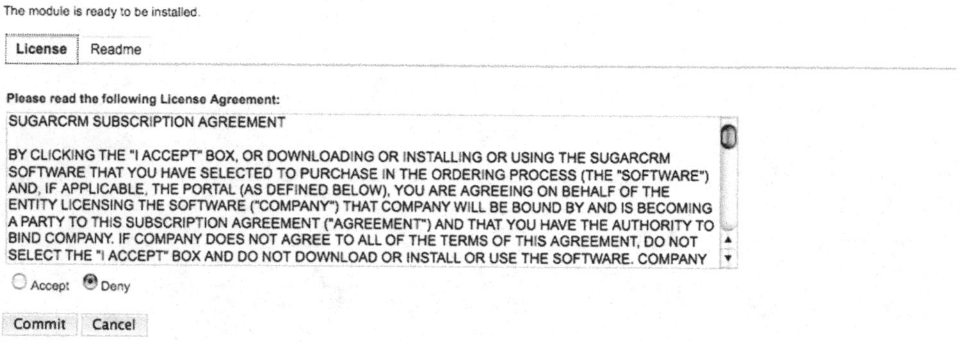

The module is ready to be installed.

License	Readme

Please read the following License Agreement:

SUGARCRM SUBSCRIPTION AGREEMENT

BY CLICKING THE "I ACCEPT" BOX, OR DOWNLOADING OR INSTALLING OR USING THE SUGARCRM SOFTWARE THAT YOU HAVE SELECTED TO PURCHASE IN THE ORDERING PROCESS (THE "SOFTWARE") AND, IF APPLICABLE, THE PORTAL (AS DEFINED BELOW), YOU ARE AGREEING ON BEHALF OF THE ENTITY LICENSING THE SOFTWARE ("COMPANY") THAT COMPANY WILL BE BOUND BY AND IS BECOMING A PARTY TO THIS SUBSCRIPTION AGREEMENT ("AGREEMENT") AND THAT YOU HAVE THE AUTHORITY TO BIND COMPANY. IF COMPANY DOES NOT AGREE TO ALL OF THE TERMS OF THIS AGREEMENT, DO NOT SELECT THE "I ACCEPT" BOX AND DO NOT DOWNLOAD OR INSTALL OR USE THE SOFTWARE. COMPANY

○ Accept ● Deny

[Commit] [Cancel]

Figure 9-23. Commit screen for installing a package through Module Loader

You'll need to agree to a license agreement, which is a stock one that is included by default on all Module Builder modules. You can replace this in the package changing the LICENSE.txt file inside the published package. If you specified a README.txt for the package during the package creation, you'll also see it here in the second tab of this form.

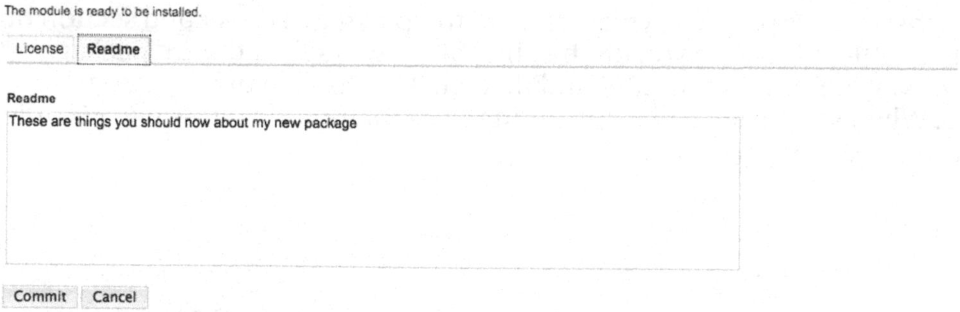

The module is ready to be installed.

License	**Readme**

Readme

These are things you should now about my new package

[Commit] [Cancel]

Figure 9-24. Readme section of the Commit screen for installing a package through Module Loader

Once you are ready to install the package, just click Commit and the installation will begin. This could take awhile, because not only will files need to be copied but also a series of SQL statements will need to be run to create the database tables that are used for the module, as well as rebuilding relationships to include any newly created relationships you have specified in Module Builder.

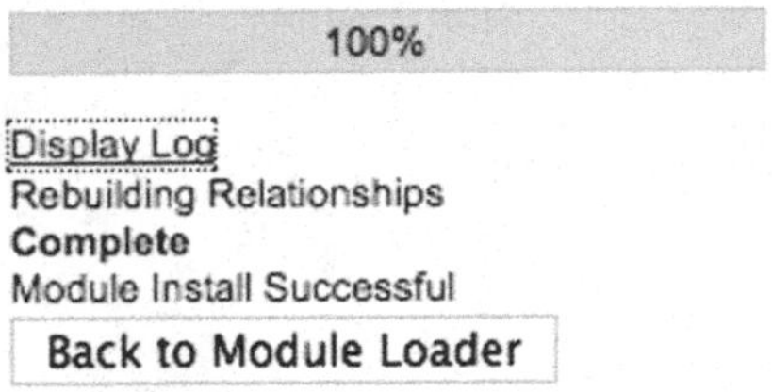

```
                  100%

Display Log
Rebuilding Relationships
Complete
Module Install Successful
  Back to Module Loader
```

Figure 9-25. Package installation through Module Loader

Once the install is complete, you can click the Back to Module Loader button and see that your module is now installed and ready to use. There are no further adjustments required, so the module is immediately available to all users with ACL rights to do so.

Exporting the Package

On the main page of the package, you can click the Export button to export the package into a module loadable zip file, which uses the same Module Loader tool used to install a published package. However when installing the package, it only puts it into Module Builder and does not make it available in the running instance to other users—to do that you'll need to deploy to the instance.

The main reason for having such an option is mostly in the cases where several developers are working collaboratively on a module and don't have a version control system such as SVN or Git at their disposal. This way one developer can work on one part of the module, and then pass it to another developer to do his part, and so on. Another possible use would be if the module may need some further customization steps in relationship to the deployed instance. For example, you may want to provide a way for instances that are missing a particular module to remove any relationships to it before deploying.

Removing an Installed Package

No matter what deployment option you choose to go with, the package installed will be shown in the Module Loader, as you can see in Figure 9-26.

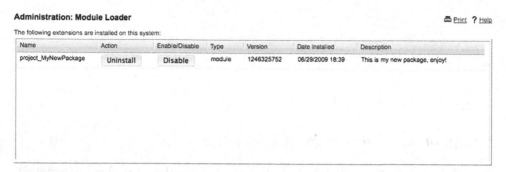

Figure 9-26. Module Loader after you install a package

From here, uninstall your package if you no longer wish to use it at all or disable it if you want to remove it for the time being but keep it installed in the system. Disabling is a good option if you can see it being used again in the future, but need it removed for the time being. A possible reason could be that there is some performance issue, so you want to disable it until you can fix it. Uninstalling it is the best option if you no longer want to use the package at all. When you click the Uninstall button, you'll go through a quick wizard that will check the system to make sure it can uninstall the package, as shown in Figure 9-27.

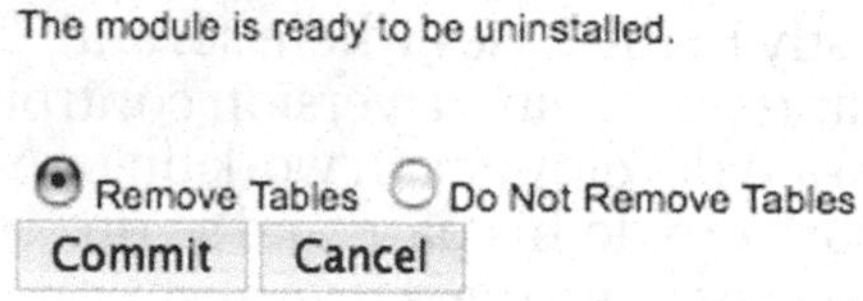

The module is ready to be uninstalled.

⊙ Remove Tables ○ Do Not Remove Tables

Commit   Cancel

Figure 9-27. Dialog for uninstalling a package using Module Loader

You have an option here to remove the tables created by the module or not to. Typically, you'll want to remove these tables since keeping them would leave extra, unused tables in your database. However, your DBA may not want you to run several DROP TABLE commands on a running SQL database, but rather do so themselves. Therefore, the option to skip this step is also given.

You just need to click Commit and the screen in Figure 9-28 appears, which removes the module from the Sugar instance.

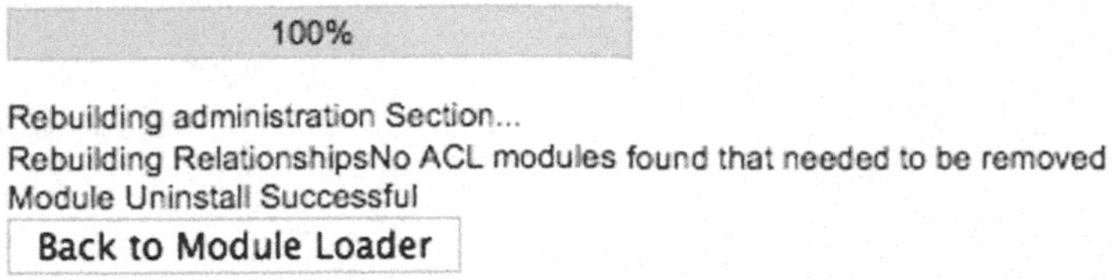

```
                100%

Rebuilding administration Section...
Rebuilding RelationshipsNo ACL modules found that needed to be removed
Module Uninstall Successful
┌─────────────────────┐
│ Back to Module Loader │
└─────────────────────┘
```

Figure 9-28. *Uninstalling a package using Module Loader*

The same steps are used when a module is installed, only doing the reverse actions. At this point, all traces of the module are no longer available to any users, and clicking the Back to Module Loader button will take you back to the main Module Loader screen. You'll notice the package will move back down to the lower grid which lists packages to be installed in case you would want to reinstall it later. If you are done with it for good, click the Delete Package button in that grid and the package will be removed from that list.

Summary

In this chapter, you learned all about Module Builder, a handy tool for building new modules for SugarCRM using an easy-to-use point and click interface. You looked at building a module piece by piece, beginning by seeing how to construct the initial package and then scaffolding for your module using the built in SugarObject templates. You walked through customizing all the parts of the module, from the available fields and their user-visible labels to all the metadata-driven views that compromise the core of your module. You then looked at deploying your module out to the world and what options you have available. Here you could use deploy right to your current instance or export it out to a zip file where it could be installed on other instances as well.

While Module Builder works great for your typical CRUD style module, many times you need to perform more customized tasks inside a module that only can be done through custom PHP code. Have no fear, Sugar has you covered here. In the next chapter, you'll look at building a module manually.

CHAPTER 10

■ ■ ■

Building a Custom Module Manually

In Chapter 9, you looked at Module Builder, which is a very easy-to-use tool that you can use to build a module. Using Module Builder you can build the most common kinds of modules with ease, which are typically those that employ some sort of CRUD interface for maintaining the records in the module. For many module needs you'll have, this is probably all that is required, but remember that you can use the logic hooks and workflows you learned about in Chapter 7 to add in the missing business logic pieces to your custom module just like you can with the built in modules. With these powerful tools at your fingertips, you'll find yourself ready to build modules for yourself rapidly in no time at all.

What if your module doesn't fit this mold? What if you need to construct some sort of special functionality that Sugar doesn't provide out of the box? Then building a module manually is definitely the course of action you'll need to take to accomplish your goals, and in this chapter you'll take a step-by-step journey on how to do this. We'll begin this journey by first looking at the reasons you would want to do something like this.

Why Would You Do This?

The first question any practical programmer asks themselves is why? Why go through the trouble of building a module bit by bit instead of going the easy route and just using Module Builder? The following are some reasons:

- You really want to learn about the internals of SugarCRM. This isn't really the most far-fetched reasoning. Recently, I spent some time building a few modules by hand and learned a wealth of information about how the innards work, which gave me a lot of insight into the platform that I've used for writing this book.

- Your module isn't the normal CRUD-style module (i.e., a module that contains a Detail, Edit, and List views). For example, the Import module doesn't have any data entry screens, but rather it's just a step-by-step wizard interface that performs an operation on another module.

- Your module has some customized data entry screens. The Roles module is a pretty good example of this, because it has Detail and Edit views that use widgets not included with Studio or Module Builder.

There's also a middle road here as well. You could use Module Builder to do the dirty work of setting up the initial views, creating the needed fields, and building relationships. After that half is done, you could deploy your module and then customize it in the instance using many of the techniques you looked at in Chapter 8, such as adding additional views or customizing the metadata in ways you cannot do with Studio or Module Builder. I would recommend this approach if possible since you'll be able to skip several of the initial steps that create the general scaffolding of the module and its file structure, and just concentrate on what you need to add to accomplish your goals.

However, if your module isn't the typical data- driven module (like the Imports module), then it's best to adhere to the following instructions and build your module by hand. Or, if you are just curious about how a module is built from the ground up, follow along to learn what needs to be done to make this happen.

What You Need to Do

If you have got to this point then you have decided that building a module by hand is exactly the course of action you wish to embark on, for one of the many reasons previously outlined. The process to do so requires a bunch of steps that are important, so that your module is properly recognized by the Sugar instance. Missing any one step could potentially result in your module not functioning as expected, whether it because of errors in the application or data loss.

For this example, you'll assume you're building a module called Parts, which will be used to build a parts database for your Sugar instance. The Parts module will be mostly a normal CRUD-style module, with a few twists along the way. Let's jump right into the process, beginning with construction of the directory structure.

Construct Directory Structure

The directory structure for the module is the first component in building your own module. Your newly created module will exist inside the modules/ directory at the root of the application, so for the Parts module that you are building the directory name would be modules/Parts/. That directory will contain all the files that will be used in your module. Table 10-1 contains a breakdown of these items.

Table 10-1. Breakdown of the Contents of Any Module

File and/or Directory	Description
Language/	Contains all the language strings for a given module.
Dashlets/	Contains any dashlets for the given module.
metadata/	Contains all the metadata files (for EditViews, DetailViews, searches) for the module. These include metadata/editviewdefs.php, metadata/detailviewdefs.php, metadata/searchdefs.php, metadata/listviewdefs.php, and metadata/SearchFields.php.
metadata/studio.php	File exists if you can customize your module via Studio. It does not have to have anything in it, just be there.
metadata/subpanels/	Contains the metadata files for the subpanel view of this module inside other modules.
views/	Contains any view files for the module.
tpls/	Contains any Smarty templates used in the module.
javascript/	Contains any javascript code included by the views in the module.
Forms.php	Contains any code you wish to be included with any access to your module, such as helper functions. Please note this file must exist, even if it's empty for the module to function correctly.
Menu.php	Contains any array that is used to build the module's menu, which is typically located in the left sidebar and contains links to common module actions, such as creating new records.
Beanname.php	The main bean class for the module.
vardefs.php	Contains the table structure, including fields, indices, and relationships to other modules.

I'll outline the contents of the directories listed in Table 10-1 and what the contents of the files mentioned in there are throughout this chapter. It's important to note that naming convention is important for the module not only for the sake of consistency within the application, but also since many platform- related components expect files to exist in certain locations and cannot function correctly if they aren't there. For example, the EditView metadata template is always expected to be located at modules/*modulename*/metadata/editviewdefs.php, as the EditView handler code expects to find it there.

At this point, it's most important to have all the file and directories listed in Table 10-1 created, minus the Menu.php, *Beanname*.php, and vardefs.php files which you'll build later on. Once that's all done, you can move on to getting your module registered inside of Sugar.

Register Module with the Instance"

You built the structure of your shiny new Parts module, but there's one problem: Sugar has no idea it exists. In order to help Sugar figure this out, you'll need to register your newly created module with the Sugar instance.

The first part of the registration involves the include/modules.php file. If you look at this file in your instance, you'll notice it contains references to every module that exists in the system. Your Parts module needs to be included in this as well. However, you can't just add your module in there if you ever expect your module to be upgrade safe. Instead, you'll add it to this file by adding it through the custom/ directory— the file that gets read by the include/modules.php file is located in the custom/application/Ext/Include/modules.ext.php file. Listing 10-1 shows what needs to be in this file in order for it to work.

Listing 10-1. custom/application/Ext/Include/modules.ext.php file that Contains Additions to the include/modules.php File

```php
<?php


$beanList['Parts'] = 'Part';
$beanFiles['Part'] = 'modules/Parts/Part.php';
$moduleList[] = 'Parts';


?>
```

There is one issue you could potentially run into when adding the parts directly to the custom/application/Ext/Include/modules.ext.php file. If you load any modules into your running Sugar instance then your changes would be wiped out. The best way to avoid this from happening is to also add the code listed in Listing 10-1 into a file in the custom/Extension/application/Ext/Include/ directory with any file name of your choosing ending with the .php extension, like additions.php. This way, whenever a new module is installed into your instance, your additions to the custom/application/Ext/Include/modules.ext.php will continue to be incorporated into that file.

There are also a few other options you can set for your module, as shown in Table 10-2.

Table 10-2. All Options for a Bean in the modules.ext.php File

Array name	Description
$beanList	List of available beans; key is the module name.
$beanFiles	List of bean file paths of all available modules; key is the module name.
$moduleList	List of available modules; no key specified.
$modInvisList	List of module which shouldn't ever be shown in the module list tabs typically at the top of the screen; no key specified
$adminOnlyList	List of modules that are for Admin use only; no key specified. The value is an array in the form of: `'modulename' => array('all' => 1)`

The next piece is to add the module into the language pack with the correct localized name for it. You'll add it to two keys in the $app_list_strings, as you can see in Listing 10-2.

Listing 10-2. custom/Extension/application/Ext/Language/en_us.parts.php File that Contains Additions to the include/languages/en_us.lang.php File

```php
<?php

$app_list_strings['moduleList']['Parts'] = 'Parts';
$app_list_strings['moduleListSingular']['Parts'] = 'Part';


?>
```

The two keys you'll add it to are `'moduleList'` and `'moduleListSingular'`, both with the keys being the module name. The moduleList key has the value of the module name itself, while the moduleListSingular specifies the module name in singular form (versus the normal name of the module which is most often in plural form).

Now that your module is properly registered into your Sugar instance, you can now begin to build the bean class file for your instance.

Add Bean Class File"

In Chapter 2, you learned that the bean class file represents the model portion of the Model View Controller design pattern used within Sugar. Its goal is to provide an interface into the backend data structures used by the module, as well as providing simple methods for any data transformations that need done as a part of the module execution. Listing 10-3 shows the bean class file you'll be using for the Parts module that you are building.

Listing 10-3. Part.php Bean Class File

```php
<?php

class Part extends Basic
{
    var $new_schema = true;
    var $module_dir = 'Parts';
    var $object_name = 'Part';
    var $table_name = 'parts';
    var $importable = true;

    var $id;
    var $name;
    var $date_entered;
    var $date_modified;
    var $modified_user_id;
    var $modified_by_name;
    var $created_by;
    var $created_by_name;
    var $description;
    var $deleted;
    var $created_by_link;
    var $modified_user_link;
    var $team_id;
    var $team_set_id;
    var $team_count;
    var $team_name;
    var $team_link;
    var $team_count_link;
    var $teams;
    var $assigned_user_id;
    var $assigned_user_name;
    var $assigned_user_link;
    var $part_reference_number;

    var $part_location;

    public function __construct()
```

```php
    {
        parent::Basic();
    }


    public function bean_implements($interface)
    {
        switch ($interface) {
            case 'ACL': return true;
        }

        return false;
    }

    public function fetchImageURL()

    {

        if ( !empty($this->part_reference_number) )
            return 'http://partimageserver.local/getImage/'↵
. $partBean->part_reference_number;


        return 'include/images/blank.gif';

    }

    public function save(
        $check_notify = false
        )

    {

        // Default the part_location field if it's not otherwise specified

        if ( empty($this->part_location) ) {

            if ( strpos($this->part_reference_number,'790-') !== FALSE )
                $this->part_location = 'Warehouse';

            elseif ( strpos($this->part_reference_number,'890-') !== FALSE )
                $this->part_location = 'Stockroom';

        }
        return parent::save($check_notify);

    }
}


?>
```

For this module you will inherit from the Basic template, so you'll also subclass the Basic template's bean file for your bean file to properly include any logic from it. The main parts to the bean file you need to specify include:

- The main bean properties such as the module directory, object name, table name, and whether the module will allow importing into it.

- Bean properties for each field in the table for this bean. This isn't absolutely required, but makes writing any PHP code for your module much easier.

- The bean_implements() method, which indicates to Sugar whether this module will use ACL to control access or not.

- Any other new methods or overridden methods you need.

For the last item in the list, you'll add one method and extend another existing method in the bean class. The save() method, which is used to save a record to the database, is the method you'll override with logic to set the part location based upon the given part reference number that the user has provided in case a part location is not specified. Then you'll add a method named fetchImageURL(), which will fetch a URL that contains image of the part based upon the part reference number. You'll use this method later on to create a view that will specifically do this. This example assumes that the server http://partimageserver.local/getImage/ is a REST Web Service that provides images for the various parts.

Build vardefs

You'll also remember from Chapter 2 that the vardefs files are used to define the underlying table structure for a given module. One nice thing is that you've based your newly created module upon one of the built-in templates that come with Sugar, so you don't have to specify all the fields that you need, just those that aren't already a part of the template that you are basing your module on.

For the parts module you are building, you are going to be adding two fields to it. The first field is a varchar field called 'part_reference_number', which will specify a reference number you'll use for your part and will also be used for image lookup as you saw in the Part bean class method previously. You'll also add an enum field named 'part_location', which gives the user a dropdown selection of the current location of the part. You'll define all the options for this enum field in the "Add Language Strings" section later on in this chapter.

Putting it all together, you have the vardefs.php file shown in Listing 10-4.

Listing 10-4. vardefs.php File for the Parts Module

```php
<?php


$dictionary['Part'] = array(
    'table' => 'parts',
    'audited' => true,
    'fields' => array(
        'part_reference_number'=>
          array (
            'name' => 'part_reference_number',
            'vname' => 'LBL_PART_REFERENCE_NUMBER',
            'type' => 'varchar',
            'len' => '255',
        ),
      'part_location'=>
          array (
            'name' => 'part_location',
            'vname' => 'LBL_PART_REFERENCE_NUMBER',
            'type' => 'enum',
            'len' => '50',
            'options' => 'parts_part_location_dom',
        ),
    ),
    'indices' => array(
        array('name' => 'idx_parts_part_ref_id', 'type' => 'index', 'fields' =>↵
array('id', 'part_reference_number')),
        array('name' => 'idx_parts_part_location_id', 'type' => 'index', 'fields' =>↵
array('id', 'part_location')),
    ),
    'relationships' => array (
    ),
    'optimistic_lock' => true,
);


require_once('include/SugarObjects/VardefManager.php');
VardefManager::createVardef('Parts', 'Part', array('basic', 'assignable'));


?>
```

You also add a few additional indices as well, so that your newly added part_reference_number and part_location can be queried in an optimal way, meaning that the database can use these indexes to speed up the execution of the various queries made to the underlying tables. At the bottom of the vardef file is where you include the additional field definitions from the basic template you are inheriting from, as well as the assignable template which adds in all the assigned to user fields to your module.

Remember that before you can use your module, you'll need to go to the Admin ➤ Repair ➤ Repair Database before you attempt to use your module so the backend parts table will be built for your module. You should do this every time a change to the vardefs.php is done as well, even if a database change is not required, since it will also refresh the cached copies of the vardefs.php file for your module at the same time. After you do this, your database will have the added or updated fields that are defined in the vardef files available for your module to use.

Now that you have the module framework built, the bean class created, and the database structure specified, you will move forward with building all the templates for the various metadata driven views in your module.

Build Any Metadata Templates

With the module bean all in place, you can now build the metadata templates. You saw back in Chapter 3 what the basic design of these are and all the options available. Since your module will be the normal CRUD style module, you'll need to be sure that it contains all of these metadata views in it as well. In order to do this, you'll need to build all of the metadata templates for each of the views you'll use in your module.

Let's start by building the DetailView in Listing 10-5.

Listing 10-5. detailviewdefs.php File for the Parts Module

```php
<?php


$viewdefs['Parts']['DetailView'] = array(
'templateMeta' => array(
    'form' => array(
        'buttons'=>array(
            'EDIT',
            'DUPLICATE',
            'DELETE',
            array (
                'customCode' => '<input title="{$MOD.LBL_VIEWPARTIMAGE_TITLE}"
accessKey="{$MOD.LBL_VIEWPARTIMAGE_BUTTON_KEY}" type="button" class="button"
onClick="open_popup(\'Parts\', \'600\', \'400\',
'&action=Image&record={$fields.id.value}\');" name="image"
value="{$MOD.LBL_VIEWPARTIMAGE}">'
            ),
        ),
    ),
    'maxColumns' => '2',
    'widths' => array(
        array('label' => '10', 'field' => '30'),
        array('label' => '10', 'field' => '30')
        ),
    ),
    'panels' =>array (
```

```
        array (
          'name',
          'assigned_user_name',
        ),
        array (
          array (
              'name' => 'date_entered',
              'customCode' => '{$fields.date_entered.value} {$APP.LBL_BY}↵
{$fields.created_by_name.value}',
              'label' => 'LBL_DATE_ENTERED',
              ),
          array (
              'name' => 'date_modified',
              'customCode' => '{$fields.date_modified.value} {$APP.LBL_BY}↵
{$fields.modified_by_name.value}',
              'label' => 'LBL_DATE_MODIFIED',
          ),
        ),
        array (
          'part_reference_number',
          'part_location',
          ),
        array (
          'description',
          ),
      )
);
?>
```

Here you can see your DetailView is pretty basic, with the basic fields for the
module such as the part name, description, the assigned username, date entered and
modified, as well as the module specific fields of part reference number and part
location. You've also modified the buttons that appear at the top of this form to add a
button that will launch the image popup for each part based upon the part reference
number. You'll build the view in the "Add Any Additional Views Needed" section a bit
later in the chapter.

Now let's move on to the EditView, as shown in Listing 10-6. The EditView is
pretty much the same as the DetailView, with fields for part name, assigned
username, description, as well as your module specific fields of part location and part
reference number.

Listing 10-6. editviewdefs.php File for the Parts Module

```php
<?php


$viewdefs['Parts']['EditView'] = array(
    'templateMeta' => array('maxColumns' => '2',
                            'widths' => array(
                                            array('label' => '10', 'field' => '30'),
                                            array('label' => '10', 'field' => '30')
```

```
                                        ),
                                        ),

        'panels' =>array (
        'default' =>
        array (
          array (
            'name',
            'assigned_user_name',
          ),
          array (
              'part_reference_number',
              'part_location',
          ),
          array (
            'description',
          ),
        ),

    ),

    );
?>
```

Let's move on to the ListView. Again, if you pull from your knowledge of the metadata templates you learned in the Chapter 3, you know that there are three different metadata templates you need to build all the components on this form. The first is the listviewdefs.php file, as shown in Listing 10-7.

Listing 10-7. *listviewdefs.php File for the Parts Module*

```php
<?php

$listViewDefs['Parts'] = array(
'NAME' => array(
    'width' => '32',
    'label' => 'LBL_NAME',
    'default' => true,
    'link' => true
    ),
'PART_REFERENCE_NUMBER' => array(
    'width' => '30',
    'label' => 'LBL_PART_REFERENCE_NUMBER',
    'default' => true
    ),
'PART_LOCATION' => array(
    'width' => '30',
    'label' => 'LBL_PART_LOCATION',
    'default' => true
    ),
'ASSIGNED_USER_NAME' => array(
```

```php
            'width' => '9',
            'label' => 'LBL_ASSIGNED_TO_NAME',
            'default' => true
        ),
    'DATE_MODIFIED' => array(
            'width' => '5',
            'label' => 'LBL_DATE_MODIFIED'
        ),
    'DATE_ENTERED' => array(
            'width' => '5',
            'label' => 'LBL_DATE_ENTERED'
        ),
    'CREATED_BY_NAME' => array(
            'width' => '10',
            'label' => 'LBL_CREATED'
        ),
    'MODIFIED_BY_NAME' => array(
            'width' => '10',
            'label' => 'LBL_MODIFIED'
        ),
);
?>
```

You'll have four fields displayed in your ListView, name, part reference number, part location, and assigned username with the option for users to also add the date created and modified fields as well as the fields representing the user who created or modified the record. As you may remember from Chapter 3, any of these fields can be sorted by the user using the ListView interface, but you can also make any other of these fields searchable from the basic and advanced search interfaces. You have two files needed to do this. The first is the searchdefs.php file which defines the search interface you see on this ListView form, as shown in Listing 10-8.

Listing 10-8. searchdefs.php File for the Parts Module

```php
<?php


$searchdefs['Parts'] = array(
    'templateMeta' => array(
        'maxColumns' => '3',
        'widths' => array('label' => '10', 'field' => '30'),
        ),
    'layout' => array(
        'basic_search' => array(
            'name',
            array('name'=>'current_user_only', 'label'=>'LBL_CURRENT_USER_FILTER', ↵
  'type'=>'bool'),
        ),
        'advanced_search' => array(
            'name',
            'part_reference_number',
            'part_location',
```

```
                    array('name' => 'assigned_user_id', 'label' => 'LBL_ASSIGNED_TO', 'type' =>↵
    'enum', 'function' => array('name' => 'get_user_array', 'params' => array(false))),
            ),
    ),
        );
    ?>
```

Remember you have two layouts to edit here. The basic search interface is the primary one, which should contain the most often used search fields for the module, while the advanced search page is the secondary one and is used for more customized searching of the module fields.

The second metadata file used to search for a module is the SearchFields.php file, shown in Listing 10-9. You'll remember from Chapter 3 that you use this file to define how to do this search against the module, such as if the display field in the Search form interface is different from the field you are actually searching against.

Listing 10-9. *SearchFields.php File for the Parts Module*

```
<?php
$searchFields['Parts'] =
array (
    'name' => array( 'query_type'=>'default'),
    'part_reference_number' => array( 'query_type'=>'default'),
    'current_user_only'=> array('query_type'=>'default','db_field'=>array↵
('assigned_user_id'),'my_items'=>true, 'vname' => 'LBL_CURRENT_USER_FILTER', 'type' =>↵
    'bool'),
    'assigned_user_id'=> array('query_type'=>'default'),
);
?>
```

Now that you have all the basic views done for the module, let's look at a few extra ones that you'll be using with your module. One is the subpanel view, which is shown on the DetailViews of any related modules to your Parts module. You can see the metadata layout for this in Listing 10-10.

Listing 10-10. *subpanels/default.php File for the Parts Module*

```
<?php


$subpanel_layout = array(
    'top_buttons' => array(
        array('widget_class' => 'SubPanelTopButtonQuickCreate'),
        array('widget_class' => 'SubPanelTopSelectButton', 'popup_module' => 'Parts'),
    ),
    'where' => '',
    'list_fields' => array(
        'name'=>array(
            'vname' => 'LBL_NAME',
            'widget_class' => 'SubPanelDetailViewLink',
            'width' => '45%',
```

```
        ),
    'date_modified'=>array(
        'vname' => 'LBL_DATE_MODIFIED',
        'width' => '45%',
        ),
    'part_reference_number'=>array(
        'vname' => 'LBL_PART_REFERENCE_NUMBER',
        'width' => '45%',
        ),
    'edit_button'=>array(
        'widget_class' => 'SubPanelEditButton',
        'module' => 'Parts',
        'width' => '4%',
        ),
    'remove_button'=>array(
        'widget_class' => 'SubPanelRemoveButton',
        'module' => 'Parts',
        'width' => '5%',
        ),
    ),
);


?>
```

Subpanel definitions typically have three parts to them. The first is the definition of the buttons at the top of the Subpanel, which for your Parts module you'll just need a Create button and a Select button. You'll use the QuickCreate option here, which shows the Create form inline instead of a subsequent browser window, since your EditView is pretty simple. (You'll remember from Chapter 3 that you could have created a separate quickcreatedefs.php if you needed to simplify the form.) You then have a 'where' key to specify any where options you need to do in order to further filter down the records shown, followed by the actual list of fields that will be a part of the module.

One more metadata template you'll add for your module is a Side QuickCreate template, which is used for the quickcreate form that is shown in the left sidebar during the ListView of the module and provides a way to quickly add new record to a module. For the Parts module you're building, you'll use a simplified EditView with only the name, description, and assigned user fields present, as shown in Listing 10-11.

Listing 10-11. sidecreateviewdefs.php File for the Parts Module

```
<?php


$viewdefs['Parts']['SideQuickCreate'] = array(
    'templateMeta' => array(
        'form' => array(
            'buttons' => array('SAVE'),
```

```php
                    'button_location' => 'bottom',
                    'headerTpl' => 'include/EditView/header.tpl',
                    'footerTpl' => 'include/EditView/footer.tpl',
                    ),
            'maxColumns' => '1',
            'panelClass'=>'none',
            'labelsOnTop'=>true,
            'widths' => array(
                array( 'label' => '10', 'field' => '30' ),
                ),
        ),
        'panels' =>array (
            'DEFAULT' =>
                array (
                    array(
                        array('name' => 'name', 'displayParams' => array( 'required' =>↵
true, 'size' => 20 )
                        ),
                    ),
                    array (
                        array('name' => 'description', 'displayParams' => array('rows' =>↵
3, 'cols' => 20)),
                    ),
                    array (
                        array('name' => 'assigned_user_name', 'displayParams' =>↵
array('required' => true, 'size' => 11, 'selectOnly' => true)),
                    ),
                ),
            )
    );
?>
```

You'll also add a menu file named Menu.php which is located in the root of the module directory (modules/Parts/) that will have a list of links to the various views you want the user to have direct access to. Listing 10-12 shows an example of what you would add here.

Listing 10-12. Menu.php File for the Parts Module

```php
<?php

global $mod_strings, $app_strings, $sugar_config;

if(ACLController::checkAccess('Parts', 'edit', true))$module_menu[]=Array↵
("index.php?module=Parts&action=EditView&return_module=Parts&return_action=index",↵
 $mod_strings['LNK_NEW_PART'],"CreateParts", 'Parts');
if(ACLController::checkAccess('Parts', 'list', true))$module_menu[]=Array↵
("index.php?module=Parts&action=index&return_module=Parts&return_action=DetailView",↵
 $mod_strings['LNK_PART_LIST'],"Parts", 'Parts');
if(ACLController::checkAccess('Parts', 'import', true))$module_menu[]=Array↵
("index.php?module=Import&action=Step1&import_module=Parts&return_module=↵
Parts&return_action=index", $app_strings['LBL_IMPORT'],"Import", 'Parts');
```

The above Menu.php file you've built will provide links to create a new part, the Parts ListView, and to import new records into the Parts module. You've added ACLController::checkAccess() call to make the current user have access to the option list—if he doesn't then the menu option will not be listed.

You now have all the metadata driven views done, so let's define the language strings you will be using in your module.

Add Language Files

The language strings are a very useful part of Sugar, since it allows you to very easily internationalize your module (referred often as i18n). It does this by having language string definitions files for each of the languages you are supporting in your instance, named like *language*.lang.php in the languages/ directory of your module, which automatically gets loaded based upon the current language selected for the user. If there are not language strings available in your module for their current language, then it will fall back to using the en_us language strings for your module, so it's important to always have these defined above any other language strings.

Let's go ahead and see the language strings for your Parts module, as shown in Listing 10-13.

Listing 10-13. en_us.lang.php File for the Parts Module

```php
<?php

$mod_strings = array (
  'LBL_TEAM' => 'Team',
  'LBL_TEAMS' => 'Teams',
  'LBL_TEAM_ID' => 'Team Id',
  'LBL_ASSIGNED_TO_ID' => 'Assigned User Id',
  'LBL_ASSIGNED_TO_NAME' => 'Assigned to',
  'LBL_ID' => 'ID',
  'LBL_DATE_ENTERED' => 'Date Created',
  'LBL_DATE_MODIFIED' => 'Date Modified',
  'LBL_MODIFIED' => 'Modified By',
  'LBL_MODIFIED_ID' => 'Modified By Id',
  'LBL_MODIFIED_NAME' => 'Modified By Name',
  'LBL_CREATED' => 'Created By',
  'LBL_CREATED_ID' => 'Created By Id',
  'LBL_DESCRIPTION' => 'Description',
  'LBL_DELETED' => 'Deleted',
  'LBL_NAME' => 'Part Name',
  'LBL_CREATED_USER' => 'Created by User',
  'LBL_MODIFIED_USER' => 'Modified by User',
  'LBL_LIST_FORM_TITLE' => 'Parts List',
  'LBL_MODULE_NAME' => 'Parts',
  'LBL_MODULE_TITLE' => 'Parts',
```

```
        'LBL_HOMEPAGE_TITLE' => 'My Parts',
        'LNK_NEW_RECORD' => 'Create Parts',
        'LNK_LIST' => 'Parts',
        'LBL_SEARCH_FORM_TITLE' => 'Search Parts',
        'LBL_HISTORY_SUBPANEL_TITLE' => 'View History',
        'LBL_ACTIVITIES_SUBPANEL_TITLE' => 'Activities',
        'LBL_TEST_PARTS_SUBPANEL_TITLE' => 'Parts',
        'LBL_NEW_FORM_TITLE' => 'New Parts',
        'LBL_PART_REFERENCE_NUMBER' => 'Part Reference Number',
        'LBL_PART_LOCATION' => 'Part Location',
        'LBL_VIEWPARTIMAGE' => 'View Part Image',
        'LBL_VIEWPARTIMAGE_TITLE' => 'View Part Image [Alt+P]',
        'LBL_VIEWPARTIMAGE_BUTTON_KEY' => 'P',
);
?>
```

You'll also remember that you have an enum field, parts location, defined in your module. The enum field will use an array to specify the options you have for the value of this field, and it draws it from the $app_list_strings language string array. To define these options, you'll add a key to the app_list_strings named 'parts_part_location_dom' with the array options for the enum field specified, as shown in Listing 10-14.

Listing 10-14. *custom/Extension/application/Ext/Language/en_us.partsdom.php File that Contains Additions to the include/languages/en_us.lang.php File*

```
<?php


$app_list_strings['parts_part_location_dom']= array(
    'Warehouse' => 'Warehouse',
    'Stockroom' => 'Stockroom',
    'Supplier' => 'With A Supplier - Must Order',
    'Unavailable' => 'Unavailable',
    );


?>
```

Create a Dashlet

One more thing you'll want to do for your Parts module is to create a configurable ListView that users can drop on their homepage or Dashboard. This is a really easy task, as you recall from Chapter 5, where for this kind of Dashlet you just need to define a few files and it will be available for all users to use.

The first thing you'll create is the Dashlet definition file, which is named PartsDashlet.meta.php and storied in the module's Dashlets/PartsDashlet/ directory, as shown in Listing 10-15.

Listing 10-15. PartsDashlet.meta.php File

```php
<?php

$dashletMeta['PartsDashlet'] = array(
    'module' => 'Parts',
    'title' => translate('LBL_HOMEPAGE_TITLE', 'Parts'),
    'description' => 'A customizable view into the Parts module',
    'icon'       => SugarThemeRegistry::current()->getImageURL('icon_Parts_32.gif'),
    'category'   => 'Module Views'
    );
?>
```

You then need to define the search fields and ListView components of the dashlet.
You'll recall that Dashlets don't have the typical search and customization forms that
the ListViews inside the modules have, but rather do this from a configuration popup
screen instead. The metadata files, however, are built the same, but you'll combine
them within one file instead of two separate ones, and store them in your module's
metadata directory inside the partsdashletviewdef.php file (see Listing 10-16).

Listing 10-16. partsdashletviewdef.php File

```php
<?php

global $current_user;

$dashletData['PartsDashlet']['searchFields'] = array(
    'date_entered'      => array(
        'default' => '',
        ),
    'date_modified'     => array(
        'default' => '',
        ),
    'assigned_user_id' => array(
        'type'    => 'assigned_user_name',
        'default' => $current_user->name,
    ),
);
$dashletData['PartsDashlet']['columns'] =  array(
    'name' => array(
        'width'   => '40',
        'label'   => 'LBL_LIST_NAME',
        'link'    => true,
        'default' => true
        ),
    'date_entered' => array(
        'width'   => '15',
        'label'   => 'LBL_DATE_ENTERED',
        'default' => true
```

```
    ),
    'date_modified' => array(
        'width'    => '15',
        'label'    => 'LBL_DATE_MODIFIED'
    ),
    'created_by' => array(
        'width'    => '8',
        'label'    => 'LBL_CREATED'
    ),
    'assigned_user_name' => array(
        'width'    => '8',
        'label'    => 'LBL_LIST_ASSIGNED_USER'
    ),
);


?>
```

Finally, you'll define the PartsDashlet class, which extends from the DashletGeneric class and controls all of the actions of the dashlet. You need to override one method, the constructor, which is only needed to point the DashletGeneric object to look in the right places for the various metadata definitions of your dashlet, as shown in Listing 10-17, and also stored in the module's Dashlets/PartsDashlet/ directory.

Listing 10-17. *PartsDashlet.php Class File*

```php
<?php


require_once('include/Dashlets/DashletGeneric.php');
require_once('modules/Parts/Part.php');


class PartsDashlet extends DashletGeneric
{
    public function PartsDashlet(
        $id,
        $def = null)
    {
        global $current_user, $app_strings;
        require('modules/Parts/metadata/partsdashletviewdef.php');


        parent::DashletGeneric($id, $def);


        if(empty($def['title'])) $this->title = translate('LBL_HOMEPAGE_TITLE', 'test_parts');


        $this->searchFields = $dashletData['PartsDashlet']['searchFields'];
        $this->columns = $dashletData['PartsDashlet']['columns'];
```

```
        $this->seedBean = new Part();
    }
}
?>
```

You may need to clear your dashlets.php cache file, stored in the cache/dashlets/ directory, for your newly created Parts dashlet to be available to users. The cache file is used to avoid the constant lookup of the available Dashlets by the application.

Let's now move forward and create the custom view need for your module Parts module.

Add Any Additional Views Needed

The biggest area where Sugar module developers need to add custom PHP code is custom views. They are needed when your module does more than just implement a simple CRUD-like interface to the data and perhaps a custom button is needed to allow data to transfer from one module to another (an example of this is the Convert Lead view in the Leads module), or maybe a different representation of the data is required (such as with the gantt chart and grid views in the Projects module). One common need for those building custom modules for their own Sugar instance is to interface into an external system.

For your Parts module, this is exactly the need you have, as you'll grab images of your parts from an external system that provides them via REST calls. You'll recall that earlier in this chapter you added a method to your Part bean class named fetchImageURL() that gets the URL, and a button on your DetailView to invoke a view which displays the image in a popup window. In Listing 10-18, you'll add the actual view to your module that is called which will display the part image to the user. You'll save the contents in the modules/Parts/views/view.image.php file.

Listing 10-18. Image View for the Parts Module

```php
<?php

require_once('include/MVC/View/SugarView.php');

class PartsViewImage extends SugarView
{
    /**
     * Constructor
     */
    public function __construct()
    {
        parent::SugarView();
    }
```

215

```php
/**
 * display the form
 */
public function display()
{
    if ( !isset($_REQUEST['record']) )
        return;

    $partBean = new Part();
    $partBean->retrieve($_REQUEST['record']);

    ' echo '<img src="' . $partBean->fetchImageURL() . '" />';
}
}
?>
```

You simply just fetch the record with the given record ID (passed in the record request variable), and then echo the HTML image element to the end user with the 'src' attribute specified with the URL returned from the Part::fetchImageURL() method.

Remember that you need to register your view as well. In Chapter 2, you covered two different ways to do this, either through a controller.php file with a method that invokes it, or by adding an action_view_map.php with the view specified. Since there isn't any additional controller code needed for your module, you'll go the easy route and just add an action_view_map.php file, as shown in Listing 10-19 in the modules/Parts/ directory.

Listing 10-19. action_view_map.php File

```php
<?php


$action_view_map['image'] = 'image';


?>
```

After running Repair Extensions in the admin panel under the Repair option, users can begin using the newly built module. With that, you have a fully built module. You should now see it listed in the module list in the header section of the application.

Summary

In this chapter, you took the long and winding road of learning how to build a module piece by piece. You first looked into why anyone would actually choose to do something like this, illustrating the common use cases for custom module development. You also mentioned that a middle ground exists as well, where you could use Module Builder to build all the tedious items, such as metadata and vardefs, but take the package that it built and customize it by hand to meet your needs. Next you went step-by-step through all of the components of the module and learned how to create them, using a sample module named Parts as the model for the code examples shown along the way. In fact, you can find all the code samples for this book in the Source Code/Download area of the Apress web site at `http://www.apress.com`.

Now you have all the background on SugarCRM to move forward with building your own application on top of it. We'll go through the process of doing so using all of the knowledge you've learned so far.

CHAPTER 11

■■■

Designing a Complete Application

Congratulations! You've made it through all of the nitty, gritty details of the internals of SugarCRM, learning how it all goes together. You saw MVC, metadata, and Web Services frameworks. You learned about user and team management, Dashlets, and themes. You worked with the rich developer tools of Studio, Workflows, and Module Builder. You even looked at doing code level modifications to make Sugar look and act just like you want. With all this knowledge, you can now put all of it to practical use.

One thing the engineering and product management teams at SugarCRM realize is that CRM is never a "one-size-fits-all" solution. For that matter, there is no exact definition of what a CRM application should have and shouldn't have. Each vertical business market has different requirements and use cases they need covered. For example, a CRM application that would be designed for a doctor's office is very different than one designed for a call center. Yet both applications seek to accomplish the same overall goals of being a tool to manage your customer relationships and business activities and fit well inside the CRM definition. SugarCRM has customers and partners all over the world that are pushing the CRM definition in this way, designing CRM applications that fit in perfectly with their business or market needs.

The ability to build entirely new applications on top of SugarCRM is what really sets it apart from the pack. Businesses used to have to write their own custom applications to do just this kind of thing, but that proposition was a very costly and time consuming one, and often brought very mixed results. I used to do just this kind of development in a past company, and looking back I could have turned out applications much faster with a strong CRM tool, such as SugarCRM, available for me to build applications on top of. I know I wasn't alone. I bet every person that reads this book has done this sort of development and relates to all the tedious and time consuming steps you must go through to get an application up and going. As you have seen, SugarCRM removes those steps due to the ease of building new modules on top of Sugar and modifying the existing ones to meet your needs. In this final chapter, that's just what you'll do—build a business application on top of SugarCRM in a fully upgrade-safe way. You'll skim over the details you learned about in previous chapters for brevity, concentrating on the design of the application itself and the value of using SugarCRM to do this.

Background of the Application

The application you build will be for the mythical company Easter Pools, which is in desperate need of an application to help manage their growing pool and spa sales and service business. One of the biggest issues they have involves customer management, trying to answer questions such as what products their customers own or when they have last serviced them. Right now, much of this knowledge is stuck in the minds of those who most often work with them, but it becomes a problem when an infrequent customer slips everyone's mind. Having a complete snapshot of a customer at their fingertips is definitely one thing that could help them service their customers more effectively. It's important as well to distinguish between their corporate accounts and their retail customers, since each group will get treated differently.

It would also be helpful for them to be able to manage their service business more effectively. Right now, they use job sheets and a big corkboard to organize everyone's day, along with all the jobs that need to be done. The problem here is it requires a lot of manual attention. Every day the service managers sit down and organize all the crew's jobs, which require specific knowledge of the jobs (like how long they take, where they are located, etc). It also requires attention to priority. For example, a pool at a major customer being down requires the highest priority while someone needing a hot tub opened may be of a lesser priority. To top it off, it would be nice to be able to have estimated and actual times needed to complete a job so they can better optimize their service scheduling to help them through the busy seasons of spring and fall without having to push their crews into working long hours.

Just like many businesses, Easter Pools has many different vendors it deals with for products, parts, and other supplies. They would find it helpful to be able to be more in tune to what their vendors provide them and which parts work with certain products. For example, it would be nice to be able to see what replacement parts are available for a hot tub. It would also be helpful to be able to associate parts with a service call, so that it is easier to know what needs pulled to send out on the service trucks, as well as provide accountability for parts used in the field. If certain supplies are almost depleted, those in charge of ordering would like to be notified of this so they can reorder them.

With all of this in mind, you can begin to design an application based upon SugarCRM that will fit their needs, and provide the ease of use and intelligence that will help them manage their business as it grows. Let's begin to design this application piece by piece, and with it see how easy it is to use SugarCRM for building such an application.

Breakdown of the Various Components

We'll use the Module Builder tool to design the base of your application. Therefore, the modules will all be normal CRUD-style modules based upon existing SugarObject templates that provide the generic functionality you need. Table 11-1 gives a breakdown of the modules you will build.

Table 11-1. Modules Built for the Easter Pools Application

Module	Description
Customers	This module will be based upon the Person template and contain all of the Retail Customers they work with.
Jobs	Based upon the Issue Template, you'll use this module to track all of the service calls Easter Pools does.
Vendors	Contains all of the vendors they work with, and is based upon the Company Template.
Vendor Contacts	Contacts at the various vendors they work with, based upon the Person template.
Vendor Orders	Tracks orders for various supplies you have made, based upon the Sale template.
Supplies	A basic module with information about the products sold, parts used with those products, and other supplies Easter Pools stocks and sells.

From the out-of-the-box Sugar Community Edition install, you'll be using the Accounts and Contacts module for managing their corporate customers and the Documents module for easy access to any product documentation for all employees. You'll also be integrating in with the Activities modules (Calls, Meetings, Tasks, Notes, Emails) with your Customers and Vendors modules, so they have a way to track all of the communications Easter Pools has with them.

With an outline of what components you'll be using in your Easter Pools application, let's now move through creating each of these components using SugarCRM and see what customizations you need to build this.

Studio

Since you are going to be using several out-of-the-box modules with your application, any needed customizations must be done through Studio in order for your changes to be upgrade-safe. For the most part, you won't need to do much customization here.

You'll reuse the Accounts and Contacts module from the main application, since they very well define the B2B (Business-to-Business) sales management data structures that will work with Easter Pools' corporate customers. As for the data structures of these modules, they will largely remain unchanged, save for a few additions to the field lists and changes to the relationships that come out of the box with Sugar CE. Let's look at what you'll be doing for them.

Accounts and Contacts

The first thing you'll be doing is adding fields to the Accounts module that will be read-only and report customer billing information, such as total outstanding invoice balance, date of last invoice, and the date of the last payment received, as well as a popup window that can give a more detailed breakdown of invoicing history. You won't have any data entry inside of Sugar itself for this, but instead use Easter Pools existing accounting system and some custom scripts to push this data to Sugar. You'll look more into how this would work later on when you talk about the external interfaces to your product.

You'll also add a few more fields for the ease of Easter Pools. One issue they had was planning service calls, in particular planning time estimates for travel time to their service crews, as well as giving them a way to find their way there. A quick and simple way to do this is to embed a map right into the DetailView for a customer. You can do that by adding an iFrame field to the Accounts module, and specifying the default URL as a template which the DetailView handler will fill in automatically. The URL to use is `http://maps.google.com/maps?f=q&q={shipping_address_street}+{shipping_address_city}+{shipping_address_state}+{shipping_address_postalcode}+{shipping_address_country}&source=embed&output=embed`. You can see the results in Figure 11-1.

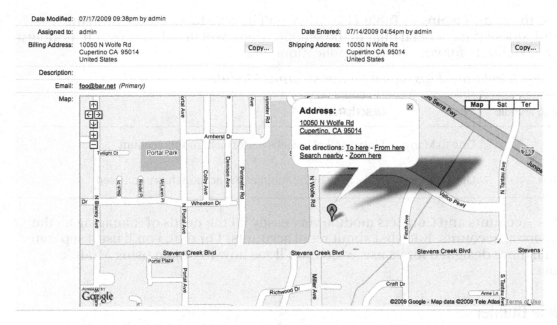

Figure 11-1. Embedded Google Map on the Accounts DetailView

You'll need to also adjust the size of the iFrame field on the DetailView template so it displays fully—anything over 200 as the max size should work nicely. Also, make sure there isn't another field in the adjacent column in the view, so the map can stretch to take up both columns.

Tables 11-2 and 11-3 provide a summary of the fields and relationships you will be adding to the Accounts module. You won't need to add any to the Contacts module.

Table 11-2. Fields Added for the Accounts Module

Fields	Description
invoice_balance_c	Currency: Stores the current outstanding invoice balance (read-only)
last_invoice_date_c	Date: Date of last invoice (read-only)
last_payment_date_c	Date: Date of last payment made (read-only)
map	iFrame: Use for embedded Google Map

For the relationships in Table 11-3, you won't be able to add them until the custom modules have been built in the section where you detail the custom modules you'll be building for your custom application.

Table 11-3. Relationships Added for the Accounts Module

Relate to Module	Type	Description
Jobs	One to Many	Links to all of the jobs performed for this account
Supplies	One to Many	Links to all of the supplies the account has purchased

The Accounts and Contacts module very easily fill the needs of managing all the commercial accounts. But what about retail accounts? For that, you'll use a separate module more designed for its use, which you'll see how to design using Module Builder.

Module Builder

You'll now look at building the new modules needed for your application. To make it simple, you'll use Module Builder to get it up and going first then add the custom code later. You'll name your package in Module Builder EasterPools, with module prefix ep (so the various modules you create will have the ep_ prefix on them).You'll begin by looking at the Customers module.

Customers

B2C (Business-to-Consumer) transactions are not really dealt with from a design standpoint in SugarCRM. The big reason for this is purely because the historical CRM market is more B2B than B2C, and CRM in the B2C landscape is an evolving market. However, with the flexibility of Sugar and the strong yet easy-to-use developer tools that come with it, you can easily build an application supporting these kinds of interactions.

You'll base your module upon the Person template, which will provide us with all the fields needed to match an individual very well. For consistency, you'll also make the same kinds of customizations you made to the Accounts module as well to the Customers module.

Tables 11-4 and 11-5 outline the fields needed and the relationships you'll add, respectively.

Table 11-4. Fields Added for the Customers Module

Fields	Description
invoice_balance_c	Currency: Stores the current outstanding invoice balance (read-only)
last_invoice_date_c	Date: Date of last invoice (read-only)
last_payment_date_c	Date: Date of last payment made (read-only)
Map	iFrame: Use for embedded Google Map

Table 11-5. Relationships Added for the Customers Module

Relate to Module	Type	Description
Jobs	One to Many	Links to all of the jobs performed for this customer
Supplies	One to Many	Links to all of the supplies the customer has purchased
Activities	One to Many	Links to all of the activities for this Customer (Calls, Meetings, Tasks, Notes, Emails)

From an end user's standpoint, B2C customer is largely the same as a B2B customer as it relates to the rest of the application. They both have the same relationships to the other modules and many of the same fields in common (minus those specific to being a company or a person). The biggest reason for the separation of modules, other than the field differences between them, is that Easter Pools can manage their corporate clients and retail customers separately. Each group is different in the way you manage them. Corporate customers tend to be more full service than the retail ones, and require a lot more attention and priority when they have service requests. Retail customers often are more apt to do certain things on their own, like many simple maintenance tasks and noninvasive repairs (of course, this isn't true for everyone). They also tend to be lower in the priority scale, simply because the corporate customers have contracts with Easter Pools that dictate service-level guarantees, something that very few retail customers have. Because of this, the corporate customers are higher revenue than the retail ones so doing apples-to-apples comparisons between them isn't very fair.

Having this separation enables them to manage the business better. It does pose a few problems when you are doing the relationships between these modules and the Products and Jobs ones. You'll see your solutions to these issues as you go on in this chapter when you look at adding custom code for the Jobs and Products modules.

Jobs

A big part of the original assessment of requirements for such an application was the ability to manage the service aspect of the Easter Pools business. You noted a lot of coordination and management is done in this area, and having the tools to help stay on top of this would be very helpful to the business as a whole.

The basis of your Jobs module will be the Issue template, which provides just about all of the fields you will need to help manage your module. You'll make a few modifications to the fields as they come defined so the module better fits what they would like to do. First, you'll modify the Status field to have more service-related dropdown values, namely New, Scheduled, Dispatched, Canceled, and Completed. You'll also adjust the Resolution field to give it the same values as the Status field to better match a service call rather than a software bug, as the Issues template is designed to handle. This can be handled by modifying the ep_jobs_status_dom and ep_jobs_resolution_dom arrays that will be added in the custom/Extension/application/Ext/Language/en_us.test.php file by SugarCRM after the module is deployed. You'll also add a Flex Relate field with a custom defined list of modules to relate the job to only include the Accounts and Customers module. For this one thing, you'll need to add some PHP code in order to do as Module Builder and Studio do, but not all the customizations you need here are out of the box (you'll see how to do this in the "Custom Code" section of this chapter). Table 11-6 outlines what you'll need to add through Module Builder for this module.

Table 11-6. Fields Added for the Jobs Module

Fields	Description
Flex Relate (internally consists of parent_name, parent_id, and parent_type)	Used for relating a job to either an account or a customer
time_required_c	Decimal: Amount of time needed to complete the job

Supplies

Easter Pools' main business involves the products, parts, and other supplies they sell to their customers. These come in a multitude of different forms. For example, they sell full-size spas and pool kits to their customers. With that they sell the chlorine and other chemicals used to treat the water in their pools and spas. Then, if something breaks on their pool or spa, they can get the replacement parts needed to fix it. These are all also very interrelated, with each one of the major products they sell (spas, pool kits, pool heaters, pool filters) having many replacement parts that go with them. Most replacement parts work on multiple different products, so this complicates the correct design of the relationships as well. You'll base this module upon the Basic template, and add a relationship which will enable you to expand upon this goal with custom code later on (see Table 11-7).

Table 11-7. Relationships Added for the Supplies Module

Relate to Module	Type	Description
Jobs	Many to Many	Links to all of the jobs where this supply is used
Supplies	Many to Many	Links to all of the related supplies to this supply

Table 11-8 outlines the lone field you'll add for this module, which will track the vendor's part reference number. This field will come in handy later on in the chapter in the "Custom Code" section when you add a business process for reordering supplies from the vendor.

Table 11-8. Fields Added for the Supplies Module

Fields	Description
vendor_ref_no	Text field: Part reference number for the vendor; will use when reordering.

Vendors, Vendor Contacts, and Vendor Orders

Easter Pools' vendors are also a critical part of its business workflow. A lot of coordination must take place in terms of product management, inventory control, and system updates. Without proper management the entire supply and service chains fall apart, wrecking havoc on all their customers by not having available the parts and supplies they need, or causing them to keep extra inventory on hand that may take months to deplete. When you design the Vendors module, you need to make it more than just a rolodex of who they are, but also must provide enough intelligence to give insight on what they provide to the business.

The base part of this module is the Vendors module, which will be based upon the Company template. You'll also track the contacts Easter Pools has at their vendors' offices, so you'll have a Vendors Contacts module as well, based upon the Person template. You'll also add the Vendor Orders module now (based upon the Sale template), which will track the order you have made to the Vendor for replenishing their inventory. You won't need to add any additional fields for any of these modules since the templates provide everything you need to record all of the vital facts about your vendors, including phone, address, email information, and the orders placed. However, you will need to add relationships here to pull everything together, as shown in Tables 11-9, 11-10 and 11-11.

Table 11-9. Relationships Added for the Vendors Module

Relate to Module	Type	Description
Vendor Contacts	One to Many	Links to all of the contacts for this vendor
Vendor Orders	One to Many	Links to all of the orders made to this vendor
Supplies	One to Many	Links to all of the Supplies this vendor provides
Activities	One to Many	Links to all of the activities for this Vendor (Calls, Meetings, Tasks, Notes, Emails)

Table 11-10. Relationships added for the Vendor Contacts Module

Relate to module	Type	Description
Activities	One to Many	Links to all of the activities for this Vendor (Calls, Meetings, Tasks, Notes, Emails)

Table 11-11. Relationships added for the Vendor Orders module

Relate to module	Type	Description
Supplies	Many to Many	Links to all of the supplies ordered with this given vendor order

Custom Code

The last piece of the puzzle for your Sugar application is to add some custom code to make things act just the way you want them to. These are things that are currently out of the scope of what the Studio and Module Builder tools provide, but nonetheless show the flexibility of the platform since all of these modifications are upgrade safe.

This means that when you upgrade your Sugar version or apply maintenance patches, your customizations will not be overridden.

Let's begin by looking at the modifications you'll make to two of the out-of-the-box modules you are working with: Accounts and Contacts.

Accounts and Contacts

You'll need to update the subpanels listing, where you'll hide the subpanels for the Opportunities, Cases, Bug Tracker, Projects, Campaigns, and Leads modules in the Accounts and Contacts modules. None of these modules will be in use by your application, so it makes most sense to remove them. There are two ways to do this. One way is by using the ACL management features you learned about in Chapter 5 to disable access to these modules. Another option is to modify the layout definitions for the modules, so you could drop an updated layout defs file inside the custom/Extension/modules/*modulename*/Ext/Layoutdefs/ directory such as the RemoveExtraSubpanels.php showing in Listing 11-1.

Listing 11-1. RemoveExtraSubpanels.php for Removing Unneeded Subpanels for the Contacts Module

```php
<?php

$layout_defs['Contacts']['subpanel_setup']['opportunities'] = null;
$layout_defs['Contacts']['subpanel_setup']['leads'] = null;
$layout_defs['Contacts']['subpanel_setup']['cases'] = null;
$layout_defs['Contacts']['subpanel_setup']['bugs'] = null;
$layout_defs['Contacts']['subpanel_setup']['project'] = null;
$layout_defs['Contacts']['subpanel_setup']['campaigns'] = null;


?>
```

The example shows how this is done for the Contacts module. For the Accounts module, simply substitute Contacts for Accounts in Listing 11-1.

You'll also be adding some new subpanels to the module, namely ones for Jobs, which will show listings of all completed and upcoming service events for an account and the Products the customer has purchased.

Jobs

For each of the Accounts and Customers module, you'll need to add a relationship to the vardefs to enable the Jobs subpanel to appear correctly in that module, as shown in Listing 11-2.

Listing 11-2. *Accounts Jobs Relationship*

```php
<?php


$dictionary["Accounts"]["fields"]["accounts_ep_jobs"] = array (
  'name' => 'accounts_ep_jobs',
  'type' => 'link',
  'relationship' => 'accounts_ep_jobs',
  'source' => 'non-db',
);


$dictionary["Accounts"]["relationships"]['accounts_ep_jobs'] = array (
  'lhs_module'=> 'Accounts',
  'lhs_table'=> 'accounts',
  'lhs_key' => 'id',
  'rhs_module'=> 'ep_Jobs',
  'rhs_table'=> 'ep_jobs',
  'rhs_key' => 'parent_id',
  'relationship_type'=>'one-to-many',
  'relationship_role_column'=>'parent_type',
  'relationship_role_column_value'=>'Accounts',
);
```

You'll need a similar relationship in the Customers module as well. Listing 11-3 shows how this would work.

Listing 11-3. *Customers Jobs Relationship*

```php
<?php


$dictionary["ep_Customers"]["fields"]["ep_customers_ep_jobs"] = array (
  'name' => 'ep_customers_ep_jobs',
  'type' => 'link',
  'relationship' => 'ep_customers_ep_jobs',
  'source' => 'non-db',
);


$dictionary["ep_Customers"]["relationships"]['ep_customers_ep_jobs'] = array (
  'lhs_module'=> 'ep_Customers',
  'lhs_table'=> 'ep_customers',
  'lhs_key' => 'id',
  'rhs_module'=> 'ep_Jobs',
  'rhs_table'=> 'ep_jobs',
  'rhs_key' => 'parent_id',
  'relationship_type'=>'one-to-many',
  'relationship_role_column'=>'parent_type',
  'relationship_role_column_value'=>'ep_Customers',
);
```

You'll also add a relationship to the Products module here, to indicate any parts or supplies needed for this job. This helps fulfill the requirement of letting the crews know what they need to take on the service trucks with them out to the service call. Another requirement mentioned earlier was a way to help manage part and supply inventory more easily. You can use the Jobs modules relationship to help with this. An easy way to do so would be to add a logic hook that fires on the save event. Listing 11-4 has an example of one, which should be saved in the custom/modules/ep_Jobs/ directory and named ep_JobsHooks.php.

Listing 11-4. after_save Logic Hook for the Jobs Module

```
require_once('modules/ep_Jobs/ep_Jobs.php');
require_once('modules/Accounts/Account.php');


class ep_JobsHooks
{
    public function updateProductInventory(
        SugarBean $bean,
        $event,
        $arguments
        )
    {
        if ( $bean->fetched_row['status'] != 'Dispatched' && $bean->status ==↵
'Dispatched' ) {
            $bean->load_relationship('ep_jobs_ep_supplies'); // load the relationship↵
between Jobs and Supplies

            foreach ( $bean->build_related_list($bean->ep_jobs_ep_supplies->getQuery(),↵
new LeadContact) as $ep_part) {

                $ep_part->on_hand = $ep_part->on_hand - 1;
                $ep_part->save();
            }
        }

    }
}
```

What this logic hook will do is check to see if the job's status has been set to Dispatched, which would be done after the truck has loaded up and left. At this point, the inventory is gone, so you can decrement each of the product's available count accordingly. If for some reason, a part isn't needed, then it can be checked back in and the supply inventory can then be updated.

You'll also add a handy button to the DetailView of the Jobs module. This button will be used to print off a map to get to the job site. You'll use the related information from the Account or Customer to build a Google Maps URL which will create the route from where the business is located to the address as it's listed in the customer's record. Building the URL is something you'll do by overriding the DetailView for the

Jobs module, as shown in Listing 11-5. (The file should be saved as custom/modules/ep_Jobs/views/view.detail.php.)

Listing 11-5. DetailView Override for the Jobs Module

```php
<?php

require_once('include/MVC/View/views/view.detail.php');
require_once('modules/Accounts/Account.php');
require_once('modules/ep_Jobs/ep_Jobs.php');


class ep_JobsViewDetail extends ViewDetail {

  public function __construct()
    {
    parent::ViewDetail();
    }

  public function display()
    {
        $business_address = '123 Main Street Anytown, OH 44444';
        $customer_address = '';

        if ( !empty($this->ep_custome5229stomers_ida) ) {
            $bean = new Account();
            $bean->retrieve($this->ep_custome5229stomers_ida);
            if ( !empty($bean->id) )
                $customer_address = "{$bean->shipping_address_address}↵
{$bean->shipping_address_city}, {$bean->shipping_address_state}↵
{$bean->shipping_address_postalcode}";
        }
        elseif ( !empty($this->ep_jobs_ac056eccounts_ida) ) {
            $bean = new ep_Jobs();
            $bean->retrieve($this->ep_custome5229stomers_ida);
            if ( !empty($bean->id) )
                $customer_address = "{$bean->primary_address_address}↵
{$bean->primary_address_city}, {$bean->primary_address_state}↵
{$bean->primary_address_postalcode}";
        }

        $this->ss->assign("MAP_URL","http://maps.google.com/maps?f=d&source=s_d&saddr=↵
{$business_address}&daddr={$customer_address}");

  parent::display();
    }
}
?>
```

You'll then add the button to trigger this action on the DetailView by making a small modification to the metadata template, as shown in Listing 11-6 (save the contents to the custom/modules/ep_Jobs/metadata/detailviewdefs.php).

Listing 11-6. Adding the Get Map to Job Button to the DetailView Metadata

```php
<?php
require('modules/ep_Jobs/metadata/detailviewdefs.php'); // include in the existing view defs
$viewdefs['ep_Jobs']['DetailView']['templateMeta']['form']['buttons'][] = array(
    'customCode' => '<input title="{$MOD.LBL_GET_MAP_TO_JOB}" ' .
        ' accesskey="{$APP.LBL_GET_MAP_TO_JOB_KEY}" ' .
        ' class="button" ' .
        ' onclick=\'document.location.href = "{$MAP_URL}"; return false;\' ' .
        ' name="button" ' .
        ' value="{$APP.LBL_GET_MAP_TO_JOB_TITLE}" ' .
        ' type="submit">'
    );
?>
```

Supplies

The design of the Supplies module will have multiple facets to it. First off, you'll allow each Supply to have a many-to-many relationship with other Supplies, which allows any supply to be related to a number of different supplies. Then you'll need to categorize each item in the Supplies module to be one of a product (meaning it is a fully fledged product they sell, such as a spa or pool kit), a part that goes to one of the products they sell or service, or a supply item, such as pool chemicals, that go along with one of the products they sell or support. With these two items in place, you can begin to build the web of how products, parts, and supplies are all related to each other.

The only issue with having the relationships setup like this is that it intermixes the products, parts, and supplies together in the Supplies subpanel in each record's DetailView, making it difficult to tell the difference between each type. If you remember from Chapter 3, you noted that each subpanel metadata definition can specify additional WHERE clause arguments to further drill down to show the records you want in the subpanel. You can use this feature to enhance the subpanel view. First, you'll create three different subpanel views, one for each of the products, parts, and supplies, as shown in Listing 11-7.

Listing 11-7. *Subpanel Metadata Files for the Products Only, Parts Only, and Supplies Only Subpanels*

relatedParts.php
<?php


```php
$module_name='ep_Supplies';
$subpanel_layout = array(
'top_buttons' => array(
array('widget_class' => 'SubPanelTopCreateButton'),
array('widget_class' => 'SubPanelTopSelectButton', 'popup_module' => $module_name),
),


'where' => 'item_type = "Part"',


'list_fields' => array(
'name'=>array(
'vname' => 'LBL_NAME',
'widget_class' => 'SubPanelDetailViewLink',
'width' => '45%',
),
'date_modified'=>array(
'vname' => 'LBL_DATE_MODIFIED',
'width' => '45%',
),
'edit_button'=>array(
'widget_class' => 'SubPanelEditButton',
'module' => $module_name,
'width' => '4%',
),
'remove_button'=>array(
'widget_class' => 'SubPanelRemoveButton',
'module' => $module_name,
'width' => '5%',
),
),
);


?>
```


relatedProducts.php
<?php


```php
$module_name='ep_Supplies';
$subpanel_layout = array(
'top_buttons' => array(
```

```php
        array('widget_class' => 'SubPanelTopCreateButton'),
        array('widget_class' => 'SubPanelTopSelectButton', 'popup_module' => $module_name),
),


'where' => 'item_type = "Product"',


'list_fields' => array(
'name'=>array(
'vname' => 'LBL_NAME',
'widget_class' => 'SubPanelDetailViewLink',
'width' => '45%',
),
'date_modified'=>array(
'vname' => 'LBL_DATE_MODIFIED',
'width' => '45%',
),
'edit_button'=>array(
'widget_class' => 'SubPanelEditButton',
'module' => $module_name,
'width' => '4%',
),
'remove_button'=>array(
'widget_class' => 'SubPanelRemoveButton',
'module' => $module_name,
'width' => '5%',
),
),
);


?>


relatedSupplies.php
<?php


$module_name='ep_Supplies';
$subpanel_layout = array(
'top_buttons' => array(
array('widget_class' => 'SubPanelTopCreateButton'),
array('widget_class' => 'SubPanelTopSelectButton', 'popup_module' => $module_name),
),


'where' => 'item_type = "Supply"',


'list_fields' => array(
'name'=>array(
'vname' => 'LBL_NAME',
```

```
'widget_class' => 'SubPanelDetailViewLink',
'width' => '45%',
),
'date_modified'=>array(
'vname' => 'LBL_DATE_MODIFIED',
'width' => '45%',
),
'edit_button'=>array(
'widget_class' => 'SubPanelEditButton',
'module' => $module_name,
'width' => '4%',
),
'remove_button'=>array(
'widget_class' => 'SubPanelRemoveButton',
'module' => $module_name,
'width' => '5%',
),
),
);


?>
```

With each of the subpanel metadata views defined, the next step is to set up the subpanel definitions for the Supplies module. You'll reference each of the above subpanel metadata files you created in Listing 11-7, adding different titles to each of them so the user can differentiate on what the contents of them are. Listing 11-8 shows how this is done (save the file as custom/Extension/modules/ep_Supplies/Ext/Layoutdefs/extrasubpanels.php).

Listing 11-8. Subpanel Definitions for the Supplies Module

```php
<?php
$layout_defs["ep_Supplies"]["subpanel_setup"]["ep_supplies_ep_supplies_1"] = array (
  'order' => 110,
  'module' => 'ep_Supplies',
  'subpanel_name' => 'relatedProducts',
  'sort_order' => 'asc',
  'sort_by' => 'id',
  'title_key' => 'LBL_RELATED_PRODUCTS',
  'get_subpanel_data' => 'ep_supplies_ep_supplies',
  'top_buttons' =>
  array (
    0 =>
    array (
      'widget_class' => 'SubPanelTopCreateButton',
    ),
    1 =>
    array (
      'widget_class' => 'SubPanelTopSelectButton',
      'mode' => 'MultiSelect',
    ),
```

```
  ),
);

$layout_defs["ep_Supplies"]["subpanel_setup"]["ep_supplies_ep_supplies_2"] = array (
  'order' => 120,
  'module' => 'ep_Supplies',
  'subpanel_name' => 'relatedParts',
  'sort_order' => 'asc',
  'sort_by' => 'id',
  'title_key' => 'LBL_RELATED_PARTS',
  'get_subpanel_data' => 'ep_supplies_ep_supplies',
  'top_buttons' =>
  array (
    0 =>
    array (
      'widget_class' => 'SubPanelTopCreateButton',
    ),
    1 =>
    array (
      'widget_class' => 'SubPanelTopSelectButton',
      'mode' => 'MultiSelect',
    ),
  ),
);


$layout_defs["ep_Supplies"]["subpanel_setup"]["ep_supplies_ep_supplies_3"] = array (
  'order' => 130,
  'module' => 'ep_Supplies',
  'subpanel_name' => 'relatedSupplies',
  'sort_order' => 'asc',
  'sort_by' => 'id',
  'title_key' => 'LBL_RELATED_SUPPLIES',
  'get_subpanel_data' => 'ep_supplies_ep_supplies',
  'top_buttons' =>
  array (
    0 =>
    array (
      'widget_class' => 'SubPanelTopCreateButton',
    ),
    1 =>
    array (
      'widget_class' => 'SubPanelTopSelectButton',
      'mode' => 'MultiSelect',
    ),
  ),
);


unset(layout_defs["ep_Supplies"]["subpanel_setup"]["ep_supplies_ep_supplies"]);
?>
```

You'll notice the addition of the unset() call to an existing subpanel. This is because you built this module in Module Builder and added the relationship there as well, so they already define one subpanel for all related Supplies. This means you'll need to disable the one created by your DetailView to avoid confusion for the end user. The easiest way to do this is simply unset() its value in the $layout_defs array.

You also have a relationship from a Supply to an Account or Customer. This relationship lets Easter Pools know what customers have purchased and what products they use. The advantages of having this link are numerous. For example, it can help the service manager to know which replacement parts need to go out to a customer if something breaks or if a supply has a recall. Easter Pools sales manager can easily find out which customers currently have the part and can schedule service calls to do any needed replacement work. To add such a subpanel, you'll need to create a collection subpanel, which is one that gathers data from multiple modules and displays them as one. The important thing here is to specify the modules you'll be pulling together (in this case, just Accounts and Customers) and then make sure you have matching subpanel metadata view for them (which you'll define as ForJobs). Listing 11-9 shows how this all comes together.

Listing 11-9. Subpanel Definitions for a Combined Customers/Accounts Subpanel

```php
<?php


$layout_defs["ep_Items"]["subpanel_setup"]['clients'] => array(
'order' => 100,
'sort_order' => 'desc',
'sort_by' => 'date_start',
'title_key' => 'LBL_ACTIVITIES_SUBPANEL_TITLE',
'type' => 'collection',
'subpanel_name' => 'activities',    //this values is not associated with a physical file.


'header_definition_from_subpanel'=> 'accounts',


'module'=>'Activities',
'collection_list' => array(
'accounts' => array(
'module' => 'Accounts',
'subpanel_name' => 'ForJobs',
'get_subpanel_data' => 'accounts',
),

                'customers' => array(
                    'module' => 'ep_Customers',
                    'subpanel_name' => 'ForJobs',
                    'get_subpanel_data' => 'ep_customers',
                ),
```

```
)
);
?>
```

Vendors

In the Vendors module, you will add some logic to the relationships and subpanels. You'll add a relationship to the existing products module so you know who the supplier is and which items that you sell. What happens when someone needs to reorder an item from the suppliers? For tracking, you'll add a Vendor Orders modules, which will link to both the Products module (so you have a history of what orders they have made in the past for the given product and which provides good insight into how often they are placing orders on a part), as well as the Vendors module to show which orders are made to the Vendor. You'll even split the subpanels into two parts just as you did for the Products subpanels in the previous section, so that you can track outstanding orders and historical orders in separate panels. Listing 11-10 shows how to do this.

Listing 11-10. Subpanel Metadata Files for the Products Only, Parts Only, and Supplies Only Subpanels

```php
currentOrders.php
<?php


$module_name='ep_VendorOrders';
$subpanel_layout = array(
'top_buttons' => array(
array('widget_class' => 'SubPanelTopCreateButton'),
array('widget_class' => 'SubPanelTopSelectButton', 'popup_module' => $module_name),
),


'where' => 'order_status != "Completed"',


'list_fields' => array(
'name'=>array(
'vname' => 'LBL_NAME',
'widget_class' => 'SubPanelDetailViewLink',
'width' => '45%',
),
'date_entered'=>array(
'vname' => 'LBL_DATE_ENTERED',
'width' => '45%',
),
'edit_button'=>array(
```

```php
'widget_class' => 'SubPanelEditButton',
'module' => $module_name,
'width' => '4%',
),
'remove_button'=>array(
'widget_class' => 'SubPanelRemoveButton',
'module' => $module_name,
'width' => '5%',
),
),
);


?>


previousOrders.php
<?php


$module_name='ep_VendorOrders';
$subpanel_layout = array(
'top_buttons' => array(
array('widget_class' => 'SubPanelTopCreateButton'),
array('widget_class' => 'SubPanelTopSelectButton', 'popup_module' => $module_name),
),


'where' => 'order_status = "Completed"',


'list_fields' => array(
'name'=>array(
'vname' => 'LBL_NAME',
'widget_class' => 'SubPanelDetailViewLink',
'width' => '45%',
),
'date_entered'=>array(
'vname' => 'LBL_DATE_ENTERED',
'width' => '45%',
),
'edit_button'=>array(
'widget_class' => 'SubPanelEditButton',
'module' => $module_name,
'width' => '4%',
),
'remove_button'=>array(
'widget_class' => 'SubPanelRemoveButton',
'module' => $module_name,
'width' => '5%',
),
),
);
```

```php
?>

SubPanelDefintions
<?php
$layout_defs["ep_Vendors"]["subpanel_setup"]["ep_vendors_ep_vendororders_1"] = array (
  'order' => 110,
  'module' => 'ep_Vendors',
  'subpanel_name' => 'currentOrders',
  'sort_order' => 'asc',
  'sort_by' => 'id',
  'title_key' => 'LBL_CURRENT_ORDERS',
  'get_subpanel_data' => 'ep_vendors_ep_vendororders',
  'top_buttons' =>
  array (
    0 =>
    array (
      'widget_class' => 'SubPanelTopCreateButton',
    ),
    1 =>
    array (
      'widget_class' => 'SubPanelTopSelectButton',
      'mode' => 'MultiSelect',
    ),
  ),
);


$layout_defs["ep_Vendors"]["subpanel_setup"]["ep_vendors_ep_vendororders_2"] = array (
  'order' => 120,
  'module' => 'ep_Vendors',
  'subpanel_name' => 'previousOrders',
  'sort_order' => 'asc',
  'sort_by' => 'id',
  'title_key' => 'LBL_PREVIOUS_ORDERS',
  'get_subpanel_data' => 'ep_vendors_ep_vendororders',
  'top_buttons' =>
  array (
    0 =>
    array (
      'widget_class' => 'SubPanelTopCreateButton',
    ),
    1 =>
    array (
      'widget_class' => 'SubPanelTopSelectButton',
      'mode' => 'MultiSelect',
    ),
  ),
);
```

You'll also add a way to simplify the reorder process by adding a button to the Supplies DetailView named Reorder that will request an item be reordered. Clicking this button will trigger a reorder action in the Products module that will add the product to Vendor Orders module, assigning it to the reorder user who can then go through and actually do the reordering. Listing 11-11 shows how you can add your action through modifying the controller for the Products module.

Listing 11-11. Reorder Action in the Supplies Controller

```php
<?php


require_once("modules/ep_VendorOrders/ep_VendorOrders.php");


class ep_SuppliesController extends SugarController
{
public function __construct()
    {
parent::SugarController();
}

    public function action_reorder()
    {
        global $current_user;

        if ( empty($this->bean->id) )
            sugar_die("A record number must be specified to reorder");

        $bean = new ep_VendorOrders;

        $bean->name   = $this->bean->name;
        $bean->status = 'Requested';
        $bean->assigned_user_id = $current_user->retrieve_user_id('reorder');
        $bean->save(true);


        $this->bean->load_relationship('ep_supplies_ep_vendororders');
        $this->bean->add($bean->id);

        $this->bean->status = 'On Reorder';
        $this->bean->save();

        SugarApplication::redirect('index.php?module=ep_Supplies&action=DetailView&record=' .
$this->bean->id . '');
    }
}


?>
```

You both add the product to the vendor orders module as well as update the product's status to On Reorder and link the product to the reorder request so that everyone at Easter Pools knows that the product is unavailable, but that it's on reorder and what the reorder status is.

Invoicing Hooks

Easter Pools already has an existing accounting system in-house that SugarCRM won't even attempt to replicate. Most accounting functions are typically considered out of the scope of what a CRM application is used for, so the requirements for Easter Pools' application is for integrating invoicing into their system calls for exporting and importing of data into Sugar, keeping the heavy accounting work safely in the confines of their existing system.

You have two goals to accomplish here in regard to working with accounting. The first is to provide a way to get job information over to the accounting system so the customer can be invoiced. There's a number of solutions here, from writing a custom interface between the two that will actually create the invoice to just giving the account receivable analysts a report daily of jobs ready to be invoiced. Right now Easter Pools still have a lot of human intelligence to deal with in billing a customer, so the best way to handle this is by simply reporting the information to accounting. But you can save a tree and make the process move much faster by having a workflow email go out when the job is marked Ready to Invoice, which would allow possible same day billing of a customer for services rendered. This also gives the analysts the ability to use their email as a workflow for billing. You can even add an option in the email that would trigger the job to be marked as Invoiced to better streamline the process (see Listing 11-12).

Listing 11-12. Invoice View that Will be Used by the Customers and Accounts Modules

```php
<?php


require_once('include/MVC/View/SugarView.php');


class ViewInvoices extends SugarView
{
    public function __construct()
    {
        $this->options['show_title'] = false;
        $this->options['show_header'] = false;
        $this->options['show_footer'] = false;
        $this->options['show_subpanels'] = false;
        $this->options['show_search'] = false;
        parent::SugarView();
    }
```

```
    public function display()
{
        global $mod_strings, $app_strings;

        $this->ss->assign("MODULE_TITLE",
                get_module_title(
                    $mod_strings['LBL_MODULE_NAME'],
                    $mod_strings['LBL_MODULE_NAME'] . ': ' . $app_strings['LBL_INVOICES'],
                    true
                    )
                );

        // Get the invoice data from our accounting system; it uses XML to do so
        $returnXML =
file_get_contents("http://accounting.local/getInvoiceHistory?customer_id={$this->bean->accounting_id}");

        $xml = new SimpleXMLElement($returnXML);

        $invoices = array();
        foreach ( $xml->invoice as $invoice ) {
            $invoices = array(
                'date' => $invoice->date,
                'amount' => $invoice->amount,
                'due' => $invoice->due,
                );
        }

        $this->ss->assign('invoices', $invoices);
        $this->ss->display('custom/include/MVC/tpls/invoices.tpl');

    }
}
```

Now in Listing 11-13, you define the Smarty template used to display this data. It's nothing more than a simple HTML table.

Listing 11-13. invoices.tpl file

```
{$MODULE_TITLE}
{foreach from=$invoice key=key item=item name=rows}
{if $smarty.foreach.rows.first}
<table class="other view">
<tr>
    <th>{$APP.LBL_INVOICE_DATE}</th>
    <th>{$APP.LBL_INVOICE_AMOUNT}</th>
    <th>{$APP.LBL_INVOICE_DUE}</th>
</tr>
{/if}
<tr>
    <td>{$item.date}</td>
    <td>{$item.amount}</td>
    <td>{$item.due}</td>
```

```
</tr>
{if $smarty.foreach.rows.last}
</table>
{/if}
{foreachelse}
{$APP.LBL_NO_RECORDS_FOUND}
{/foreach}
```

Just as you've built a way for looking at the outstanding invoices that a customer has, you'll also need to define a way to get invoices to your Accounting system. You've done the first part of this in the Jobs module by defining a checkbox field Ready to Invoice to indicate to your Accounting system that you are ready to invoice a customer for the service work you've performed for them. I mentioned earlier in this chapter when you looked at the Customers module that the invoicing process for Easter Pools has human logic in it, and they have chosen not to include that in their SugarCRM-based application. However, automating the transfer of information to accounting is definitely a part of this process. You can automate this using logic hooks. First, you'll add a logic hook, so that where the Ready to Invoice checkbox is checked you'll automatically assign the invoice to the invoicing user account (which will need to be created separately). Listing 11-14 shows what this logic hook would like.

Listing 11-14. *Jobs before_save logic Book*

```
require_once('modules/ep_Jobs/ep_Jobs.php');
require_once('modules/Accounts/Account.php');


class ep_JobsHooks
{
    public function assignToInvoicing(
        SugarBean $bean,
        $event,
        $arguments
        )
    {
        global $current_user;


        if ( !$bean->fetched_row['ready_to_invoice'] && $bean-> ready_to_invoice )
            $bean->assigned_user_id = $current_user->retrieve_user_id('invoicing');
    }
}
```

Next you'll turn on notifications inside the email settings. This will automatically send an e-mail notification when a record is assigned to a user, which in this case will notify the invoicing user (you'll set this to be whomever is handling invoicing for Easter Pools) to be notified that a Job is ready for him to invoice.

Final Touches

Now that you've built all of the modules for your application, and configured your outside accounting system to integrate with your newly designed application made just for Easter Pools, let's now clean up a few remaining pieces. The first thing you'll want to do is configure the available modules to users of the Easter Pools SugarCRM application. You can do so in two different ways: the first is to just hide the tabs you are not using from the user interface through the Configure Tabs option. The only problem with this approach is that it only hides the tabs, but doesn't truly disable the modules. Any user could just type the URL to access any module in the system. The only way to truly block access to those modules you are not using is through ACL Roles, so you'll add a new one called Users in the Role Management admin panel to do this.

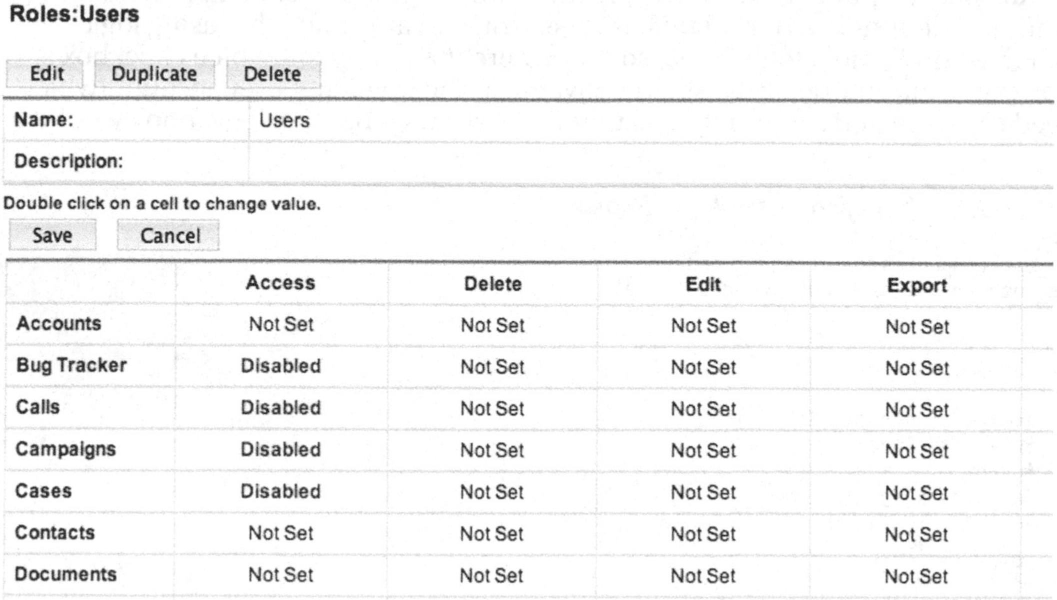

Roles:Users

Edit	Duplicate	Delete

Name:	Users
Description:	

Double click on a cell to change value.

Save	Cancel

	Access	Delete	Edit	Export
Accounts	Not Set	Not Set	Not Set	Not Set
Bug Tracker	Disabled	Not Set	Not Set	Not Set
Calls	Disabled	Not Set	Not Set	Not Set
Campaigns	Disabled	Not Set	Not Set	Not Set
Cases	Disabled	Not Set	Not Set	Not Set
Contacts	Not Set	Not Set	Not Set	Not Set
Documents	Not Set	Not Set	Not Set	Not Set

Figure 11-2. Users role

You also should personalize the application a bit to make the branding match what is used in the rest of the company. The single most important part of the success of any business application is user acceptance. A good way to achieve this is to make the application not only easy to use, but visually appealing and have the appearance that it integrates flow into the rest of the company. Your first task in achieving this is to first set the company logo image that is used in the application and displayed in the header of the page. You can do this very easily through the System Settings in the

Admin panel by just uploading the image you wish to use to your instance (see Figure 11-3).

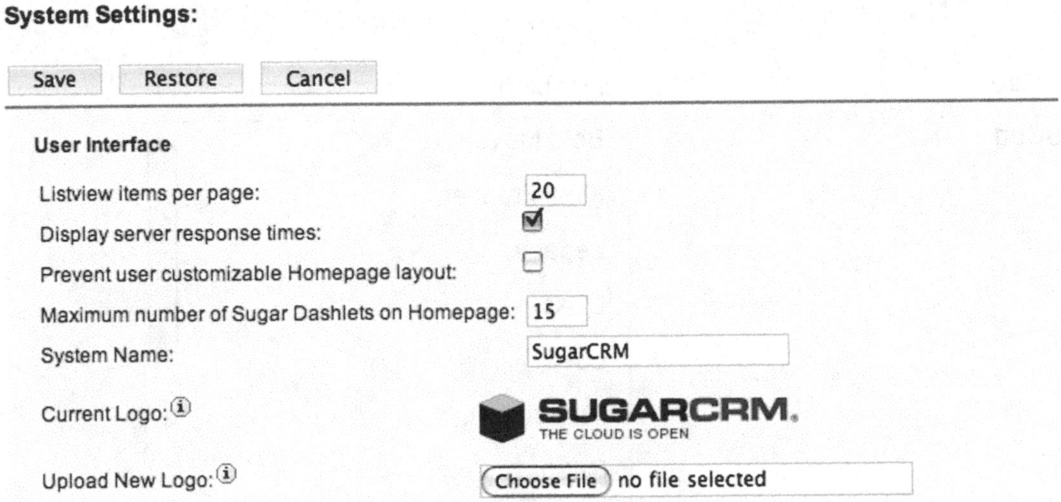

System Settings:

Save	Restore	Cancel

User Interface

Listview items per page: `20`

Display server response times: ☑

Prevent user customizable Homepage layout: ☐

Maximum number of Sugar Dashlets on Homepage: `15`

System Name: `SugarCRM`

Current Logo: ⓘ ◆ **SUGARCRM.** THE CLOUD IS OPEN

Upload New Logo: ⓘ (Choose File) no file selected

Figure 11-3. System Settings Section for Changing the Company Logo

You can also make this change by dropping the image in the custom/themes/default/images directory, naming it company_logo.png (or company_logo.gif if it is a GIF image). One nice feature here that has been added with the new theme framework introduced in Sugar 5.5 is that you can upload an image of any size and dimension, and it will be automatically resized correctly to fit in the header without making the image look disproportional.

You also want to customize your theme selection as well. To keep end user training consistent for all those who will use the Easter Pools' new application, they have decided to standardize on the RipCurl theme (mostly due to its aquatic-like theme, since they are a pool business). To do this, you'll change the config.php file, which stores the default configuration setting for Sugar to specify the default_theme setting to RipCurl instead of the default Sugar theme. Then you can disable all the other themes in the Theme Settings section of the Admin panel, as you see in Figure 11-4.

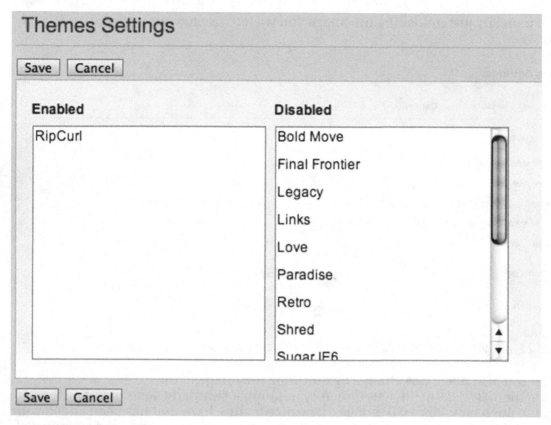

Figure 11-4. Themes Settings of the Admin Panel

These simple changes may seem like minor things (and they are for the most part) but it's the details like this that make the difference to any business. I mentioned earlier in this section the idea of user acceptance, and its role in the success of any deployment of an application whether it be SugarCRM-based or not. The difference with SugarCRM is it gives you as a developer the tools to enable customization of your application, making these final touches easy to do.

Summary

In this chapter, you used all the knowledge accumulated throughout the entire book and put it to practical use by designing a business application for a business. The mythical business named Easter Pools had the requirements of creating an application to manage their growing business. In particular, they needed management of their diverse customer base which covered both commercial customers as well as retail customers needing products, parts, supplies, and service for their pools and spas, and the ability to easily and quickly be able to tell what products they own and the history of service appointments they have made. They also needed better management of their service business, including parts inventory, scheduling and prioritizing requests, and automating the notification of when to invoice a client. Vendor management was also critical, needing both insights into the parts, products, and supplies relationships, as well as tracking orders made.

Piece by piece, you saw the versatility of SugarCRM shine here, showing how easy is it to extend and build upon it to meet any needs. You built several new modules and reused a few as well, adding fields and additional relationships to fulfill the requirements for the application as well as add some nice new abilities. In addition, you added external integration, first with Google Maps to provide mapping information to Easter Pools' service crews to help them get to their job sites. You added integration into an already existing account system using REST Web Services and the built-in push notifications system that comes with SugarCRM. You then also took a moment to add a few last changes to your application to clean it up by hiding the modules you won't be using and have it match the already existing branding used by Easter Pools.

The example application you looked at how to build in this chapter is a good blueprint on how to customize Sugar to meet your needs. The developer's tools that come with Sugar enable you to get your application off the ground easily, and from there you can add your own code level customizations to have the application meet your requirements. If there's one thing that sets SugarCRM apart from the pack is its versatility, and with the ever changing needs that all companies have its one of the most important features to have so your application can grow with your company.

Index

■ ■ ■